Roger D. Stone's
The Voyage of the Sanderling

"The Voyage of the Sanderling is a classic—the tale of an important adventure, a lengthy cruise under sail dedicated to a new kind of exploration and discovery. Roger Stone is uniquely equipped to sail the coasts of North and South America, and to report on what we are doing to destroy, and sometimes save, those vital parts of our planet. Approaching the land from the sea, he offers an entirely new and dramatic picture of the way our shore-based activities are killing our oceans. He names the villains, the heroes and heroines, in the battle between pollution and ecological sanity. An important, timely, beautifully written warning to us all."

—Charles Bracelen Flood

"A thorough and balanced picture of the regional environment—one that confirms the enormity and seriousness of [coastal decline] but also details that progress that has been made in recent years, thanks largely to individuals with the grit and determination to fight modern-day coastal pirates."

—*Christian Science Monitor*

"Stone and his youthful crew know how to make a good time out of their mission, as anyone who loves a brisk wind or a good strip of beach would do....*The Voyage of the Sanderling* is part travelogue, part history, part adventure and part environmental report....While the *Sanderling*'s discoveries are discouraging, Stone is instinctively upbeat and looks for the favorable possibilities...."

—*Los Angeles Times Book Review*

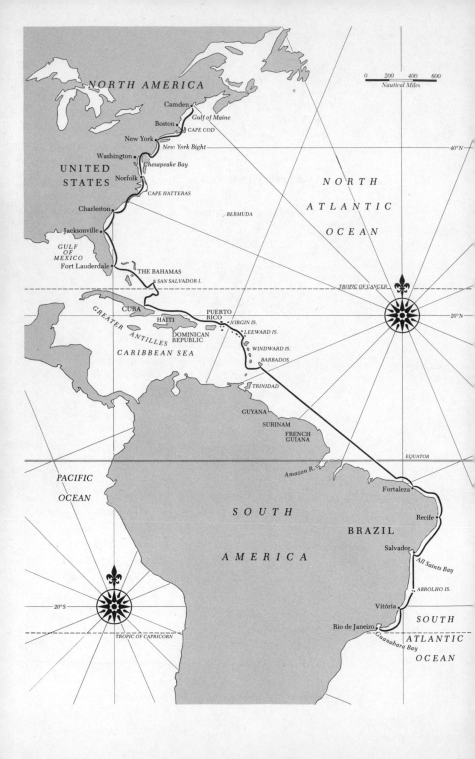

The Voyage
of the
Sanderling

—◦—

Roger D. Stone

Vintage Books
A Division of Random House, Inc., New York

VINTAGE DEPARTURES

First Vintage Departures Edition, March 1991

Library of Congress Cataloging-in-Publication Data
Stone, Roger D.
The voyage of the Sanderling / Roger D. Stone. — 1st Vintage
departures ed.
p.   cm. — (Vintage departures)
Reprint. Originally published: New York : Knopf, 1990.
Includes bibliographical references and index.
ISBN 0-679-73178-4
1. Marine pollution—Environmental aspects—Atlantic Coast (U.S.)
2. Marine pollution—Environmental aspects—Atlantic Coast (South
America) 3. Coastal ecology—Atlantic Coast (U.S.) 4. Coastal ecology
—Atlantic Coast (South America) 5. Coastal zone management—
Atlantic Coast (U.S.) 6. Coastal zone management—Atlantic Coast
(South America) 7. Sanderling (Sailboat) I. Title.
[QH545.W3S83   1990b]
574.5′2638′0974—dc20   90-55668
CIP

Manufactured in the United States of America
10 9 8 7 6 5 4 3 2 1

For Flo

THE DIFFERENCE BETWEEN INDIANS AND EURO-
PEANS WAS NOT THAT ONE HAD PROPERTY AND THE
OTHER HAD NONE; RATHER, IT WAS THAT THEY
LOVED PROPERTY DIFFERENTLY.

—WILLIAM CRONON,
Changes in the Land

THE HUMAN BEING IS A WEED SPECIES.

—S. DILLON RIPLEY

Contents

Contents

Part III
THE BRAZILIAN MIRACLE

Acknowledgments

My foremost thanks must go to those whose support was the *sine qua non* for the project of which this book is an account. These include Sue and Gerrit Van de Bovenkamp of the Armand G. Erpf Fund, whose establishment of an endowed Conservation Fellowship at the World Wildlife Fund lay at the root of it all. In turn I owe the Fund's chairman, Russell E. Train, and its then president, William K. Reilly, my profound appreciation for their decision, early in 1986, to award the fellowship to me. Receipt of this honor enabled me to set aside my previous management responsibilities at WWF and concentrate on *The Voyage of the Sanderling*. Thirdly, as I specify in the first chapter, the project would not have floated had it not been for the extreme generosity of Bill Anderson in his contributing *Sanderling* to WWF for my use.

Two principal lieutenants greatly eased the skipper's task. For research ashore, I am particularly indebted to Hope Patterson, who tracked down a remarkable volume and variety of information about Atlantic coastal life during the sixteenth and seventeenth centuries, and who quietly but firmly made invaluable comments on my texts. Aboard, no one was a more dedicated participant in the project than Peter Walsh. He spent more than a year on the boat, attacked our various mechanical and logistical problems with grit and determination, and remained throughout a valued friend and counselor. "You bet" is the phrase I associate most clearly with Peter's role as first mate and chief engineer.

Mauricio Obregón served not only as a spirited crew member but also as a key source of insight into the world and travels of Christopher Columbus. The library at Island Resources Foundation on St. Thomas, as well as the prolific and excellent writings of its principal figures, Judith and Edward Towle, were especially significant to my understanding of the Caribbean. In Rio de Janeiro, Márcio Moreira Alves opened to me his excellent library, which contains many original works by pioneer visitors to Brazil. Georgette Dorn at the Library of Congress and Susan Danforth at the John Carter Brown Library in Providence, Rhode Island, provided kind and courteous assistance.

Ed Towle, who gave *Sanderling* the use of a mooring in Red Hook Bay during her Virgin Islands layover, was one of many who eased the boat along her route. At the head of this list is Ed Simmons of Greenpeace, who not only found the boat but helped register, insure, and equip her; was an ongoing source of wise advice about nautical matters; and as the project ended was still fussing with *Sanderling* as she lay at the dock in front of his Fort Lauderdale house. Jim Sharkey of the excellent Zahniser's marina in Solomons, Maryland, took wonderful care of *Sanderling* during the time she was berthed there. Bob Heinemann and Barry Willson co-skippered the boat all the way from Rio back to the Bahamas; when I joined Barry in Nassau for a final sail across to Florida, the boat was in better condition than when I had left her. To all the crew members who joined *Sanderling* for various stages of the voyage, particularly Matt Huntington and Steve Riehemann, I owe profound thanks: they were superb companions, and they made it possible for me to concentrate on research and writing while they did the lion's share of the sailing and grunt work. No one was more enthusiastic about being aboard than my daughter Leslie; I wish her many fine sails in the future.

Nicholas Stancioff and Alex Cook helped me achieve adequate mastery of the word-processing system called WordPerfect, which is wonderful once tamed. World Wildlife Fund's computer expert Tim Sivia and his assistant, Kathy Dale, were also most helpful in this regard. Paige MacDonald and Julia Moore at WWF greatly eased the pain of dealing with financial and administrative matters. Bob McCoy, also at WWF, read my scripts and cheerfully provided thoughtful and useful advice. I sent sections of the book to many other people for comment, and to all of these I extend warm thanks for their invaluable reactions. Elisabeth Sifton, my gifted editor, lobbed shots of enthusiasm across the waters when they were most needed, and handled my manuscript with discerning sensitivity. Her "Eh?" is worth a thousand words.

I extend the deepest appreciation to all those out there on the coastal frontiers, fighting often lonely and frustrating battles against degradation and destruction, whose stories and programs and challenges lie at the heart of this narrative. Without exception they received me with gracious warmth, gave unstintingly of their time to tell me what they were trying to do, and offered many suggestions of other sources

Acknowledgments

and things to read. I only wish that there was sufficient room in this volume to explain their activities in greater detail, and I hope someday to be able to write a sequel, describing how their dreams came true. No one combed through this script with deeper attention, lightly decorating pages with little blue dots wherever she sensed problems, than my toughest critic and most loyal supporter: my wife, Flo, to whom, despite her preference for dry land, I dedicate this work.

Roger D. Stone
Washington, D.C.
May 1989

The Voyage
of the
Sanderling

Introduction:

Sanderling's Mission

I STOOD FACING THE JAMMED HORSESHOE HARBOR OF CAMDEN, Maine. At summer's end it was so tightly packed with glistening yachts that some, for want of swinging room, were tied up alongside makeshift rafts anchored out in the middle. Over my left shoulder, condos. Straight ahead, the town's traditional stores and its trim little yacht club, now engulfed by newer buildings offering the tourist throngs ice cream, guitars, croissants, lobster. Even the harbormaster (harbormaster? in Camden?) had a spanking-new office down near where various cap'ns in traditional sailboats picked up their greenhorn passengers for day- and week-long outings in Penobscot Bay. The high, round Camden Hills loomed beyond. They have been applauded for their spectacular beauty by navigators from Captain John Smith to the author and yachtsman Alfred F. Loomis, who in his classic 1939 work *Ranging the Maine Coast* called them "among the finest of God's creations that may meet the eye of the cruising man." Late in the 1940s, when I first came here to visit a school friend, Camden was a placid resort and lobstering town, barely recovered from the quiet gas-rationing years of World War II. Several of us, none older than sixteen, chartered a leaky double-ended cutter called *Roaring Bull* and got her as far away as Bar Harbor. Camden figured again in my travels during the summer of 1955, when upon graduation from college I shipped out as a paid hand aboard the small Alden schooner *Seaward* and rode this bucking vessel, with a determined skipper and one other crewman, on a chilly two-month round trip through the fog from Massachusetts to Newfoundland and back. Alden-designed yachts and Camden figured prominently in my many subsequent Maine coast cruises. Now I was back in this newly crowded,

3

diversifying community to pick up yet another Alden boat and sail her southward from there to Brazil via the East Coast of the United States, the Bahamas, the Greater and Lesser Antilles.

"Do what?" my wife, Flo, asked when the subject first came up.

"A book about the current environmental crisis along the Atlantic coast, about how it has changed over the last five hundred years since the first European discoverers arrived, and about its prospects," I said. "Sail the whole way or as much of it as possible, to be able to describe it from up close, and see things it would be hard to get to any other way."

To establish a baseline, I planned to look into the early explorers' logbooks and journals (often called "relations") for descriptions of the abundance of species and resources they encountered, the hardships they endured and the reasons for these. I would try to factor out sob stories and Panglossian exuberance expressed in the hope of future expedition commissions from kings or entrepreneurs, and reach a close approximation of the coast's real condition as the sixteenth century began. With that information in hand, I would survey the degradation that has been occurring ever since small numbers of aboriginal peoples were first dislodged by European explorers or settlers from their homes or campsites along the shore; and the coastal waters, reefs, beaches, wetlands, harbors, estuaries, and rivers—along with their bountiful resources—first subjected to careless misuse by colonists and migrants. At close range I would witness examples of the continuing decline that, as the 1980s ended, was finally attracting the attention it had long deserved. I would also seek evidence of recovery.

Before the beginning of the current century, quietly at first, with only a few observers paying close attention, then at an accelerating rate with the boom in "development," the U.S. coast started to die. The bottoms of major harbors became lined with dissolved heavy metals, oil and grease, and nonbiodegradable toxic chemicals. As the use of fertilizers and herbicides grew, runoff from nearby farms started to poison the waters. Human and animal wastes drained, sometimes from far inland, into rivers and bays and estuaries, supplying them with growing amounts of nitrogen, phosphorus, and other nutrients. (In moderation, these help plants to grow; in excess, they encourage the spread of surface algae, which sop up oxygen as they decay and replace it with hydrogen sulphide. Gasping, fish perish and litter the shores, and their numbers dwindle.) Cities spread, second homes and condominiums proliferated along the bays and beaches, more and more roads were built. Bulldozers trampled over life-nourishing salt marshes and head-waters, pavement replaced sand dunes and their stabilizing grasses. Erosion, instability, and sedimentation all increased.

Now we are learning routinely about algal blooms and dying dolphins, of tanker accidents and oil-soaked cormorants, of used hypodermic needles washing up on beaches, of marine life that in some estuaries has all but vanished, of beach erosion and new buildings toppling into the rising sea before they are even completed, of large areas closed to shellfishing because of pollution, of coastal waters so poisoned that they have become virtually devoid of life, of fish and shellfish found with gaping lesions caused by toxic poisoning. Acid rain, previously thought to kill fish in fresh water only, is now also said to be yet another cause of nutrient pollution and diminishing resources in bays and estuaries. In 1988 the Environmental Defense Fund, a privately supported research and conservation agency, asserted: "One-fourth of all nitrogen contributed by human activity to the Chesapeake Bay originated in acid rain." Airborne nitrate deposition, its report continued, represents a larger share of the problem than either sewage outflow or runoff of animal waste.

A more remote but deadly additional threat to coastal welfare is the rapid man-made buildup of carbon dioxide, methane, nitrous oxide, low-level ozone, and other "greenhouse gases" in the atmosphere. To an extent not yet known to science, they are increasing its ability to entrap the earth's heat and prevent it from radiating into space. Predictions of how much warmer the earth will consequently become vary widely, from three to nine degrees Centigrade by the middle of the next century; fully reliable data from comprehensive global computer models will not be available for another decade or two. Not even the most powerful machines can affordably pinpoint the consequences of the warming trend at the regional or local level. But among the likeliest outcomes of the greenhouse warming, scientists agree, is that it will be accompanied by a general sea level rise largely attributable to the thermal expansion of the oceans and the conversion of ice to water.

In 1989 the Canadian physicists W. R. Peltier and A. M. Tushingham reported that the enhancement of the greenhouse effect has brought about a "globally coherent" increase in the current rate of sea-level rise, to "2.4 plus or minus 0.90 millimeters per year," or perhaps a foot per century. The "best guess" of another scientist, James Broadus of the Woods Hole Oceanographic Institute, is a rise of between four and seven inches over the next forty years. Multiple dangers accompany a vertical rise of these modest-seeming dimensions. Damage to coastal areas from storm flooding will greatly increase; brewing in warmer air, storms themselves are likely to become more severe. With construction blocking many wetlands and other critical areas from simply "migrating" up along the shore as the waters rise, salt marshes that now thrive will soon become lagoons terminating in embankments for highways, railroads, or buildings. Over the very long range, plate tectonic actions will exaggerate local or regional distortions.

At a meeting of coastal conservationists held in Rhode Island late in 1987 to discuss the plight of bays and estuaries (places where salt and fresh water meet), I was to hear much about the economic and biological magnitude of the assault upon these especially important regions. An acre of salt marsh, said the conference proceedings, is "2 to 6 times more productive" in terms of useful organic material produced than most fertile fields; up to 125 pounds of commercial fish can be harvested from each acre of the Atlantic coastal wetland and estuary system. The report also stressed the coastal wetlands' role as a buffer protecting higher ground from storms, as an absorbing filter for pollutants, and as a focal point for hunting, fishing, and other activities generating billions of dollars in annual revenues. Yet participants in the meeting, which was organized by Save the Bay (a private group whose concern is Narragansett Bay) and funded in large part by the federal Environmental Protection Agency, could see little ahead but further degradation without major change. They urged adjustments in both human behavior and the institutional framework. In the United States, regulations to arrest most aspects of this decline hardly existed prior to 1972. In that year, serious federal action belatedly began with the enactment of the Federal Water Pollution Control Act (better known as the Clean Water Act), whose idealistic goal was to eliminate all discharges of water pollutants by 1985. Under the terms of that act, a National Pollutant Discharge Elimination System (NPDES) was established, and the EPA was empowered to administer it in partnership with other federal and local agencies. In 1972 the Congress also enacted the prescient Coastal Zone Management Act (CZMA), which, recognizing that land use and coastal water quality are related issues, called for the establishment of federal-state partnerships to develop long-term integrated management plans. Administrative responsibility was invested in the National Oceanic and Atmospheric Administration (NOAA), a division of the Department of Commerce. In subsequent years came refinements to these benchmark statutes, as well as new ones such as the Coastal Barrier Resources Act of 1982, and numerous laws and regulations having to do with the complex subject of solid-waste disposal in the ocean and elsewhere.

As of now, however, the coastal crisis has still not been countered by a cohesive national stabilization effort. The system remains a patchwork, riddled with contradictions, plagued by inadequate funding for federal and local enforcement agencies, constantly under attack in the courts and still suffering from years of harassment by Reagan ideologues. Administrative responsibility for the key section of the Clean Water Act that deals with the discharge of dredged materials, for instance, remains in the hands of the U.S. Army Corps of Engineers, a dig-we-must agency long known for ham-handed insensitivity to environmental considerations in its determination to widen, deepen, and expand the nation's navigable waterways. For all CZMA's noble intentions, Congress also enacted a National Flood Insurance Program that was continuing to provide huge subsidies for coastal development. EPA's effectiveness suffered greatly, despite valiant efforts by survivors within the agency, from lack of adequate funding and political support during the Reagan administration. Reagan's anti-environmental stance, particularly with regard to offshore oil and gas development, also inhibited CZMA planning. While many local agencies were addressing local issues with great vigor and effectiveness, the largest private organization solely devoted to any aspect of coastal policy on a national scale—the Washington-based Oceanic Society—had in 1987 a total of six employees. For all the huffing and puffing, the national response remained woefully inadequate to the challenge.

The crisis was by no means limited to U.S. waters. In the Bahamas and the Caribbean, overconcentrated resort development has resulted in coastal deterioration—counterproductive, to say the least, on islands whose livelihood had come to depend in large part on their pristine beauty. Sewage from hotels has clouded and polluted the very crystal waters that attract visitors. On some islands, excessive hotel construction jeopardizes the supply of scarce fresh water. Fishermen have killed coral reefs by using Clorox and even dynamite to flush crawfish (or spiny lobsters) out of holes; under such assaults, the crawfish themselves have grown scarce in many areas. Other staple foods such as the conch and white sea urchin, or "sea egg," have begun to disappear because of overharvesting.

In Brazil, which until recently had no controls on pollution whatever, key places along the coast went from virginity to death within only a few years, as the population grew and new industries dumped lethal torrents of waste into yesterday's pure seawater. Shrimp vanished from Rio de Janeiro's once glorious Guanabara Bay, now littered with refuse and iridescent with oil slicks and industrial runoff. All Saints Bay, alongside beautiful Salvador, Brazil's colonial capital in the northeastern state of Bahia, is not much better off. Outward from the center of almost every city on Brazil's coast stretches a lengthening band of disorderly development.

A vigorous reaction to the mounting tragedy has at last sprung up. Fishermen, nature lovers, and conservationists are joined in their dismay by frustrated swimmers and sunbathers, those squeezed out of coastal areas by high taxes or property values, and plain citizens fed up with the untidy, unhealthy scene and apprehensive about its dangers. By the summer of 1988, when a prolonged heat wave coincided with an unprecedented number of New York area beach closings because of dangerous filth washing ashore, the U.S. press was in full cry. *Time*'s editors, often quick to say that the magazine has "already covered" many a timely subject, devoted its second cover story in a year to coastal woes. *Newsweek* and even *Business Week* (in 1987) also dealt with the issue at cover length. Politicians—Governors Kean of New Jersey, Schaefer of Maryland, Baliles of Virginia—spoke out ever more shrilly (though still not always following words with actions). Environmental concern is "good politics," Governor Michael Dukakis told me—before, ironically, Republicans began to use his state's foot-dragging on cleaning up filthy Boston Harbor as a principal element in their "negative" campaign against him. George Bush, heir to the dismal Reagan record, in one of his first major speeches as the Republican candidate, pledged to bring to the White House a "new conservation ethic." State and local governments began to propose tough new regulations against ocean dumping and other forms of coastal pollution, and tighter restrictions on real estate development in coastal areas. In the Caribbean the concept of coastal management spread "down-island." Even in Brazil, whose citizens considered the coast an inexhaustible resource, an awakening was under way.

Hopeful signals—"comebacks" on the part of the osprey, the brown pelican, the Atlantic salmon, the now better protected rockfish or striped bass—give us encouragement. So have improvements in the water quality of some of our rivers—the Hudson, the Potomac, even the hard-pressed Delaware. In some corners of the United States, the Nature Conservancy and other organizations, usually just a step ahead of the developers, have succeeded in locking up critical coastal areas through outright land purchases or conservation easements negotiated with individual owners. At the regional level, creative public/private approaches such as the multi-state Chesapeake Bay Agreement have begun to bear fruit. Local laws have already become stricter. Maryland's "Critical Areas" program, for example, all but rules out development in ecologically important coastal or wetland areas.

In some ways, biological factors enhance the chances of coastal survival. Many marine creatures are tough as nails to begin with. In tenacity the blue crab rivals the cockroach. No great adjustment in human behavior would be needed for these marine populations to begin growing again. So, while other changes would come a lot harder, the essential question is whether people will give even an inch or simply continue their profligate habits and their helter-skelter march to the sea. Between 1950 and 1984, the U.S. population in coastal areas almost doubled. The Census Bureau expects that by the early 1990s, 75 percent of the U.S. population—more than 180 million people—will reside within fifty miles of a coastline.

Are the positive indications strong enough to suggest a coastal bottoming out and the beginning of a recovery? Or is the slide likely to continue and even accelerate in the face of population growth and other pressures? I would submit a gloomy assumption. In some places, I think, a combination of will and money and political power could in fact arrest the ecological decline, but for most of the Atlantic coast, no such good fortune can be foreseen.

By including the Eastern Caribbean and the east coast of South America in my study, I have hoped to establish useful contrasts. Differences between ecological circumstances, cultural values, and the economic imperatives of poor Third World nations vis-à-vis the wasteful profligacy of behavior in the well-off United States might come clear. Perhaps there would be parallels as well. What might Guanabara Bay's defenders learn from the Chesapeake, or vice versa? In the mid-1960s, then a journalist, I lived in Rio de Janeiro for several years, traveling widely throughout the South American continent and achieving some understanding of what makes the region not tick. A decade later I assumed the presidency of the Center for Inter-American Relations, a private organization in New York that attempted to inform a yawning U.S. public, then hardly conscious of the region's geography, let alone of the power of its now best-selling literature, about Latin America's people and cultures. I stayed on watch there for seven lean but fascinating years. Subsequently, as a staff member and Erpf Fellow at the World Wildlife Fund, I at last learned something about biology and ecology. My background, in short, gave me a head start with regard to the non-U.S. end of the project. While time-consuming and possibly arduous, a sailboat voyage down the Atlantic coast, which I defined as including the Eastern Caribbean as well as the U.S. shoreline and that of Brazil, would provide the book with an organizing principle, and result in a lot of information that it would be hard to get in any other way. A boat would give me access to remote places along the coast where nature still prevails. Along the way I would encounter many people—scientists, conservationists, fishermen, residents, and vacationers—who were trying hard to maintain and improve the coast's quality. Seeing them at work, and hearing them talk of life near the sea, was an essential part of the knowledge I sought.

Arranging this ambitious scheme proved more difficult than dreaming about it.

"That's one I won't have to worry about," Flo would say to friends.

But by mid-1986 most of the pieces somehow came together. The exception was that I had no boat and could not just go out and buy one. This considerable handicap would be overcome, I hoped, by means of a yacht donation to the World Wildlife Fund, which could then make the boat available to me. Over the summer, guided by the resourceful Ed Simmons at Greenpeace, I canvassed the East Coast in search of a willing donor with an appropriate vessel. One proffered prospect, aptly named *Wild Goose Chase*, failed to pass muster when it was found that, unbeknownst to absentee owners, she had sunk at a slip in Annapolis and incurred extensive damage, including a "pickled engine." By the time I reached him, Walter Cronkite had just committed his handsome 42-footer to the U.S. Naval Academy. The big old *Cyrano*, once owned by the luxury yachtsman William F. Buckley, Jr., briefly flickered as a possibility but on closer inspection seemed a bit much to handle. Other opportunities cropped up, then vanished like mirages.

Just before Labor Day, word arrived that William Anderson, a seasoned sailor from South Natick, Massachusetts, was willing to surrender his spanking-new 38-foot cutter and had judged my cause to be worthy. Carefully designed by the Alden firm, the boat was built in 1983 by Hank Hinckley of Maine's illustrious boatbuilding dynasty. She was said to be lavishly equipped, meticulously maintained, and in the water at Camden and ready to go. I needed only to get myself there, look her over to make sure she would do, shake hands with Mr. Anderson, sign a few papers, and take command.

Here now, at the busy Wayfarer marina on the north side of Camden Harbor, I scanned a long row of handsome sailboats and tried to spot this prize. Bill Anderson, so familiar a figure around this yard that he was not hard to find, welcomed me aboard. Without delay he commenced a brisk explanation of how to work her:

About 2,100 rpm on the diesel should keep it cool and give you seven knots of speed.

Leave the radar on standby for two and one-half minutes before switching to "on."

A single red marker on the anchor chain gives you 75 feet of scope.

The fuel and water tanks hold 85 gallons apiece, not the 75 gallons indicated as maximum on the gauges under the floorboard at the after end of the dining table in the main cabin.

Operating instructions and manuals for electronics and other gadgets are in the forward port drawer in the main cabin.

We continued in this manner for some time, discussing the winches and the autopilot, and how to stow the dinghy atop the main cabin, and where extra sailing gear was located (in a cardboard box marked "office supplies"). Then we moved ashore for signing and notarizing and photocopying. But Anderson's mind was still aboard. Back we went. "What else have I forgotten to tell you?" he kept asking. He knew full well that trial, error, and experience, rather than even the most rigorous note-taking, are how a skipper really gets to know a new command. Even so, we picked through drawers and manuals and went over the switches on the panel for a second time. He was still passing along information as he shook hands, wished me luck, and crossed the gangplank to the shore. Once there, he turned and gave a quick wave, took a final look at his ninth sailboat, then disappeared around the corner of a building. Several times I had mumbled words of appreciation for his great generosity, but found it difficult to rise fully to the level of eloquence needed for this quietly, almost gruffly, emotional moment of transition.

Now at last I was alone aboard what would be my compact home for much of the next two years. Originally called *Wind Song*, the boat would be renamed *Sanderling* in honor of the pale-colored *Calidris alba*, a shorebird that breeds in North America and migrates southward as far as Argentina. Working the beaches, this nimble sandpiper eats where sea meets sand, then briskly scuttles away from rising waters and back when they recede. While *Sanderling* is undeniably a central character in the narrative that follows, this book is not so much about boats and sailing as it is about the coast itself. Yet it's perhaps worth pausing at the outset for a closer look at the vantage point from which you will get most of the story.

Along with coasts and harbors, sailboats too have changed dramatically over the years. As a child on Long Island, I spent rainy summer afternoons in the cozy paneled library of my family's next-door neighbor, browsing through bound volumes of *Yachting* from the 1930s to the 1950s. The cruising boats featured in its ads and design sections were usually built of wood, had wooden masts and booms and classic lines with moderate overhang at both bow and stern (in other words, the length on deck was considerably greater than the waterline length). They had long keels with rudders faired into their after ends. Power was provided by four-cylinder gasoline engines and was used for little other than to move the boats along at a modest pace when the wind blew lightly or from the wrong direction. Loomis called his engine "the mill" and used it only when all else had failed. Anchoring and weighing anchor were strictly manual activities involving the unleveraged horsing around of heavy gear.

Below, one cooked with kerosene or alcohol, lit small kerosene lamps after dark, and slept on hard pipe berths—often no more than strips of canvas strung across metal frames. Cabin heat, if any, came from simple little charcoal or wood-burning stoves. Food storage was in poorly insulated iceboxes. Though the enclosed head with a hand-pumped flushing system had become standard, some still went off cruising with only a toilet-seated bucket in the forward cabin. The skipper of my 1955 Newfoundland venture habitually surprised his more modest young crew by dropping his drawers after breakfast and—like a crewman aboard the *Santa María*—extending his bottom outboard from the leeward (downwind) rail. Among the few amenities aboard a 1950s sloop we once chartered in Hadleys Harbor, Massachusetts, a boat that boasted a scant four feet of headroom in the main cabin, was a selection of Elizabethan songbooks.

Life aboard, in short, was on the primitive side even when everything worked; breakdowns of simple equipment were endemic. One almost assumed that leaks would require vigorous pumping, that the fuel pump or voltage regulator or some other part of the engine would fail when power was most urgently needed, that the stove's failure to ignite would deny chilled crew members their hot soup at the end of a long wet day.

Close to shore, where I remained until much later, navigation was usually accomplished by means of dead reckoning—reasoned guesses about where one was, based on estimates of speed through the water, current, and drift and confirmed by visual observations of buoys, lighthouses, or other prominent landmarks. In fog one ran the buoys under power (if it worked), cutting the throttle to idle from time to time in order to listen (earball) for the groan of a whistler or the blast of a diaphone. At times one even noseballed—sniffed the wind for the scent of nearby spruce—and bore smartly away when it was detected. Though loran had just come in, the principal electronic aid to navigation was still a radio direction finder that could, after painstaking manipulation of an antenna, be pointed more or less in the direction of a fixed radio beacon.

Aficionados who loved the simplicity of this sort of yachting and didn't mind its rigors tended to resent the novelties—radars, autopilots, electric windlasses, hot-water showers—that the yachting industry began to add in the 1960s. Fiberglass construction was dismissed as "plastic," advanced hull and rudder designs that often increased speed as ugly, innovations in electronics and sheer comfort as more for the marina habitué than for the blue-water salt. Inevitably, though, the frills became standard as yachting technology zoomed forward under heavy pressure from the intensely competitive racing sector. By the 1970s none but a diehard fringe of those who could afford the new conveniences turned them down.

Sanderling, I discovered after only a few minutes of inspection, admirably combines the solid virtues of older cruising sailboats with the newer comforts. Designed for handling ease rather than the speed of a racer, she is rigged as a cutter, her single mast stepped handily further aft than a racing sloop's would likely be. Forward is a genoa jib that easily winds around the forestay when the breeze is too strong for all of it. The mainsail rolls up around a cable inside the hollow mast; all, or as much of it as one cares to use, can be cranked out along the boom. To carry out these operations, you need never leave the shelter of a canopy, called a dodger, that covers the forward end of the cockpit and offers protection from spray, wind, and rain. The spacious cockpit area boasts benches of solid teak. Underneath are storage bins for sails, winches, and other deck gear. In an older boat, to gain access to these spaces, you would precariously hold the bin open with your head while sorting through the stuff inside. Not on *Sanderling*: her bin doors have wonderful springs that snap taut to hold them open but give instantly when nudged.

On deck, many winches ease the hardship of setting and trimming sails. Forward on the starboard (right-hand) side is an electric windlass, which at the touch of a toe to a black button obligingly hauls up the 35-pound plow anchor and its heavy chain. Just forward of the aluminum mast, at its foot, an enclosed radar antenna is linked to the unit below: no more noseballing. *Sanderling*'s modern fiberglass hull hardly eliminates all leakage, as we were to discover; but surely she is far less porous than most wooden boats.

Below deck, the sturdy Perkins diesel engine is but one of many amenities. In the main cabin, on the starboard side, is a spacious icebox with a refrigeration unit (it works when the engine is running or when the boat is plugged into shore power) and even a separate freezing compartment that makes ice cubes. The icebox top doubles as the navigation station. Here you spread out your chart and have room for plotting with the assistance of a Fathometer and two electronic navigation aids—a loran and a satellite navigation receiver—that are close at hand along with VHF and single-sideband (SSB) radios, and an electrical panel leading to a battery- or alternator-powered system of uncommon strength. Across the way to port is a three-burner stove fueled by LP propane gas carried in four ample tanks placed way aft behind the cockpit. The mere application of a lighted match, not the technical wizardry sometimes required for older versions, is sufficient to ignite this stove's top burners; firing off its spacious oven and broiler is scarcely more complex.

Next, moving forward, comes a classic main-cabin sleeping design. Two comfortable slide-out single bunks flank a central fold-up table; additional passengers crawl into pilot berths up and out from the lower bunks. Between the main and forward cabins the washroom features not only a head but a compact shower offering, after the engine has been running, hot fresh water. Clothes lockers also separate the main from the forward cabin, which contains two wide V-bunks as well as room to stow the anchor chain and other ship's gear.

What this nutshell tour cannot fully convey is the sense of order and loving care that I found aboard *Sanderling*. Nor have I yet mentioned the traditional elements of her design: the moderate sheer at each end, with the graceful gull-like lift to the stern found on many Alden boats; the long stable keel for ease of handling under sail or power; the distinctive sweep of the bowsprit supported by the traditional dolphin striker with its carved design. I was luckily the possessor of a handsomely fitted vessel admirably combining old and new virtues, fully able to carry out the designated assignment. If I failed, I could hardly blame the tools.

During the afternoon my initial crew arrived—John and Caroline Woodwell (brother and sister) from Woods Hole, Massachusetts, Bill Perkins from Washington. We visited the supermarket and did other chores, cooked fresh haddock aboard as a crisp clear night fell and a quarter-moon arose amid piercing points of starlight. Before sunrise the following morning I turned the engine starter key and was thrilled by the instant response. I rousted the crew to slip the docking lines. Soon, on this glassy windless morning, we were gliding almost wakeless out of Camden Harbor and into West Penobscot Bay. The first streaks of the morning sun began to dry the dew from our decks and sprinkled gold onto the green of the Camden Hills, high on our starboard quarter, as we turned south and headed for the sea.

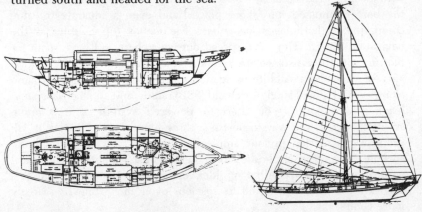

Part I

———— ❦ ————

REDISCOVERING
AMERICA

1

Maine Coasting

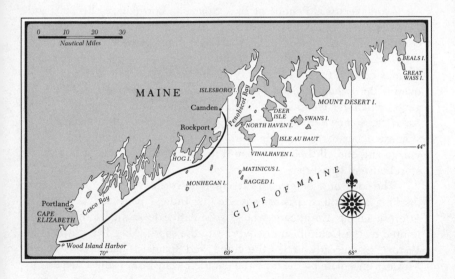

WITH THE EXCEPTION OF GULLS AND A FEW LOBSTERMEN WORKING
their pots, we had Penobscot Bay, the legendary paradise of Norumbega,
all to ourselves. Ahead lay the resort islands of North Haven and
Vinalhaven, whose rocky wooded shores and hidden harbors have
concealed generations of well-off summer folk from Boston and New
York. To port, northward, was the old town of Castine, where a vastly
superior U.S. naval force, led by a sluggish Paul Revere and a stray

Saltonstall, took a bad drubbing from the British in 1778. Even farther north, passing Searsport, narrowed the Penobscot River, explored in 1525 by a Portuguese seaman named Estevão Gomes, who thought it might lead to the Pacific and gave it the Spanish name Río de las Gamas (River of the Deer), in deference to his Spanish employers. Closer by, between stretches of clean blue-black water, lay spectacular smaller islands named Islesboro, Great Sprucehead, Barred, and Eagle. Talented outsiders—the IBM magnate Thomas Watson, the photographer Eliot Porter, the writer Ved Mehta and his family—maintain summer sanctuaries in this bay. To starboard was the promontory of Owls Head and, beyond, the Atlantic—or, more precisely, a large and highly productive estuary called the Gulf of Maine. Offshore islands lying beyond: Ragged, Matinicus, Monhegan, signposts marking the way into the most important estuary, roughly midway along Maine's crinkly 4,000-mile coastline.

Norumbega was the earliest name for New England and indeed, some say, for the entire Atlantic coast of the United States; its focal point for mapmakers was Penobscot Bay. Spanish, Portuguese, French, and Dutch fishermen may have touched here frequently during the fifteenth century and even before; the coast was later crowded with foreign visitors coming to summer. Periodically someone offers evidence that Vikings cruised this coast as early as the year 1000; but no one is sure even if the Italian seaman John Cabot made it as far west as Maine in 1498, when he commanded the first British ship to explore North America. Somewhere along the discovery chain, several historians have suggested, an early explorer stumbled upon a well-developed Indian village and embellished the account he brought back to suggest a great storehouse of treasure.

The idea of a bejeweled city in the North Atlantic, one perhaps marking a northern passageway to the Indies, provoked a flurry of interest among Europeans whose speculative fever had already been ignited by the Columbian discoveries to the south. Magellan's little ship *Victoria* had already circled the globe, and Spaniards had already tasted Mexican chocolate by the time the parade began. Now came a succession of sixteenth-century efforts to explore or settle Norumbega. Cruel realities and severe hardship befell almost all of these pioneers. Yet well into the seventeenth century, after a number of chilled, dampened, sickened, and enfeebled visitors had scotched the myth with dour assessments of the region's development potential, others were still expressing high hopes for its future. The good news somehow traveled faster and more durably than the bad. All the news was spread-

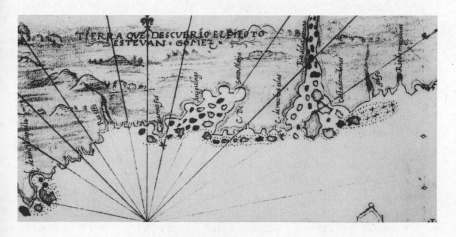

The Maine coast, drawn in 1545 on the basis of Estevão
Gomes' descriptions. Owl's Head, at the mouth of
Penobscot Bay, is called "C. de muchas islas." Opinions
vary as to whether the prominent bay shown to
the west of Penobscot is Muscongus Bay or Casco Bay.

ing remarkably fast, considering the state of communications technology,
and people kept coming over and trying.

In 1524, the skilled Florentine navigator Giovanni da Verrazano
became the first explorer to take a serious look. By the time he reached
Maine, he had already cruised, aboard his France-backed vessel *La
Dauphine*, from the Carolinas to New York and New England. Though
he noted "excellent harbors" and islands "of pleasant appearance" along
the Maine coast, encounters with Indians left him so apprehensive that
he called it the "land of bad people." The following year Gomes,
representing Spain's interests, took a close look at the Penobscot in
search of gold; after determining that none was to be found, he quickly
sheared away. Relying on data gathered by those and other pioneers
sufficient to convince him that the land around the Penobscot was arable
and the water "never subjecte to the Ise," Sir Humphrey Gilbert
attempted to found a "Norumbega Colony" in 1583. But his expedition
never reached shore: when one of his ships was lost off Newfoundland,
the rest of his small fleet beat a retreat back toward Europe.

Samuel de Champlain passed Penobscot Bay several times during
the course of three voyages between 1604 and 1613, spiking the
Norumbega myth with his reports of cold weather producing scurvy and
a rocky coast not suited for settlement. Not even Gilbert's misfortune

and Champlain's disclaimer were sufficient to discourage British enthusiasm for the region—particularly that of Sir Ferdinando Gorges, a well-heeled crony of Gilbert, Sir Francis Drake, and Sir Walter Raleigh. In 1605, Gorges commissioned a further exploration that was led by Captain George Waymouth. He reported stands of tall trees, a profusion of wild fruits, swarms of edible seabirds, and "great Cods and Hadocks" that were "well fed, fat, and sweete in taste." Waymouth anchored that summer in a narrow bight that is now called Georges Harbor, between what are now named Burnt and Allen islands. Though the holding ground is poor and a swell sometimes rolls in from the southwest, this place remains a favored haven for yachtsmen transiting the coast. There Waymouth found sweet water, ample supplies of pine trees for turpentine and pitch, and good soil to plant peas and barley. Later he ventured to an anchorage just inside the mouth of the Kennebec River a bit further to the west, and returned with a glowing report to King James I. "I would boldly affirme it," he wrote, "to be the most rich, beautifull, large and secure harboring river that the world affordeth." Stressing habitability as well as economic potential, he encouraged the king to authorize Gorges to lead a movement to establish in New England a "second colony" to rival the new Jamestown settlement.

Thus came about the first serious European effort to found a settlement along Maine's coast. In June 1607, some 120 colonists, led by George Popham and Raleigh Gilbert (son of Sir Humphrey), set forth from England aboard a ship called the *Mary and John* and without incident anchored off Burnt and Allen islands. There, the author of an anonymous journal found among Sir Ferdinando's papers after his death was dazzled by the size ("of greatt bignesse") of the lobsters and by how easily they could be caught in large numbers. A shore party, he reported, "kild near 50 great Lopsters. You shall See them Whear they ly in shold watt'r nott past a yeard deep and with a great hooke mad faste to a staffe you shall hitch them up."

In mid-August, Popham moved to a small island at the mouth of the Kennebec. Though it was too late to plant, before winter set in they "began to fortefye" their campsite and built there a "storhouse to reserve our vyttual." The weather held fair through October. Then came the usual succession of winter northeasters and severe frontal passages, weather "soe extreame unseasonable and frosty" that "noe boat could stir upon any business." Cold, their food supplies dwindling, and with no idea how to hunt, the settlers began to suffer from pneumonia and scurvy. By spring most had died, including Popham; the survivors hastened back to England.

Not even this grim episode was enough to warn off Captain John

Left: Giovanni da Verrazano. *Right:* Captain John Smith

Smith. Cruising the coast in 1614, he failed in his efforts to find whales or gold and copper mines, just as he had failed in other enterprises elsewhere. But this irrepressible adventurer had many positive things to say. The shore he encountered, he wrote, "Is all Mountainous and Iles of huge Rocks, but overgrowen with all sorts of excellent good woodes for building houses, boats, barks or shippes, with an incredible abundance of most sorts of fish, much fowle, and sundry sorts of good fruites for mans use."

No less enthusiastic was a chronicler named William Wood, who in a 1634 volume entitled *New England's Prospect* mentions lobsters up to twenty pounds, whose "plenty makes them little esteemed and seldom eaten." Quoting a fulsome poem that advertised the range and quality of Maine's water life, Wood could not resist the temptation to augment it with a few lines about equally magnificent species that had somehow been omitted.

No further effort to establish a European settlement in Maine was made until toward the end of the century. To insulate themselves from Indian attacks, summering fishermen frequented offshore islands such as Damariscove near Boothbay Harbor, where as many as 150 vessels gathered at the height of the season. Later deforested and overgrazed by sheep, the island now lies bare and unused except by lobstermen who set their pots along its shores and sailors and motorboaters who, on fair summer days, anchor here for lunch breaks.

The fate of Damariscove suggests something of what happened all along the Maine coast during the eighteenth and nineteenth centuries, a period when exploitation was the rule and work the ethic. Industrious men—working through severe winters when waves break over the tops of hundred-foot islands in screaming gales, blanketed in fog one in every two days—spent two centuries depleting the region's resources. They severely reduced the populations of cod and herring and haddock, brought to a standstill the run of Atlantic salmon up the Penobscot River, caught and ate all but the oiliest-tasting birds. Once heavily wooded, each with a crown of spruce around its rock-strewn edge, the islands were denuded as the trees became the spars, boats, and houses that Captain Smith had foreseen; the evergreen forests were felled to make way for farms and pastures. At Hurricane Island, on Vinalhaven and elsewhere, men of the mid-Maine coast began to quarry granite and, in perilous (often fatal) voyages aboard overloaded coastal sloops or schooners, carry it to the growing ports of Boston and New York. By the turn of the twentieth century the offshore islands were left with little but their cobble beaches—even these in some places harvested to pave city streets—and the odd blueberry bush.

A recovery of sorts is in progress. Maine's fisheries remain troubled. But many of the islands today have become reforested, even overgrown, closer in appearance to five hundred than to a hundred years ago. On the mainland, summer camps and cottages dot the shoreline, and shorefront development threatens every place with a nice view. Merchants dependent on heavy summer trade have little interest in controls of any sort. But in a state that still values individualism, the conservationist spirit has grown as well, and the believers have become more powerful. Housing starts had doubled in southern Maine since 1980, and developers were casting eager eyes eastward along a coast that still had many wild stretches, when voters reacted in 1987 by approving, by a wide margin, a $35 million bond issue for public land acquisition.

Some long-absent species have returned to the Maine coast. On Matinicus Rock, a little lump of granite to seaward of the mouth of Penobscot Bay, the U.S. Fish and Wildlife Service and the National Audubon Society have mounted a sustained effort to restore several severely threatened bird species that were prevalent there five hundred years ago. One such is the arctic tern, a small if sometimes raucous seabird that during the nineteenth century suffered badly along the Maine coast because milliners prized its feathers. Traditionally, about half of all arctic terns in the United States nested on Matinicus Rock. Though lighthouse keepers protected these nesting grounds from human predators, they could do little to ward off attacks on the terns' eggs and chicks by more recently arrived swarms of powerful herring and black-backed gulls. In the fifty years between 1936 and 1986, the Matinicus colony declined from 3,000 to 774 pairs. But by poisoning a small number of the ubiquitous garbage-eating gulls, which have prospered in Maine as human activity has increased, conservationists have brought about a rapid turnaround for the terns. Between 1985 and 1986, the first season after the program began, the number of nesting terns and their chick production both showed dramatic increases.

The unlamented removal of the gulls has also been helpful to the razorbill, a species of auk that has traditionally roosted on Matinicus Rock, as well as to the Atlantic puffin. The puffin, a bright-billed little black-and-white bird that Champlain called the "perroquet," or sea parrot, though it is not related to any tropical species, once burrowed at many locations along the coast of eastern Maine. Though the razorbill and the puffin managed to avoid extinction (the fate of the larger and clumsier great auk in the Canadian Maritimes), they suffered greatly from human and animal predation. Down to a handful of breeding locations in Maine, the colorful puffin was reduced to a single breeding pair on Matinicus Rock before the comeback began.

The effort to save the puffins has come along well, and a major reason is the persistence of its director, Stephen Kress, a Cornell professor who since 1973 has been working at the task from his summer base at a popular Audubon Society camp on Hog Island in upper Muscongus Bay. From here Kress and his field staff fan out each May, carrying with them puffin chicks imported from Newfoundland, to deposit them on several carefully selected offshore islands for fledging. "It's a high-risk business," Kress told me when I visited Hog Island. "Most of the birds we raise we never see again. Our average return rate is twenty percent, and of these less than half breed. But from zero we've had as many as eighteen breeding pairs at Eastern Egg Rock. Seal Island was historically the largest puffin colony in the United States, and in 1984 we began to reestablish it. Matinicus Rock is back up to more than a hundred pairs."

The success Kress has enjoyed with the tern and puffin programs prompts him to think more broadly about how to bring about conservation in Maine. "We have established successful colonies," he said. "We have the techniques, we have the experience. I'd like to apply these skills to the job of managing species before they become endangered, not just when the whistle blows." He has started working with other kinds of birds—egrets, herons, the glossy ibis— at one location. He husbands the dream of employing terns and puffins, fitted with radio devices, to help manage the coast's dwindling fisheries: "The herring industry around here is in terrible shape. Most of the canneries are shut down because

Left: Philip Conkling of the Island Institute.
Right: Stephen Kress and Atlantic puffin.

foreign supplies are so much more reliable that domestic producers lose their shelf space in the markets. Still, the pressure on our inshore herring schools is tremendous. Every one has a spotter plane on it and a fleet of purse seiners in hot pursuit. Think of it—there are no quotas on these fish, only restrictions like exclusive breeding areas and net size limits. Somehow, we need to do a better job of managing these resources, and maybe there's a way that the puffins and terns can help. It's all part of the same problem, though. The fate of the fish and the seabirds depends on human values. That's why I'm so interested in environmental education, and in what we do at this camp we have here." As Kress spoke, a staff member announced the impending arrival of a new boatload of students from the mainland. "Maybe, sometime, all this will make a real difference," he said with a small sigh.

If Kress manifests a new spirit abroad in Maine, so too does the energy of a group called the Island Institute, whose concern is the welfare and balanced use of Maine's 3,000 islands, and its determined leader, Philip Conkling. En route to Camden the morning I picked up *Sanderling*, I paused in Rockland, the Institute's headquarters, to talk with Conkling. He was destined for law school after graduating from college in 1970. But his draft number came up and he opted for alternative service, ending up teaching in a Quaker settlement in a remote corner of the western U.S. mountains. The experience, he said, totally changed his life. Later he lived off the land in forest camps, walked the woods for the Southern Pacific Railroad, and in all respects became a convert to ecological soundness. Returning East, he enrolled in what was later to become the environmental sciences program at the Yale School of Forestry. Upon graduation he gravitated toward Maine. "I wondered what in the East was something like the West," he said. "I found there was only one choice."

Once in Maine, Conkling, then boatless, spent a summer inventorying a few islands under a contract with the Nature Conservancy. "I spent most of that summer waiting for rides," he said as we sat in his small office overlooking Rockland Harbor. "I hung around a lot of wharves and talked to a lot of people." Still single, he later took a job as a forester in the northern Maine woods, "where you worked hard from Monday to Friday, and everybody spoke French, and the major weekend activity was to get drunk and fight. If there had been two of us I could have stood it. But I was alone, and I had to get out." Beginning in the late 1970s Conkling was once again making inventories of Maine islands and trying to plan their future. While at this in 1982, he ran into Tom, a Bostonian Cabot, who was concerned about a neglected lighthouse way down east. With financial help from Cabot, the Island Institute was born. It first existed as a branch of Outward Bound, which maintains a training station on Hurricane Island off Vinalhaven, where Conkling had worked as a naturalist. Later it became an independent nonprofit organization with its own board of directors, staff, and diversified program.

While not ignoring the aspirations of the summer people who use and generally respect the islands, Conkling tries hardest to develop ways for people living on them year-round to make a decent living. "He hopes they won't all fall into the hands of people like us," said his father-in-law, Richard Morehouse, a Boston architect who summers in a remodeled hotel on Lane Island off the south end of Vinalhaven. Tirelessly patrolling the coast in a sturdy twin-engined outboard, Conkling counsels with island dwellers about grazing practices and livestock reintroductions (sheep, cattle, even a botched caribou effort), sustainable timbering, cottage agriculture, aquaculture, kelp. His staff will, for a small fee, perform for island owners services that range from simple resource inventories to comprehensive management plans. Then Conkling lobbies hard for implementation of the plans.

Can this work succeed in keeping the Maine islands—currently far more popular than at any time since concrete replaced granite and several key fisheries collapsed late in the nineteenth century—out of the clutches of the condo developers? Conkling does not know the answer. But he finds reason for some hope. "It's not an either/or situation," he said. "These islands are like boats. The Pleistocene glaciers receded and the waters rose and people came aboard them, and one way or another they stayed. Several factors are working in favor of their sticking around some more. For one thing, the resources of these islands have been underutilized for most of this century, so we have some capital accumulated. Second, you should never underestimate the robustness of the natural communities along here. And third, we're learning some pretty sophisticated management techniques."

A year later I met Conkling at Deli One on Portland's Exchange Street. It leads from the revitalized downtown, now featuring a handsome new art museum, toward the renovated wharf district. Here art galleries and boutiques and bars and restaurants have sprouted in what not many years ago was a seedy neighborhood. New condos extend out into the harbor along one pier. The waterfront seemed ripe for further development of this sort. But, said Conkling, a group called the Working Waterfront Coalition had recently won, by a surprising two-to-one margin, a local referendum banning residential construction along a major stretch of the city's shoreline. Though pleased at this outcome, then already under attack in the courts, Conkling was worried that the Coalition might have overstated the point in order to make it.

The Island Institute, he added, was currently trying to launch a new statewide Working Waterfront program. While most of Maine's working harbors are unlikely to be taken over by outsiders, he said, the danger lurked here and there; and the state's fishermen face other sorts of problems as well. In Burnt Coat Harbor on Swans Island, a lobsterman soon to retire sold off his dock to an off-islander on the condition that he and several other watermen could continue to have access to it. Soon after the sale had been completed, the new owner sheepishly phoned to say that, for insurance reasons, his lawyer had advised him not to let them use the dock after all: Through a land acquisition program, legal actions, and pressure to apply already existing regulatory controls, Conkling, in partnership with local fishermen, would seek to prevent such losses in working harbors along the coast. "People seem to like the idea," said Conkling. "But it's not easy to get it organized. On a nice day like this fishermen don't go to meetings even if they said they would. They're out on the water."

Summer people, not universally popular among fishermen or developers, have also done much to foster Maine's new conservation ethic. In the mid-nineteenth century the economy of Mount Desert Island had achieved a fever pitch. Settlers, largely Scottish and Irish, had begun methodically peeling the virgin trees away from the forests on the island's high hills; by 1870 they were all gone. Fisheries were well

Carvers Harbor on Vinalhaven Island: still a working port.

established and the island's three principal harbors all had flourishing fleets. Trade between the island and Boston and New York was growing fast; on clear days hundreds of commercial sailing vessels could be seen from a viewpoint on the island. Farmers cleared land to raise grain and potatoes. Sheep grazed and poultry pecked on the new open spaces. Soon after the Civil War, the delights of the island were also attracting a summer colony. First came the Bishop of Albany and Harvard's president, Charles W. Eliot, later to be joined by the banker J. P. Morgan and his fabled steam yacht *Corsair*, and still later by bevies of Rockefellers and others from New York, Boston, and Philadelphia. The summer colonies created a new service industry. Over the years, caring for the "cottages," their inhabitants, and their boats overtook farming, fishing, and tree harvesting to become the principal factor in the island's economy. As wider job opportunities lessened the pressure on the island's resources, the summer folk—with a stake in preserving rather than using them—began tugging in the other direction. Forest reserves and formal gardens were established. In 1926 the Rockefellers, having accumulated most of the undeveloped acreage on Mount Desert Island, turned it over to the federal government to form the basis of Acadia National Park.

In a sense the strategy backfired on them, for the amenities the summer elite created quickly began to attract a broad public. The results now include a gaudy motel strip just across the narrows in Ellsworth; overcrowding at campsites in Acadia National Park, now visited by four million people a year; hordes of summer pedestrians along the once hallowed streets of Bar Harbor, the island's principal town. No wine-sipping Harvard aesthetes these: their tastes run more to nachos, mozzarella sticks, Amaretto, and Kahlúa. But if their presence during the vacation season is bothersome to the summer old guard and an increasing number of year-round residents, they have been a bonanza to local businessmen, who vigorously oppose all measures to limit their access to the island. And on balance, not even a quick burst of summer gridlock can do much to dent the basic character and beauty of this grand island. The late historian Samuel Eliot Morison, who first visited Mount Desert in 1890 and published a breezy little history of the island seventy years later, offered therein this timeless conclusion about the matter:

> We who love this Island say that it can never be ruined while the tide ebbs and flows twice a day and an offshore wind turns the sea to an incredible blue, or the east wind brings wreaths of fog that clothe the coasts and hills in soft white. It can never be ruined while the Acadia National Park keeps up the trails; while the Northeast Harbor Fleet continues its good work of indoctrinating the rising generation in the arts of oar and sail. . . . Mount Desert is not merely an island; it is a way of life to which one becomes addicted; and if we are permitted in the hereafter to enter that abode where the just are made perfect, let us hope that it may have some resemblance to Champlain's Isle des Monts Deserts.

Without the stabilizing influence of the summer residents, on the other hand, Mount Desert might have become too degraded even for the rapt Morison. The effects of the preservationist spirit that flourishes there, moreover, are now being felt throughout the state. Mount Deserter Peggy (Mrs. David) Rockefeller has assumed the lead in a movement to maintain traditional values and safeguard the entire coast from unseemly development through promoting conservation easements and other tactics to preserve wildlands. The Maine Coast Heritage Trust, which she was instrumental in founding in 1970, has secured many key islands and headlands. Currently, the developers at its heels, the increasingly powerful Trust is focusing particular attention on the little-touched and beautiful "Bold Coast" at the state's eastern end; overall, it could claim as 1988 ended to have helped to arrange the permanent protection of "24,000 acres of important coastal property and 130 entire islands." One of Peggy Rockefeller's daughters, Margaret

Rockefeller Dulany, continued the family's tradition by leading a movement to repopulate the town of Frenchboro, on Long Island, by handing out free land to people stating good enough reasons to want to settle there.

SANDERLING ROUNDED OWLS HEAD and turned westward toward Muscongus Bay. We navigated carefully from buoy to buoy through the Muscle Ridge Channel. Along here, even in clear, calm daylight weather, mistaking one channel marker for another could quickly bring a boat to a crunchy halt on barely submerged rocks close by. While negotiating the buoys bound westward, I mourned our inability to sample the coastal wonders that we were leaving in our wake. Even if we were not to experience it aboard *Sanderling*, the unspoiled shore that lies between where we were and the Canadian border, 120 miles eastward as the crow flies, merits here a backward glance and a few tales from previous summers.

Astern already was Enchanted Island, a sprig forming part of a chain called Merchants Row at the south end of Deer Isle. Enchanted is not much to look at on the chart—a dot. Years ago, on a vacation cruise, Flo and I and our daughter Leslie anchored there at noon one quiet sunny day and ran the dinghy ashore. There, tucked between a V formed by granite ledges, we found an exquisite little beach made of tiny bits of shell ground down by swirling seas, and, above the high-water mark, a ten-yard stretch of real sand held in place by beach grass, and beyond, just in the woods, an abandoned lobsterman's wooden shack. We shrieked as we left warm air for 55-degree water, diving from the adjacent rocks, then sunning on the warm sand. As time passed, this eloquent little place, with its bold shore and deep woods and shell beach and tide pools, became a prime destination whenever we cruised nearby and weather allowed.

Schoodic Point, the first major headland east of Mount Desert, is where "down east" really begins. From here to Canada old values remain, though in recent years the beginnings of summer-tourist development have begun to offset both the previous purity and the severe deprivation occasioned by the decline of the sardine industry at Jonesport, Eastport, and Lubec. For years, every time we've passed the Schoodic landmark heading east on family cruises, we have made a ritual of reading aloud the stirring passage from the venerable Duncan & Blanchard (now Duncan & Ware) *Cruising Guide to the New England Coast* that warns of the bracing thrills ahead:

To be headed east by Schoodic whistle before a summer sou'wester with Mt. Desert fading astern and the lonely spike of Petit Manan light just visible on the port bow is about as close to perfection as a man can expect to come on this imperfect earth. Astern lie supermarkets, yacht clubs, water skiers, high-charged power cruisers, the pageantry associated with racing and day sailing. Ahead lie cold waters, racing tides, the probability of thick fogs and delightful scale-ups. . . . For the experienced navigator with a touch of the explorer, this country is the Promised Land, and for the "cricker" it is a happy hunting ground. The gregarious, the inexperienced navigators, and those who like to dress up and go ashore for dinner at the yacht club every evening will be happier west of Schoodic.

If you go, the authors continued,

be prepared to stay awhile. You may be fog-bound or wind-bound, but be sure that you will have to wait out tides. A tide setting against the wind on this coast can raise a dangerous sea in short order. To beat against a Fundy tide in a light breeze is a losing battle.

Back in the 1970s, during one of the many cruises we have undertaken with our friends the Walshes, we glimpsed the perils of this tricky coast. Powering through thick fog toward Great Wass Island on a windless afternoon, we wrapped a lobster-buoy line tight around our propeller shaft. The engine shuddered to a halt. Since we could not sail and would otherwise have drifted backward through the murk, toward myriad rocks and shoals, we had no choice but to tie together all the extra line we had—and anchor in 300 feet of water. Then we tried, with boat hook and knife, finally swimming to get a better look at its clenched grip, to pry loose the offending line. To no avail: we spent the night bobbing in the ocean. The next morning it cleared a little and a tiny breeze sneaked in from the southeast. It was enough to enable us to hoist sails, wrestle in the distant anchor, and ghost past Mistake Island light, and its bellowing horn, to the beautiful anchorage around the corner.

From there I rowed our dinghy three miles to the town at Beals Island, to summon a scuba diver to cut away the debris. Finding one, I returned to our anchorage with him in his fast boat, leaving three junior crew members, aged twelve and thirteen, to make the return trip in the dinghy. Soon after they cast off, thick fog shut in, obscuring all landmarks. With no compass aboard, and only their ears to guide them back toward the Mistake Island horn, three increasingly scared kids groped their way seaward. Aboard our chartered sailboat, now again operational after the professional made one quick dive and cut away the line and buoy with a sharp knife, I faced withering accusations of irresponsibility from the dinghy crew's parents—particularly my wife— as the afternoon waned and it began to grow dark. We tooted on the boat's foghorn and hoped for the best. Not soon enough, we heard a faint yell, then welcomed three tired and cold small oarspeople. They were no more relieved to be aboard than we were to have them back.

Late in the summer of 1988, Flo and I revisited the Bay of Fundy as guests of the seasoned Maine cruisers Beth and Don Straus aboard their rock-solid cutter *Sea Otter*. For a week refreshingly free of fog the four of us were able to glimpse the wild majesty that persists in the region. We saw right and humpback and finback and minke whales, and great flocks of white-sided dolphins, gray and harbor seals, gannets and shearwaters, razorbills and puffins and guillemots, graceful red phalaropes resting daintily on calm waters, great flocks of Wilson's storm petrels. A humpback swam right under our boat. We were only the fifth cruising boat of the summer to make it across to the tide-wracked harbor at Brier Island off the Nova Scotia coast, where in a recent winter northeaster two heavy cars parked on a strong high pier in the harbor were swept into the pounding sea. Now we had reached an end, a Nirvana. Would this, too, succumb to change?

In 1925, the town of Beals, which encompasses several islands, won independence from Jonesport, on the Maine mainland. Six hundred people lived in Beals. It had five boat shops to serve the lobstermen, its own school, and a manageable economy. Those unsupported by the island could cross Moosabec Reach to work at one of myriad sardine-packing plants lining the shore. Even though a bridge connecting Beals to the mainland was built in 1957, by the 1980s I expected to find this small archipelago in decline. Not so. The traditional wooden-boat industry has hung on despite heavy competition from large yards turning out fiberglass boats. Musseling, unheard of in Maine a decade ago and now the state's third-largest fishery, is particularly good along the coast near Beals. Whereas Jonesport's sardine plants are almost all defunct, Beals is doing rather well. A thousand-acre tract recently acquired by the Nature Conservancy safeguards Great Wass Island, scenically and biologically the most important of the group, from random shoreline construction. "Beals is like a Maine coastal community of twenty-five years ago," Conkling said. "The low bridge has kept most of the yacht traffic out of the Reach. That in turn has helped keep the area out of the eye of the development storm. But the old characters have held on pretty well, and the Conservancy program helps with ecological balance."

Conservation and development in action: the balance supported around here by many lobstermen as well as by the summer residents.

Is Beals a model for other places way down east, with its fearsome swirling currents and thick fogs, twenty-foot tides and subarctic vegetation? Maybe so, but the food stamp remains a common currency at nearby towns such as Lubec and Eastport, whose economies vanished with the collapse of the sardine-packing industry. Other fisheries are in trouble too, partly because of foreign competition, partly because of overharvesting inshore, partly perhaps just because fish just come and go with their own rhythm. Even the lobster, Maine's very symbol, may be in trouble. For more than a decade, the total catch has remained steady at between eighteen and twenty million pounds a year. But the number of pots set out to achieve this catch has doubled as prices have risen, and the average lobster caught is younger and smaller than ever despite regulatory limits. According to one recent report, 90 percent of them are caught and eaten before they have a chance to reproduce.

In reaction to the mounting competition and new evidence of environmental degradation, Maine showed new concern, new approaches, new technologies. In the picture-postcard village of Cutler, near the Canadian border, researchers had initial success in "farming" captive lobsters by using, in part, a less cannibalistic species than the highly aggressive Maine natives. At Tenants Harbor, near Penobscot Bay, a businessman named Chip Davidson and several associates took the mussel industry in a similar direction. One Saturday morning during the summer of 1986, a T-shirted young foreman named Scott, in charge of things at Davidson's Great Eastern packing plant, talked about how this farming operation works in spite of the algal blooms called red tides that have begun to affect Maine as well as many other Atlantic shellfish areas. "The red tides have contaminated shellfish in some places," Scott explained. "But we place our seed mussel in enough different lease areas so we can avoid the problem at any particular time, and when the tides go away the mussels flush themselves clean. The state monitors for the tide. They use mice the way miners used canaries in tunnels. They inject the mice with extract from the mussels. If the mice die in sixty seconds or less, they know the mussels came from a red-tide area. Our mussels are placed carefully in areas where there's plenty of food available for them, and we help them grow fast by keeping them constantly below the waterline. Our mussels reach market size in only a year to a year and a half, as opposed to seven years for wild mussels. Their pearls are smaller, and the amount of meat per mussel is higher. After we pick them up from our lease sites, we truck them in here. They spend one night in a purge tank, where they clean out the grit inside them. Then we pack and ship—to as far away as Alaska and San Francisco. Our business has been growing pretty well. Chip started it in 1978. When I came here we were doing four hundred bushels a week. Now we're doing two thousand a week almost all year. It's a great business."

Sanderling now motored past Kress's Eastern Egg Rock, where several months before we had been rewarded by the sight of a pair of puffins, surprisingly long-legged, standing together on a windward perch and looking out to sea. Off Pemaquid a southwest breeze finally filled in and we had our first crack at the boat under sail, killing the quiet diesel and unfurling the mainsail and the big jib. Tranquilly under this rig, adding engine power when the fickle breeze faltered, we ran well to seaward of cluttered Casco Bay, where a beach called Popham is the sole reminder of the lost colony; an ugly power plant emits a stream of black smoke; and the urban skyline of Portland juts as a surprise from the soft green hills of Cape Elizabeth. The sprightly waterfront provides evidence of the renaissance that is in progress in Portland, where high technology and young professionals are replacing traditional activities. Here too there is enthusiasm for conservation: the outsiders came to Maine because it was different, and they do not want it to become more like every other place. Here one also finds warning signals of growing pollution. Inadequately treated sewage flowing from the city of Portland has long since compelled health authorities to close a large portion of Casco Bay to shellfishing. Dangerous concentrations of dissolved heavy metals and toxic organic chemicals were recently discovered. Local industries had dumped them into the water. Portland's new breed faces a mounting challenge if the nearby coast is to be kept clean.

Just west of Cape Elizabeth, we passed a graceful 300-acre island called Richmond, which Champlain had christened the "Isle of Bacchus" in honor of its "many vineyards bearing beautiful grapes." In its bay, called Saco, and along the banks of the river of the same name, Champlain found his first evidence of agriculture. Here he also discovered a solid dugout Indian canoe—the first he found not formed of birchbark. Though rocky coast would continue ahead—the spartan offshore Isles of Shoals and rugged Cape Ann standing as reminders of what Maine's shoreline is really like—we were now entering a new world of sand beaches and salt marshes, warmer waters, far more people.

Our last morning in Maine dawned clear, with a light southerly wind dead against us. Once out of our anchorage in Wood Island Harbor, we set a loran course direct for Provincetown at the outer tip of Cape Cod, 194 degrees magnetic, eighty-five long miles away. Now we were in a region of which William Wood had written, in his 1634 *New England's Prospect*, lurid descriptions of wildlife: black bears "which be most fierce in strawberry time," great quantities of moose a mere forty miles northeast of Massachusetts Bay, swimming geese being successfully stalked by wildcats, and so many wolves that "there is little hope of their utter destruction, the country being so spacious and they so numerous." These, Wood concluded, represented "the greatest inconveniency the country hath." Around us now was, for modern times, an equally impressive array of animal life: a seal as we left the harbor, several small whales, pelagic birds, including the shearwater and again the Wilson's storm petrel, an ingratiating little swallowlike creature that flits low among the waves, seeming almost to land feet-first upon the water as it feeds from the surface. Late on this mid-September morning a hummingbird, headed south, drilled straight past us.

Years ago Flo and I attended a wedding reception on a foggy summer Saturday afternoon at a big old beachfront house near Kennebunkport. The groom's grandmother, a Midwesterner, shivered in the damp. "This is a cold and rockbound coast," she said. "And you know what?"

"What?" we dutifully asked.

"They love it this way," she said.

2

~

Troubled Cape, Islands in Danger

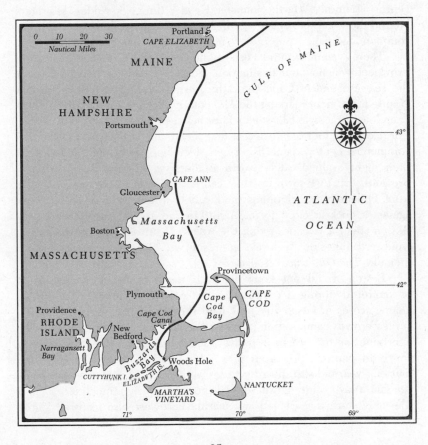

ON A CLEAR MORNING IN MASSACHUSETTS BAY, THE GLASS TOWERS OF Boston crackle sunlight reflections back to sea. A parade of passenger jets descends overhead toward Logan Airport. *Sanderling* is little removed from life ashore. Yet on this standard crossing, from Cape Ann off Gloucester to the inner elbow of Cape Cod, a sailor will seldom fail to see pelagic birds, humpback and other whales, and further evidence of abundant marine life. Working fishermen, their nets or trawls deployed, move slowly to and fro. Passenger vessels equipped for the new sport of whale-watching track their quarry with sonar gear. Oceangoing tankers and container carriers thrum along the sea lanes to or from poison-laden Boston Harbor, an infamous area at last now undergoing the beginnings of a belated cleanup. Along the North and South Shores, fanning out from Boston, are pretty beaches, inlets and rivers. Badly polluted streams flow from the coastal communities into the bay, often past remnants of salt marshes once lovingly painted by the nineteenth-century Luminist Martin Johnson Heade; the toxic-ridden seawaters around these harbors encourage liver cancer in local flounder and other common food fish.

There is similar contrast ashore, nowhere clearer than at the port of Provincetown, now our destination. Tucked under the hooked beak at the seaward end of Cape Cod, the town is dominated by a 348-foot granite monument marking the *Mayflower* Pilgrims' first landfall, which in architectural style falls somewhere between Moorish and West Point. For close to four centuries it has been an important fishing and commercial center. Tuna fishermen sleep here between trips to hunt their highly valued catch, worth as much as $10,000 per fish. On a previous visit to P-town, as they call it, I saw an elaborate quahogger from Philadelphia, all pumps and rubber tubes, still busily at work against a dock at close to midnight. In the 1930s, the writer Henry Beston spent a year observing the Atlantic from a shack on the empty windward dunes not far away; the result was his ageless natural-history memoir, *The Outermost House*.

Beston would not know what to make of the Provincetown I encountered during a cruise in 1986. Along its Commercial Street, among scores of kitsch and junk-food shops and bars and restaurants, surged crowds composed in part of solid New England burghers out for a fortnight on the beach, in part of vacationing or resident gays of both sexes, in part of spaced-out kids. "My mother sucks," snorted one fourteen-year-old skateboarder to his punk friends. A glassy-eyed teen-age girl weaved through the crowd propped up by a much older man. The only store that carried any marine hardware also featured ample

Bartholomew Gosnold, as portrayed on figurehead
of whaling ship, dated c. 1832.

stocks of German Army greatcoats, Rambo mess kits, and other paramilitary paraphernalia. In a candlelit restaurant, I feasted on salty raw oysters from nearby Wellfleet (the British explorer Bartholomew Gosnold had enjoyed them here in 1602, and Champlain in 1606 had found them plentiful and "of good quality"). It was the visit's sole redeeming feature.

Under power and dead into the wind, *Sanderling* bored across the bay toward this tawdry terminus. By midday the breeze began to pick up and our speed began to slow—from six and a half to five, then to four knots and below as our bow crunched into the crests. Neither John nor Caroline, though Cape dwellers, had seen Provincetown; both were quietly anxious to get there. But it was becoming evident that we could not make it until late evening. With the going ever less comfortable, we decided to abandon the idea. We killed the engine, raised the sails, and slanted off on port tack toward Scituate. Thus passed the afternoon. At sundown we decided not to stop anywhere, but to continue through the night to catch a favorable early-morning current at the Cape Cod Canal. Navigating with the aid of our wonderful loran, we pointed westward into a mauve sunset. Bouncing around in the galley, I cooked chicken with wine and mushrooms on the three-burner bottled-gas stove. The night turned bright and starry; after the half-moon set, the tightly bunched

Pleiades showed distinctly overhead. John and Bill stood the midnight to 4 A.M. watch, guiding us surely toward the canal entrance while Caroline and I tried to catnap.

Soon after dawn we were in the canal and barely more than an hour later out the other end of it, slamming into high steep waves from shallow Buzzards Bay, now pushed hard against the rapid current by a rising wind gusting to over 30 knots. We worked our way slowly, pitching violently, out toward Cleveland Ledge, where the bay opens a little and we could release some sail and slide off on a tack. The radio began issuing gale warnings. Even in choppy Buzzards Bay, we were able to make a decent speed of four to five knots under these conditions; with both sails rolled in about halfway, this simple rig's equivalent of a couple of reefs, the lee rail remained out of the water and only an occasional fling of spray made it past the dodger to drench the exposed person at the wheel.

"You're not going out in this shit?" a young and hardy-looking lobsterman had asked us on a similar morning earlier in the summer. But here we were, and somehow it did not seem all that bad. Small ternlike gulls now replaced the hunkering great black-backed gulls that predominate in Massachusetts Bay and eastward. Common terns reappeared as well, and as we approached Naushon and Nashawena, along the undeveloped chain called the Elizabeth Islands, we found hundreds of swallows riding the tail wind across the bay to the mainland. One veered to inspect us briefly, then turned back downwind and sailed off.

Abeam to port was the current-scoured little harbor of Woods Hole, home for its well-known Oceanographic Institute and several other scientific institutions, including the Woods Hole Research Center headed by John and Caroline's father, George Woodwell, a prominent scientist who is gravely concerned about such planetary threats as ozone depletion and global warming. We flirted with the idea of stopping at the Woodwells' house, a short walk up from the Little Harbor with its Coast Guard station, for breakfast and a hot shower and a good talk about the lamentable state of things. With the wind as strong as it was, I reluctantly decided against venturing into a current of almost six knots in the narrows, where many a seasoned skipper has ended up on the rocks in the best of weather.

A few months before, I had spent several days in the Hole talking to George and other resident scientists about conditions around "the Cape and the Islands," as the region is known. You'd think that such people would be most concerned about marine resources, and indeed they were. But at the Woods Hole Oceanographic Institute, Dr. Judith Capuzzo, a red-haired newlywed marine biologist, also had real estate issues on her mind. The entire Cape, even the most protected enclaves such as Chatham, has suffered from a population and construction explosion in recent years. The "values" have taken off. "It's gotten so that some scientists have turned down jobs at WHOI simply because they can't afford to live around here," Capuzzo told me. "But the problem goes way beyond economics. The fragility of our groundwater is a much more serious matter here than pollution along the coast, even though the public still thinks that the coastal situation is far more severe. There's been too much construction, period, and there's also been far too much shoddy construction with leaky septic tanks and the like."

The fastest-growing area anywhere in New England, its population rising at six times the national average, the Cape is dotted with former villages that have become instantly suburbanized. Retirees have swelled the previously small numbers of year-round residents, summer residents, and visitors. In the absence of strong zoning restrictions, real estate speculators have swooped down, creating shopping centers and traffic jams and many construction jobs—and also, according to a Washington *Post* report, wreaking havoc upon a delicate environment: "More than 15,000 wells have been dug into a single groundwater aquifer that is vulnerable to commercial and residential pollutants seeping through the sandy, porous soil. About 500 acres of shellfish beds have been shut down because of pollution."

By mid-1988 the situation had deteriorated to the point where former Senator Paul Tsongas, appointed by Governor Michael Dukakis as head of a state commission to advise him on the management of environmental affairs, felt the need to take action. Owner of a house in Chatham, Tsongas slipped into his commission's preliminary report a recommendation for a year-long moratorium on Cape development to gain time for comprehensive planning. Joseph Polcaro, head of the Massachusetts Home Builders Association, predictably called the suggestion "so absurd that it defies description." But polls conducted by the Boston *Globe* and the Cape Cod *Times* showed large voter majorities in favor of the ban; Tsongas called the result "a classic case of the troops being way ahead of the generals," and successfully pressed to get the issue onto the ballot for Cape voters in November. At the voting machines the Cape troops overwhelmingly supported the idea of a moratorium and also the concept of a regional commission with regulatory power over development. Though both resolutions required passage by the state legislature, which in the face of heavy opposition from real estate and construction interests would doubtless be more difficult to achieve, it was a major victory for coastal environmentalists.

Woodwell, a blunt and deeply thoughtful man who served for several years as the World Wildlife Fund's chairman, talked land use during the course of an overnight sail that we had taken several months before, with John aboard as well, from Woods Hole to Nantucket and back. About the Cape, George is so concerned that he planned to do a study of the region with Ian McHarg, author of a fine and influential book called *Design with Nature*. As for the beautiful Elizabeth Islands, which had impressed Gosnold in 1602 and are still mostly controlled by a single family from Boston, Woodwell had found evidence of overgrazing so severe that on one island, even though the sheep are long since gone, the native grass is still not able to regain a foothold.

Nowhere did Woodwell discover more signs of environmental misuse than on the old whaling and farming island of Nantucket. After we had wedged ourselves into the large but boat-cluttered harbor and paid an intimidating twenty-five dollars for the use of a mooring overnight, we settled into the cockpit. Over drinks we talked of this place as we gazed at the pachydermlike line of large power yachts tied up at the marina. "Once there were forty thousand people out here and they had real farms," George said. "Then they cut down every tree on the island. Then along came some summer people and the tourist trade. Walter Beinecke bought the waterfront and that hurt the island's fishing industry, which once was almost as important as New Bedford's or Gloucester's. Now the natives can hardly afford to live here anymore."

Ashore on Nantucket, it is not hard to find support for George's gloom. Near the busy airport, where commercial and corporate jets operate with piercing regularity, now stands a 300-room hotel and convention center anchoring a "commercial strip" whose other end is downtown. Not far away, a sad relic of older values: a dormant set of large windmills erected some years ago to harness the island's 13-mph-average wind and convert it to electricity. Now the land is more prized for "development" than for the price of the power the mills could generate for sale; and Nantucket is thus doomed to depend on imported hydro-carbons for its energy. Downtown: the harbor, into which five hundred boats had squeezed; the hordes of sightseers who step down from the Woods Hole and Hyannis steamers to comb the cobbled streets, visit the handsome old whaling captains' houses, shop, wobble off onto narrow roadways aboard rented bicycles and mopeds, and eat fresh bluefish and bay scallops and chowder. Nantucketers scorn this crowd: they arrive with a dirty shirt and a five-dollar bill and don't change either while they're on-island, the saying goes. "Don't even THINK of parking here," read a sign on an entryway, blocked by a parked car, just off Main Street. Summer houses have multiplied out beyond town on the moors, whose pristine beauty is marred by tarred roads and rooflines that jut awkwardly despite rigid building codes. Demand continues to be heavy even

A swarm of tourists on Nantucket.

though prices have soared to remarkably high levels: $175,000 for a simple "starter house," a couple of million for a simple three-bedroom dwelling on prime waterfront land, a stunning median market value of $413,000 according to a 1988 report. On one recent visit, at the height of the August vacation crush, I was pursued by a riderless moped as I drove through town.

Will Nantucket become yet another victim of speculative fever? Perhaps not. The positive side of the story centers on Beinecke, the S&H Green Stamps mogul who terrified many islanders—as well as Woodwell—when early in the 1970s he bought up most of the old downtown area and began to do it over. Eventually, his Sherburne Associates came to own two hotels, eighty-two retail stores, an entire marina with cottages on the wharf, and four restaurants. "No Man Is an Island," read the bumper stickers at the time; shopkeepers complained bitterly about the Beinecke group's unprecedented practice of asking them for a share of revenues as well as stiff monthly rental charges. Still today, some old-guard Nantucketers disparage him as a "damn fool" or worse. According to others, Beinecke turned out to be as much concerned about quality as about financial return. "He worried about it right down to the last doorknob," recalled a New Yorker whose family is a bedrock member of the summer community. "I'm a supporter of the Beinecke idea, and have been from just about Day One." The marina-restaurant-hotel-shopping area that he created did indeed push the fishing sector into a corner: today it is served by a single rickety-looking pier a long walk from downtown. But the new complex that Beinecke brought into being turned out to be a tasteful alternative to what would probably have emerged from a less tightly controlled mode of downtown renovation. The carefully cooked food at the Straight Wharf Restaurant, if expensive (no nachos here), is worth it, and the quality of the merchandise in the Beinecke-controlled stores along cobbled Main Street is first-class. The appeal of shopping downtown, where Beinecke had installed many shops as well as an A&P supermarket, helped to inhibit the growth of random satellite commerce beside the relatively unspoiled roadways leading to outer villages and beaches.

Evidence of Beinecke's success is that when he sold most of his Nantucket holdings in 1986 to a group called First Winthrop Corporation for $55,750,000, doomsayers began once again to warn of the island's demise or, at least, the replacement of the now revered downtown A&P with teddy-bear and cotton-candy stores. Whatever becomes of downtown, the rest of the island is now far better able to withstand the onslaught of disorderly development than it was a quarter-century ago. At that time an old hand named Ripley Nelson, in partnership with the late Roy Larsen, once chairman of Time Inc. and an unusually enlightened businessman, founded the Nantucket Conservation Foundation as a private organization "to preserve and protect for the public, places of natural and historic significance on Nantucket."

Early on, independent-minded Nantucket Yankees were suspicious of this project. It was dominated by summer people, who, notwithstanding their high-minded rhetoric, might at bottom have wanted to inhibit the island's development primarily for self-serving reasons. It involved requests that local residents, fully dependent on the island's economic well-being, do the unthinkable: share or surrender power and even land. But the Foundation today not only owns and manages 20 percent of all the land on the island; it and its values have also become part of the community. In the island's town meetings, where decisions affecting everybody are made by a committee of the whole, a number of conservation measures have been approved in recent years. Most notable was the creation, in 1984, of a land bank, supported by a 2 percent levy on certain real estate transactions, from which, alas, Beinecke has been largely exempt. Though accused in some quarters of being less than fully cost-effective, the land bank in its first three years generated $10.9 million and acquired 761 acres of land for conservation.

The town also created a Conservation Commission, which in 1987 produced the first comprehensive wetlands management plan ever drawn up for Nantucket. On the private side, Nantucket conservation and historic preservation groups were springing up like mushrooms on a wet night. "No Moor Development," read one recent bumper sticker promoting a group that specializes in saving the island's remaining heathland. Among Nantucketers "affordable housing" understandably became a buzzword; several new laws and rules address the issue.

If these are powerful and well-supported new forces for conservation, the question remains whether they will be adequate for Nantucket to withstand the remorseless pressure of soaring property values and high-octane real estate interests, and grow in an orderly way. Many people who are interested in conservation say no. "The Foundation has gotten too set in its ways," said one summer resident whose family arrived on the island in 1907. "They just haven't been aggressive enough. Now it's too late." Margot Larsen, Roy's widow, has given up on the village of Siasconset, a hub of the summer community since the 1870s, because "I just can't stand the noise of the big trucks." Jim Lentowski, an articulate man of just over forty who has directed the Nantucket Conservation Foundation for close to two decades, fears that changes in the tax law will drastically reduce his ability to generate land donations. "You used to be able to give just for tax reasons," he says. "But now that you have to *pay* tax to give away appreciated land, it's got to be from the heart. We may be nearing the end of what the Foundation can do as a land bank, and the time when we have to undergo a major reorientation of its mission and programs."

Lentowski offered further explanations for his gloom in his well-appointed office, a former golf clubhouse that several years ago was towed out to its present site on the edge of the moors. "What's spoiling Nantucket is its convenience," he said. "It used to be harder to get here, with the fog and poor airline service, and we had a different kind of summer crowd. Now the planes come much more regularly, even though people still complain if they are half an hour late, and many people come in their own corporate planes as well. For the past five years or so, we've been the Palm Beach of the Northeast. There's been sort of a revolution here. The new people bring their decorators and their Fifth Avenue values along with them, and it doesn't matter to them what it was like before. The Texan who arrived yesterday and paid two million dollars for a place down on Hulbert Avenue thinks it's just great the way it is." The current rate of construction, Lentowski added, is about 300 houses a year—ample to keep all the island's electricians and carpenters earning $30,000 to $50,000 a year. With some 7,000 lots left to build on, according to the Planning Commission, a straight-line projection would have Nouveau Nantucket's development ending abruptly in 2010 or so. But as long as the island can maintain its water supply and dispose of its garbage and sewage and generate enough electricity, Lentowski thought that the development will continue indefinitely. "Those are all problems that technology can and probably will deal with." He sighed. "And as long as they get solved, I just see no end to what's going on. After they run out of horizontal space, they may even start going up."

Miami Beach on Nantucket Sound? Lentowski may be right. The last evening I was there, though, I sat on a porch facing the harbor entrance as wisps of fog blowing in from the southwest began to cloud what had been a brilliant blue day. We looked out at a magnificent parade of wooden sailboats streaming into the harbor to participate in the annual Opera House race, scheduled for the next day. We ate clams freshly raked, at low tide earlier in the day, from the flats only a few yards from where we sat. Across the harbor we could see the pristine barrier island of Coatue, wholly acquired long ago for conservation. We talked of the island's rich history, as well as of the leopard-skin hot pants observed at a recent art gallery opening. Just after dark we drove into town for dinner, and found a parking place right on Main Street. For all the pressure on it, the place still felt pretty good; the best guess about this splendid and busy island's future may just be a waffle. "The bottom line," my New York friend said, "is that it's always damn hard to get to the truth when you're talking about Nantucket."

Summer people have become at least a factor in the politics of Nantucket and its neighbor island of Martha's Vineyard. Not so, except peripherally, at the fishing port of New Bedford, which dominates the mainland, or western, shore of Buzzards Bay. One of the few Portuguese-speaking enclaves anywhere in the United States, New Bedford is all business—and business was pretty bad there for a while. But something of a recovery has come about with an unprecedented new demand for fish and higher prices. My logbook says this:

> At the foot of Union Street, at Pier 3, the Portuguese tall ship *Sagres* was tied up and attracting a vigorous tourist trade, largely from the substantial local Portuguese population. On Union Street itself, though most stores are closed Wednesday afternoons (golf day for shopkeepers as well as doctors?), tourists were still

plentiful at art galleries, restaurants, and the Whaling Museum. One street has been closed for a mall, sculptures adorn the entryways of several buildings. Overall New Bedford seemed sprightlier than a few years ago, without having succumbed to quiche-and-spinach-salad tourist conformity.

Part of the reason is that this remains also a bustling fishing capital traditionally ranking number one in the nation in the value of its commercial fishery landings. The local fleet, a veteran fisherman told me, has grown from 150 vessels twenty years ago to 350 today. "That's just too many," he said. "They're all trying to cash in." Many offices downtown bear signs saying "Marine Attorneys" and "Boat Financing and Settlements." Each morning an auction is held at which the catches brought in are purchased by one or another of the packinghouses lined up along one pier. By early afternoon, when I visited, work was proceeding on many boats: welding of broken links on the big chain nets that scallopers use to drag the bottom, engine repairs, fixing rope nets. The boats varied considerably in size and quality—from a forty-five-year-old, wooden-hulled 60-footer to a bright blue steel oceangoing vessel called the *Impulse* that had cost her owner $800,000.

José Pedro, the white-haired captain of the older vessel, explained the comparative advantages. "A big boat like that can take the weather, and we have some terrible weather around here. It can come and nip you quick, and you've got to be damn careful. But a big boat also costs a lot to operate and you need a big crew. On my boat I can go down to a crew of two when the fishing is bad, or I can just stay home without it costing me much." When they can, the scallopers and the draggers embark on seven- to ten-day voyages out to the great fishing grounds at Georges Bank, recently the subject of a U.S.-Canadian dispute and a World Court ruling partitioning the region. Japanese and European factory ships also appear there, and when they show up, said José Pedro, "they sweep the bottom clean." Though other fishermen on the pier talked of the "good money" they were making despite the fierce competition, José Pedro had gloomier thoughts: "The golden days are over in this business. They're trying to tighten up on the controls now. They have to—the government has a big stake in this business because of the subsidies they've put into the boats. But they've locked the barn door too late. There's hardly any fish left." A local merchant working the piers felt the same way. "Ain't one of these men who wouldn't sell you their boat if you wanted to buy it," he said.

New Bedford hardly seemed a dying town later in the afternoon when the *Sagres* departed. A large and cheery crowd of local folk had come out to the head of the pier to wave goodbye, and several

Portuguese-owned yachts (as well as one spotless tug) hovered about the tall ship as she moved slowly away from the pier. Her crew swarmed aloft to pay a ceremonial farewell, and cheers came from the shore. "Those fellas had some good time in here," said one observer. "And we had a good time with 'em."

A good time—that's the problem, as the conservationists see it. Too much of an effort to cash in, not enough attention to the rules of the game, not enough to environmental degradation. Here is an area whose rivers and streams are so toxic that even the blue mussel and as stubborn a survivor as the blue crab have trouble getting along. For years toxic chemicals called PCBs—polychlorinated biphenyls that harm livers and other organs, may cause cancer, and are not biodegradable—have been slowly leaking into the harbor from nearby landfills. Substantial quantities were already entrenched there from as long ago as the 1950s, when one electric equipment manufacturer dumped PCB-laden transformers directly into the drink. The most intensely studied marine ecosystem anywhere along the U.S. Atlantic coast, New Bedford has the dubious distinction of having been targeted as a site for the Environmental Protection Agency's Superfund cleanup program. Inshore fisheries are in constant danger of being overharvested even though foreigners are welcome within them only if they have special permission from state authorities.

Around New Bedford, to hear Judy Capuzzo tell it, things are always on the edge: "It's very complex. Many of the stocks have become very depleted from overharvesting, but in some respects things are getting a little better. The state is slowly getting the power away from the lobbying groups. There are some encouraging signs on small cod and flounder, and even the haddock, which was almost extinct, is just now starting back. It's harder to control things beyond the three-mile limit. But we do have an inshore management plan, and we do have our legal minimum sizes so that the fish have a chance to reach sexual maturity before they are harvested. The problem is people. Legally you can't deny someone the right to enter the fishery, and there are all sorts of conflicts among the various types of fishermen. A particular size of net means something entirely different from one to the next. Sometimes the meetings I attend—I'm a member of the State Fisheries Commission—just go on and on without ever getting anywhere. Most of the fishermen aren't thinking about sustainable use. They're thinking about making the next payment on the boat. And sometimes it gets very frustrating. Someone will propose an increase in the legal minimum. Then a fisherman will

A scientist examines New Bedford harbor pollution close up.

start crying that his family will starve if we do that. Then you'll see him driving away in his BMW."

Much of the current discussion centers on domestic and international regulations and agreements. In the 1970s, New England fishermen were being badly hurt by fast-growing competition from the mammoth foreign-owned fishing and processing ships that haunted U.S. shores. The U.S. reaction was the passage of the Magnuson Act, which established a 200-mile limit for fishing or processing activity by foreigners not allowed to operate closer by international agreements or exceptions that the law provides. It came at a moment when the popularity of fresh fish, low in cholesterol, was on a rapid upswing in U.S. households. Prices were rising, and fishermen long frustrated by foreign competition made big investments to cash in on the bonanza. Before long, said Philip Coates of the Massachusetts Division of Marine Fisheries, "the market had reached the breaking point in terms of price elasticity," and U.S. producer prices were being undercut by fresh-fish imports from as far away as Iceland. Beyond the 200-mile limit, where some ventured, conditions also remained uneasy. To protect their rights on the Grand Banks, in 1987 the Canadians announced that their fishing vessels would be armed with machine guns.

I asked Coates if, later on, things had calmed down out on the Banks. "Far from it," he said.

Such are the hazards of life around Massachusetts Bay and the Cape and the Islands, from blighted P-town to bustling Nantucket to resurgent, almost irrevocably polluted New Bedford. Maybe it was that roaring southwester and our inability to stop at the anchorages I fondly remembered from years back: Hadleys Harbor and Tarpaulin Cove and Quicks Hole along the Elizabeth chain all have their own charm and clean water. This time I was just as glad to be moving along.

3

Blight Around the Bight

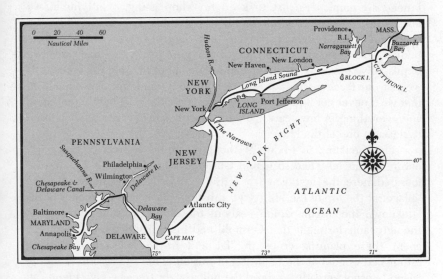

SANDERLING SLOGGED DOWN BUZZARDS BAY, POUNDING INTO STEEP little seas. We tacked first toward the Elizabeth Islands, then back toward the New Bedford side, making little westward progress. By early afternoon I was ready to call it a day and proposed to my soggy, tired, ever-willing crew that we await better weather at Cuttyhunk, western-most of the Elizabeths. All hands enthusiastically agreed. By 3:30 P.M. we were tied to a mooring in the snug basin, protected from the gusty southerly by the high bluff rising above the little village. Here, where boat gridlock is a daily occurrence during the summer season, only a handful of pleasure craft were now in evidence. The fuel dock and the places selling ice and lobsters to the summer transients were battened down tight. It reminded me of Juan-les-Pins on the Côte d'Azur when years ago my family and I arrived there for our vacation in mid-September, soon after all the French had gone home. In town, our first morning there, we saw little but iron grates slamming down. We had a wonderful time.

Ashore at Cuttyhunk the restaurants and bakeries were as abandoned as the fuel dock, and only a few townspeople were about on the single significant street. A small food market remained open. Its pale-faced young proprietress was pleased not only to sell us supplies but also to pass along her views about life on the island: "In the winter there are about thirty people here. During the summer the population goes up to about six hundred ashore, and out there in the harbor—well, look at that postcard, it's like that every day. Too many people, if you ask me. I need six employees just to keep my shop going." Cuttyhunk, we learned, offers various public-sector jobs such as garbageman ($4,000 a year) and primary-school teacher—the largest item on the village budget, even though at the time of our visit the school had only two pupils. "I've never heard anyone complain about it," said the grocer. "If we lost our teacher we'd lose our school, and you know as well as I do that we'd never get it back. And we have a good school here, computers and everything. A few years ago one of our teachers correctly diagnosed dyslexia in one of the kids."

Phil Conkling in Maine, I thought, would appreciate the gritty nature of this talk, and so would Gosnold, who during his 1602 cruise founded here the first English settlement in North America. In the village, at the top of the hill, is a tombstone marking the remains of his "unknown Indian companion"—about the only remaining evidence of the agreeable fortnight that Gosnold and his thirty-two crew members spent there planting crops in "fat and lusty" soil and expressing astonished wonder at the bountiful profusion of life and resources on the island. Gosnold greatly admired the tall straight trees he saw, found "all sorts of fowl, much bigger than ours," and "divers sorts of shellfish, as scollops, muscles, cockles, lobsters, crabs, oysters and wilks, exceedingly good and very great." If the captain admired the island's land, "in comparison whereof the most fertile part of England is but barren," he was equally struck by the "wholesomeness and temperature" of the climate and found the Indians he encountered to be "of a perfect constitution of body, active, strong, healthful and very witty."

Of all the early European explorers, only Captain John Smith would later write as rapturously of the joys of life along the New England coast. Gosnold's frustration must have been intense when shipmates insisted that they abandon Cuttyhunk in July to return to England and sell sassafras and other commodities that they had collected. Gosnold would have been disheartened too at the deforestation, which by 1858, according to one report, was total—not a stump to be found—and at the degree to which the island's other resources had been overused. But he would have admired that gritty shopkeeper, one supposes, and he would have enjoyed the Belon oysters, native to Brittany, that are raised around Cuttyhunk for local consumption and delivery to one principal off-island customer: the superb oyster house in Manhattan's Grand Central Station. According to a recent Coast Alliance study, "hardly a coastal town" in New England is safe from the threat of toxic pollution to its fish and shellfish populations, and visiting the seafood store is "a game of Russian roulette." By this standard Cuttyhunk still seemed a good bet.

For two days the southerly blew hard, sending low clouds racing across Cuttyhunk and reminding us of suggestions that this island served Shakespeare as the model for *The Tempest*. By late the second afternoon, the wind started to shift toward the west, indicating clearing and a frontal passage; flashes of blue began flecking the sky. The coming northwester would send us blasting down Block Island Sound, we figured, and if we left early in the evening we should catch the last minutes of a favorable current through the swift-flowing tidal bottleneck, called the Race, that marks the entrance to Long Island Sound. So we tossed down our Belons and the rest of our dinner, weighed anchor, and cleared the shoals around Cuttyhunk just as dark fell.

Ahead now was Rhode Island, most of whose population lives within five miles of the shore and where, at a recent conference, the governor referred to environmental protection as "a way of life." Narragansett Bay, the state's keystone, remains plagued by pollution problems of the usual sorts. Next to heavy industry, highway runoff containing large quantities of lead from gasoline is a principal contributor of toxic substances to this body of water, where hundreds of tongers, working full-time and year-round from small boats near shore, harvest one-quarter of all the littleneck, cherrystone, and quahog clams the nation consumes. Along one stretch of the bay's shore, according to one recent study, 20 percent of the toxic pollution came from a single source: Interstate Highway 95. On the order of 700,000 pounds of toxic metals—enough copper to run a wire from New York to Los Angeles, enough nickel to manufacture 60 million five-cent pieces—are being dumped into the Narragansett each year. Not surprisingly, three-quarters of all Rhode Islanders sampled in

Trudy Coxe of Save the Bay.

a recent poll felt that the bay's pollution is one of the most important issues facing the little state.

Many of them support a fast-growing organization called Save the Bay, well led by the forceful Trudy Coxe, which struggles hard and with considerable success to keep the Narragansett up to the "fishable, swimmable" standard mandated by the 1972 Clean Water Act and sufficiently clean to sustain the shellfish populations. A particularly attention-getting device for Save the Bay is "The Good, the Bad, and the Ugly"—its unique annual performance rating of wastewater-treatment plants with discharges affecting the Narragansett. In addition to monitoring the plants for compliance with their NPDES permits, Save the Bay has also lobbied for pretreatment of industrial wastes, which is in any case mandated by federal law, though it is demanded neither by federal nor by local enforcement authorities and is thought by some observers to be unworkable. The well-publicized monitoring program, the organization claims, has been a key factor in the achievement of overwhelming voter approval for more than $100 million in bond issues to improve wastewater-treatment facilities. Water quality is but one of half a dozen program areas for Save the Bay, an agency with a 1986 budget of less than $500,000 and a staff of only a dozen people.

The wind blew hard from the southwest all night, peaking at 32 knots, almost a gale, and the going was hard and wet. Then the front passed and the northwester materialized as forecast, boosting us past Newport and Block Island and through the Race on schedule early on a morning that turned storybook cloudless blue. As the breeze faded and the seas calmed, we motored westward down the progressively more polluted Long Island Sound, whose mainland shore pours ever higher quantities of poisons and raw sewage into an estuary that now shows signs of serious stress. Annual algal blooms, encouraged by nutrients from the sewage inflow, help turn once clear blue-green water a dull brown. When the algae begin to die and are attacked by bacteria, the water's oxygen supply becomes depleted. The combination of oxygen depletion and toxic substances has, in recent years, resulted in widespread die-offs of marine species even in a spacious body of water with swiftly flowing tidal currents that flush it twice daily.

At sundown we anchored in a calm and quiet corner of Port Jefferson Harbor on the Long Island side. My journal for the day concludes succinctly: "Sleep at anchor felt good." At dawn we set off again toward Hell Gate, the East River, and New York City. Early on, we passed Crane Neck and Stony Brook Harbor, a little hole where grassy mud flats occasionally give way to narrow channels, and where as a child I had learned something of sailing in open sixteen-foot Comets. Our well-organized fleet, which consisted of a dozen or so boats, had two races a week during the summer season, a committee to which to protest rule violations, and many trophies to award at the annual Labor Day finale. Despite fluky winds and currents, and the often realized threat of capsizing or running aground, we took it all very seriously and felt special delight in beating the adult skippers, who usually turned out only for the Sunday races. (Two of my contemporaries in that little world, Larry Huntington and Freddy Van Liew, later became top ocean racers with their own big boats.) All week, at least when we did not have summer jobs, we would bash around among ourselves, racing and cruising: the Comets were our hot rods, and we would ask the girls to go out with us, and our beer and cigarettes, on moonlight sails. We also went clam digging on the mud flats, listened to the quawks of the black-crowned night herons along the shore, endured stubborn gnats when it was calm, absorbed the full presence of nature in what then was still a rural place. Now the racing fleet is gone, the little harbor turned over to outboards and board sailors, water-skiers and small power cruisers. The skyline is badly scarred by a brutal high-rise building, part of the State University of New York campus at the village of Stony Brook, that now looms over one end of it. One diehard I know claims that edible oysters may still be found here. Public authorities, who I doubt have heard much lately about oysters in Stony Brook Harbor, no longer allow people to eat even its common clams.

Geologically a terminal moraine (the point marking the maximum advance of ice-age glaciers) but in appearance little more than a large sandbar, Long Island was once a showcase coastal resource, rich in salt marshes and marine life. In his *Description of the New World*, a guidebook for British traders published in London in 1651, George Gardyner wrote of its "fruitfull soil for English grain and Milet, and of a good air. The Seas about it are well stored with Fish, and the woods, with Deer and Turkeys, and it hath many quiet Indians, that live by hunting and fishing." On the island's north shore, wrote the eighteenth-century Swedish traveler Peter Kalm, "when the tide is out, it is very easy to fill a whole cart with oysters, which have been driven onshore by one flood . . . oysters here are reckoned very wholesome, some people assured us that they had not felt the least inconvenience after eating a considerable quantity of them."

Today, thanks not only to a huge population boom since World War II but to careless management as well, the region has lost most of its oysters; worse, it is fast losing its potable groundwater thanks to overconsumption and to contamination from toxic seepage. The effects of heavily polluted runoff from the shore and heavy ocean dumping into the New York Bight near the coast are horrifying. Each summer brings new grim tales of brown algae (which first appeared in the Sound in 1985 and have returned annually) and dead waters, the disappearance of shellfish-eries in polluted bays and of finfish along the seacoast. At the height of the summer 1988 heat wave, Long Island's ocean beaches—along with others in the New York area—became tidal recipients of what *Time* magazine termed a "nauseating array of waste." The debris, which included drug paraphernalia and hospital refuse carrying viruses, possi-bly including AIDS, provoked the temporary closing of long stretches of New York's public beaches—and a new wave of concern about the problems besetting the coasts.

We passed the hideous power plant marring the appearance of Eatons Neck. Soon thereafter a more agreeable sight, that of the Manhattan skyline on this sparkling morning, rose into view. "I've never seen the place looking so good," said country girl Caroline, a recent graduate of the Yale School of Forestry. "Maybe it's because we're so far away." The twinkling towers loomed as we moved through Hell Gate,

Sanderling approaches New York harbor from the East River.

then seemed almost oppressively high when we motored down the East River past a carnival at the South Street Seaport. Once out in New York Harbor, with the impressive Hudson estuary now in full view, we reveled in an afternoon so fine that it seemed barely possible to think of sludge and PCBs and raw sewage.

It was a fine day as well on April 17, 1524, when Giovanni da Verrazano, his vessel *La Dauphine* moving well across a southwester, sailed into the harbor and anchored in the Narrows. "New York never looked fairer than on this first day when European eyes gazed upon it," wrote Samuel Eliot Morison. Verrazano called it "a very pleasant place, situated amongst certain little steep hills; from amidst which hills there ran down into the sea a great stream of water." In deference to his French employers he named the region Angoulême and would have explored it were it not for the arrival of a "contrary flaw of wind" which threatened to drive his ship ashore and prompted him to weigh anchor and continue sailing eastward to Narragansett Bay, Maine, and thence back to France. Though he revisited the New World several years later, meeting his undeserved end at the hands of Carib Indian cannibals on a beach in the Lesser Antilles, Verrazano never returned to the Northeast. Nor did any other European explorer take a good look at the region until 1609, when Henry Hudson spent almost a month there. Despite several conflicts with resident Indians, Hudson succeeded in sailing the *Half*

Henry Hudson and the *Half Moon* with Indians
on the banks of the Hudson.

Moon as far upriver as Albany in a fruitless search for the Northwest
Passage.

He still came away impressed by what he had seen. "The land is the
finest for cultivation that I ever in my life set foot upon," he wrote in his
journal, "and it also abounds in trees of every description." Between
them Hudson and Robert Juet of Limehouse, a *Half Moon* officer who
also kept a journal, recorded a remarkable litany of species seen or eaten:
fish and shellfish of every description and in large numbers; pumpkins
and grapes and pigeons. Not mentioned in these journals, but doubtless
evident as well, were profusions of eagles and ospreys, harbor seals and
porpoises, bears and mountain lions and smaller mammals. Far upstream
oysters lined the riverbanks in great beds. Vast schools of shad, bluefish,
and striped bass migrated and reproduced deep into the long, wide
estuary.

If its endowment of natural resources was unequaled, the opulent
Hudson River valley soon began to score other sorts of superlatives. The
valley, well positioned to play a critical role in the Revolutionary War,
fully lived up to this promise with contributions ranging from Benedict
Arnold to the chain set athwart the Narrows near West Point to throttle
the Royal Navy. It was also the site for major enhancements of
intellectual and artistic life by Washington Irving, Thomas Cole, and the
so-called Hudson River School of mid-nineteenth-century landscape

painters that he inspired, the early-twentieth-century Woodstock communities of artists and writers. The deep river spawned the steamboat.
By means of an engineering marvel of its time called the Erie Canal, it
opened the way from the Atlantic seaboard to the West. Late in the
nineteenth century the nation's foremost plutocrats—Harrimans, Mor-
gans, Rockefellers, Roosevelts—arrayed themselves in formidable mansions with views of the riverfront's cliffs, highlands, and bold shores.
Heavy ship traffic and the cacophony of thriving industries characterized
the Hudson throughout the nineteenth century; the frenzy of deforestation to create farmland in the valley reached its climax about one
hundred years ago.

Transportation shifts from ship to train, and later from train to truck,
brought hard times. By the mid-twentieth century the river had become
an unsavory sewer for the transport of untreated human and industrial
waste. As of 1976, when the dumping was finally brought to a halt,
General Electric had burdened the river with some 500,000 pounds of
PCBs. Recently scientists have found in the fat of Hudson River snapping
turtles concentrations of this deadly stuff exceeding the legal maximum
a thousandfold. Factories spewed forth not only PCBs but vast quantities
of toxic heavy metals, particularly lead, mercury, and cadmium, as well
as astonishing amounts of oil and grease. In pollution levels as well as in
historic and artistic achievement, the Hudson had attained dramatic
heights.

The turnaround dates from the mid-1960s. At the time, Con Edison,
the New York City utility that was fashioned from J. P. Morgan's
amalgam of many small gas companies and Thomas Edison's electricity
supply firm, was seeking a means of dealing with New York City's
impending power crisis. Foreshadowed by an ominous series of blackouts
and brownouts dating from the 1950s, the situation gave promise only of
getting worse. Con Ed's solution was to propose a large pumped-storage
hydroelectric plant that would form a great gash on the slopes of Storm
King Mountain, a picturesque and often painted bastion of granite that
looms over the west bank of the river in the village of Cornwall-
on-Hudson below the highlands just north of West Point. During periods
of less than high demand for electricity, giant pumps, using power
generated by steam, would lift water from the river and store it in a
reservoir 1,160 feet above on the flank of the Harvard-owned Black Rock
Forest. When demand rose, water would be released from the reservoir
and drive the system's mighty turbines. In size the Cornwall facility,
rated at close to 2 million kilowatts at maximum capacity, would be
exceeded only by the hydro plants associated with the Grand Coulee
Dam and Niagara Falls.

The dramatic story of the community's reaction to Con Ed's 1962 announcement begins with scattered protests. They came to the attention of a few influential local citizens, including the prominent New York attorney Stephen P. Duggan and his wife, Smokey, who for years had summered in Cornwall. Early on, even Duggan expressed reservations about taking on City Hall. But the Duggans and their blue-chip associates, along with gathering grass-roots ranks of Con Ed opponents, struggled on in a *Perils of Pauline* melodrama that on several occasions seemed to have ended in defeat. In fact, construction began early in the 1970s. But with growing skill and determination the anti–Con Ed forces kept coming back with new appeals and new arguments. Along the way the Duggans figured in the establishment of two now influential organizations: Scenic Hudson at the regional level and the Natural Resources Defense Council (NRDC) at the national level, now a broadly effective environmental agency acting in the public interest. A benchmark 1965 court decision, recognizing these two entities as "aggrieved parties" even though neither had any economic stake in the issue's outcome, opened the way for citizen groups to participate directly in many other environmental cases in subsequent years.

At the moment when Con Edison seemed on the verge of winning the right to build at Storm King, Robert Boyle, author of the excellent book *The Hudson River* and a leader in the battle as founder of the Hudson River Fishermen's Association, became the NRDC's first client. The new line of arguments that he and the lawyers advanced, centering on the plant's prospective effect on migratory fish that use the Hudson, led to the unexpected victory, finally achieved in 1980. In the negotiated settlement the company forfeited Storm King in return for the waiver of an Environmental Protection Agency ruling calling for highly expensive water-cooling towers to protect fish near other riverside plants. Even this compromise broke new ground. Over and above its importance for the Hudson region, Storm King had become a bellwether for the nation. Russell E. Train, negotiator of the settlement and the former head of the Environmental Protection Agency and of the World Wildlife Fund, called it "the granddaddy of the environmental movement."

After Storm King came many other improvements in the Hudson's quality. Assisted by a push from the state's Department of Environmental Conservation, which was founded in 1970, conventional sewage-treatment programs multiplied. The program, which now extends to almost every municipality along the river, culminated in the recent inauguration, in upper Manhattan, of a Versailles of its breed called the North River Plant. Its opening ended the long-standing practice of dumping raw New York City sewage into the river. Though the Hudson remains plagued by continuing infusions of toxic chemicals from industry and an overabundance of nutrients from agricultural runoff, some of the biggest problems have been overcome. Now that General Electric has stopped dumping PCBs into the river, the continuing battle centers on the question of what to do with the 500,000 pounds of the stubborn stuff now littering the river bottom. General Electric has claimed that its lethal qualities will gradually be dispelled if it is left where it is; the state's Department of Environmental Conservation, contending that the PCBs are continuing to devastate the Hudson River fishery, is seeking approval to proceed with a dredging program.

In 1983 a fisherman named John Cronin caught Exxon ships flushing their giant oily tanks with Hudson River fresh water, and filed a complaint with the U.S. Attorney in New York. The company bought off local antagonism by committing millions to the establishment and maintenance of Hudson conservation efforts. New institutions were born, grew, took their positions as Hudson watchdogs. Cronin himself became the Hudson Riverkeeper, patrolling aboard a twenty-five-foot powerboat under the auspices of the Fishermen's Association. Meanwhile the handsome *Clearwater*, a replica of an old-time river trading vessel, operating with the close involvement of the ardent folksinger Pete Seeger, plied the river as a symbol of citizen concern and a focal point for information about actions needed to improve the river's environmental quality. The Hudson Valley now has so many advocates, say some local authorities, that aggressive developers with large dirty projects in mind usually look elsewhere for sites. One electric power transmission company voluntarily went to the expense of burying its lines in full knowledge that the well-organized Hudsonians would fight anything else. "In recent years we've filed dozens of suits on the Hudson," said the low-key but highly effective conservation superstar John Adams, the NRDC's founder and a Hudson Valley resident.

This vigorous counterattack hardly means that the river's problems have been overcome, conservationists stress. "They're nickel-and-diming us to death," said Klara Sauer, Scenic Hudson's executive director. "Land speculation is just rampant. The concerns are so multifarious that there's more than enough work for all of us." Threats range from the persistent flow of toxic substances into the river to a constant barrage of inappropriately large-scale riverfront real estate schemes; from New York City's proposal to draw off vast amounts of Hudson fresh water for the municipal system, thus jeopardizing portions already going to many communities along the river, to the proposed construction of a large coal-loading facility that would, among other things, disturb the view from Olana, a strikingly oddball mansion built as the artist Frederic

Church's home. Observers cited the need for a broad approach to the valley's management as real estate development thunders on and the regional population continues its rapid growth. Exotic plants—the purple loosestrife, the water chestnut—have squeezed out native species in some places.

Yet for all that, the overall progress made since the Storm King case sets the estuary apart from many others still on a downward course. Where twenty years ago few would have risked it, many people now sail, water-ski, even swim in the river and drink its water. With reforestation many long-absent animals, including the osprey and the bald eagle, have returned. Governor Mario Cuomo's 1988 proposal to designate the Hudson Valley as a "greenway," with especially strong environmental protection, represented the culmination of years of pressure from Scenic Hudson and many other citizens' groups. In 1988 a comprehensive long-term strategy for the management of the estuary was gaining political support in Albany. Downriver, the Rockefeller family strengthened its commitment to the region by naming a new organization, Historic Hudson Valley, to promote travel to what Laurance Rockefeller said should become a "national historic site" and a prime tourist destination. Citizen action, along with $800,000 in private donations, clinched a $13.2 million state deal to buy out a developer intent on reducing Sloop Hill, 102 areas of prime riverfront land facing Storm King Mountain, to 502 condominium units. "With every development," said Winthrop Aldrich, a veteran official in the state's Department of Environmental Conservation, "there comes a reaction of outraged citizens and artists and politicians and editorial writers. It's an extraordinary record of organizations, and really, it boils down to people."

Aboard *Sanderling* the mood was upbeat as well as we cast our last glances upriver. Sandy Hook dropped astern by late afternoon and now we continued, in a millpond sea and a light offshore breeze, down the crowded Jersey shore. Still in high spirits after a stimulating day, we dreamed of carrying these conditions for another hundred miles to Cape May. It was not to be. Soon after midnight the wind swung from west to south, forcing us back to engine power as the breeze filled in and the seas again mounted. By the following afternoon we were mired in another howler, with the wind reaching 30 knots. Great rollers tossed us around, often killing our speed as *Sanderling's* bow crunched into them and flinging torrents of spray across the cockpit. After one damp and chilly stretch at the wheel, the resolute Caroline retired below to take a hot shower. Soon after I took over, I heard a crash and a squeal from below. The door into the head had burst open when a big wave hit and Caroline fell against it. In the altogether, she bounced out into the main cabin with a hand still on the door. Shining and slippery, she sat suspended there for an instant. Then the back side of the same wave sent her sliding right back into the head to resume her shower.

The wind remained southwesterly as we finally rounded Cape May late at night and sent us screaming off at up to nine knots on a broad reach as we bore away into Delaware Bay. Here I had hoped to pause a while, to take at least a quick look at Norburys Landing, where each spring millions of northbound red knots and sanderlings pause to fatten up on eggs laid there in large quantities by the horseshoe crab, an anachronistic arthropod that, against long odds, still prospers even in this tanker-ridden region, which is also the site of an energetic EPA cleanup program. The shorebird–horseshoe crab symbiosis provides a sterling example of how nature often manages to get along despite human incursions. I was not to learn more of it at this predawn moment, with another frontal passage in progress as the wind again rose, shifting once more onto our nose. We shortened sail as its velocity increased to a high of thirty-seven knots, then tried to use power to speed our chilly passage up the wind-whitened channel to the canal from Delaware Bay into the Chesapeake. Finally we reached it in midafternoon as the wind mercifully moderated. We powered through, a large tanker in close pursuit.

The stove failed to light (our mistake in not understanding how to switch gas tanks), and we were forced back to a cold dinner as the preamble to our final evening's run down the Chesapeake to Annapolis. Given a choice between salad and cold canned corned-beef hash, John, who hates salad, chose salad. Later the wind went dead aft, once again rising. Now groggy from too little sleep as well as cold, we bundled into all the warm clothes we had and tried to navigate among the myriad confusing lighted buoys along the route. A small wind shift provoked an embarrassment, a standing jibe that caused damage aloft. From this we recovered with great help from the nimble John. ("Can't I go below for five minutes without all hell breaking loose?" he jested.) By midnight we were under the Bay Bridge and, soon after, tucked into an anchorage at Annapolis. For some months, her first passage now complete, *Sanderling* would stay in the bay.

4

Chesapeake Blues

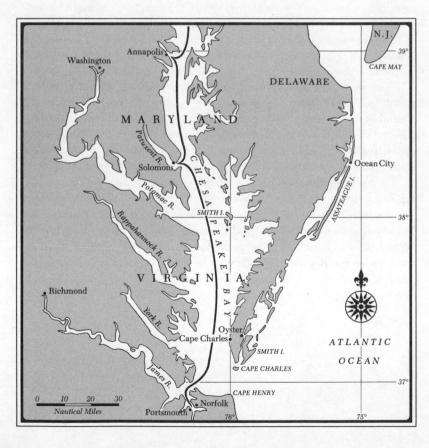

IN 1632, KING CHARLES I ACKNOWLEDGED THE CHESAPEAKE. MORE than a century after the first European explorers had ventured there, twenty-five years after Captain John Smith and his band of Virginia colonists had set up camp on a swamp at Archer's Hope near Jamestown, Britain's monarch bestowed a substantial land grant upon the London entrepreneur Cecilius Calvert, the second Baron Baltimore. The son of a wealthy convert to Roman Catholicism, Baltimore had long pursued his father's dream of founding a New World settlement that would encompass the religious pluralism then lacking in England. Now, his grant in hand, Baltimore moved swiftly. The area awarded, already well explored by Ralph Lane of the Roanoke colony as well as by Smith, covered much of the Chesapeake watershed.

To occupy it, Baltimore assembled, in 1633, a company of some 140 settlers consisting in large part of well-off Catholic investors and Protestant indentured servants. They were instructed to sail to the New World and "sett downe" on "a fitt place" somewhere in the region of the "Chesapeack" or "Patowemack," of which Smith had sent back enthusiastic reports. Baltimore's ships, the 300-ton *Ark* and an accompanying 50-ton pinnace called the *Dove*, arrived in Virginia late in the winter of 1633–34. Within six months of their arrival, the colonists had: established a settlement called St. Mary's on a high bluff eight miles up the Potomac from Point Lookout at the river's mouth; learned hunting and fishing techniques from the many friendly Piscataway Indians in the region; harvested crops from seeds they had prudently brought along with them; begun raising hogs, poultry, and cattle borrowed from their Jamestown neighbors; and in many respects established the most successful British colony up to then founded in the New World.

The Jesuit priest Andrew White, an *Ark* passenger, rivaled Captain Smith as the Chesapeake's least abashed early European enthusiast. "The most delightfull water I ever saw," White called it in his Relation. His conclusion:

> The soyle . . . is excellent so that we cannot sett down a foot, but tread on Strawberries, raspires, fallen mulberrie vines, acchorns, walnutts, saxafras, etc., and those in the wildest woods. The ground is commonly a blacke mould above, and a foot within ground of a readish colour. All is high woods except where the Indians have cleared for corne. It abounds with delicate springs which are our best drinke. Birds diversely feathered there are infinite, as eagles, swans, hernes, geese, bitters, duckes, partridge read, blew, partie coloured and the like, by which will appeare, the place abounds not only with profit, but also with pleasure.

An anonymous Relation noted the presence not far inland from the bay of "Bufeloes, Elkes, Lions, Beares, Wolves and Deare in great store," and the usual wide assortment of birds, including turkeys weighing fifty pounds. In one of the few early understatements about the Chesapeake's resources, this author dryly observed that its waters "doe abound with Fish of various sorts."

While dysentery and other illnesses felled a hundred of the colony's first five hundred occupants, nature generally provided far better for them than for any of North America's previous settlers. The great tidal estuary into which the *Ark* and the *Dove* had sailed, a river valley that "drowned" when the last ice age receded, is 5 to 30 miles in width and 180 miles long, covers 2,660 square miles, and boasts an elaborate network of bays and rivers giving it more than 8,000 miles of shoreline. The Susquehanna, draining half of what is now Pennsylvania, flows into the Chesapeake from the north; from the west a parade of wide rivers: the Patuxent, the Potomac, the Rappahannock, the York, the James. Much of the bay's western shore is lined with red-and-yellow fossil-laden cliffs and beaches; myriad creeks and streams slice cleanly into the sandy earth. The eastern shore, in sharp contrast, is shallow and mud flat and salt marsh. But it too boasts a profusion of waterways and is a place of great beauty. The soil was indeed as productive as Father White claimed. The climate came close to the prized "golden mean" between winter frosts and summer scorchings that Atlantic colonists had sought from Newfoundland to the Carolinas.

In fact as in the various Relations, the bay harbored an astounding profusion of biological resources. Vast expanses of salt marsh were ideal breeding grounds for the microscopic algae that rest at the base of the food chain for most of the principal fish species then as now used by humans. Oysters and clams and blue crabs, on which the region's reputation as a seafood capital remains centered, were instantly available during the appropriate seasons. Overall the bay produced more seafood than any similar body of water anywhere. Migrating ducks and geese blackened the skies during the spring and fall. Jamestown's settlers had occupied a brackish lowland, compounding their health problems by drinking river water that they themselves had fouled and awaiting the arrival of provisions from England rather than raising their own. Relatively speaking, Maryland's Catholics had stumbled upon Paradise, and quickly set about utilizing its resources.

Even before European colonists arrived in the Chesapeake, humans were beginning to damage this robust environment. Before Maryland was settled, according to one estimate, clearing of virgin forest to create cropland had already amounted to thirty to forty acres for each of the ten to twenty thousand Indians who then occupied the region. Increasing erosion became the handmaiden of accelerating deforestation during colonial times; the direct runoff into the bay and its tributaries was causing siltation problems by as early as 1700, when cargo ships could no longer enter Port Tobacco, a once thriving town along the Potomac. By the end of the eighteenth century the St. Mary's region had become poverty-stricken, its soils exhausted from what one observer called "imprudent methods of tobacco cultivation." Concern for the decline of the shad, a regional fish prized for its large and tasty roe, was voiced as early as 1830. The harvest of oysters peaked in 1879—at 17 million bushels extracted from what has been called "the most productive natural oyster ground on earth." The smell of decaying garbage in Baltimore's inner harbor was chronicled in 1776; its stench was pungent as the twentieth century began, when the city, still without sewage treatment of any sort, already had a population of more than half a million.

During the twentieth century mounting levels of industrial and agricultural effluents flowed into the estuary. Said the Virginia Marine Resources Commission in 1961: "Contamination of our natural waters by pollutants of various types is one of the most pressing problems facing our Commonwealth today." All the bay's ailments were compounded by the powerful Hurricane Agnes, which struck in the fall of 1972. So severe a storm that one like it can be expected to occur no more than once or twice each two hundred years, Agnes dumped eighteen inches of rain on the region over three days and caused tributaries to flow at up to twenty-five times their normal volume. The floods killed large numbers of fish and oysters, devastated many wetland regions, and did $40 million worth of damage.

Two years after Agnes, the bay again achieved its previous level of health. But if its natural communities could cope with a natural disaster, they were less able to tolerate the relentless human ravages that, by the beginning of the 1980s, dragged this splendid estuary so far down that many close observers began to doubt whether it could ever recover. One of the problems, ironically, was that its changing chemistry was encouraging too much growth of the wrong kind of vegetation. Torrents of nutrients (chiefly nitrogen and phosphorus) flowed into the bay thanks to untreated human and animal waste and runoff from overfertilized farms as far away as Pennsylvania, whose Susquehanna River basin contributes more than half the Chesapeake's freshwater supply; during droughts, as much as 90 percent of this flow consists of treated sewage. The bay's emergence as a Shangri-la for some 200,000 pleasure boaters also affects water quality. Few boaters (myself included, I blush to admit) use the

William C. Baker.

on-board sewage treatment plants that the Coast Guard requires. Overenrichment, here as on Long Island Sound, leads to abnormal blooms of algae covering the water surface; when these organisms die and decay, levels of dissolved oxygen decrease, sometimes to the vanishing point. The severe level of oxygen depletion called hypoxia is lethal to marine life and can lead to mass die-offs of fish. Hypoxia regularly occurs on 116 square miles of the Chesapeake, according to a report issued in 1987 by the Office of Technology Assessment of the U.S. Congress.

More and more population growth in the region meant urbanization and a resort and second-home development boom; streams and salt marshes were bulldozed and blasted to make way for condominiums and marinas and new roads and bridges. Farmers tended to cash in by selling their best land and working more fragile soil instead. Erosion, which leads to sedimentation in the bay, has resulted. Shallow to begin with, the bay is filling in at rates of as much as four millimeters a year in some of the headwaters. More erosion has brought greater turbidity. "In the ten years since I've been living in Annapolis," said William C. Baker, president of the Chesapeake Bay Foundation, "the decline in water clarity has been just amazing. You used to be able to see down six, eight, ten feet. Now you can hardly do better than eighteen inches." Cloudy water, as well as high nutrient levels, encourages plant growth on the surface and reduces the light available to underwater grasses. Less light below the surface, in addition to soaring quantities of farm and garden herbicides entering the system, has killed 85 percent of all the bay's subaquatic vegetation (SAV), which serves as food for waterfowl and the breeding habitat for many marine species.

Herbicides form only a small portion of the heavy dosage of toxic substances that have been inflicted upon the bay. Some flowed in semi-regulated doses through pipes; some entered the estuary in random fashion from what are known as nonpoint sources—part of the runoff from rains or storms. From densely populated and industrial zones came deadly concentrations of dissolved heavy metals: copper and zinc, lead and chromium and cadmium. Toxic organic chemical compounds (PNAs, PAHs, PCBs) settled into sediments, from which, not being biodegradable, they proved extremely difficult to remove. Creosote from the lower bay's shipyards blended into the ooze. For more than 150 years, Baltimore Harbor has been beset by such a barrage of assorted pollutants that recently one adventuresome company began thinking about mining it to reprocess its concentrations of heavy metals. "Pick up a piece of Baltimore Harbor," said the biologist L. Eugene Cronin, former director of the Chesapeake Research Consortium and a leading authority on the bay. "It'll stand up like a bowl of black Jell-O."

Large companies and military installations—Bethlehem Steel, Allied Chemical, the U.S. Army's Aberdeen Proving Grounds, and many other government facilities, even Gwaltney of Smithfield, a ham-and-bacon-processing company—were among the principal violators. Over nine years Allied dumped more than 100,000 pounds of a pesticide called Kepone, so poisonous that it caused illnesses in 133 company employees, into the James River at Hopewell, Virginia. From the sewage system the substance, which according to Cronin is so "highly persistent" that the least expensive plan to get rid of it, or isolate it, would cost $3 billion, settled into the river bottom. The result was the closing of the river indefinitely to most fisheries and the death of many species, from fish to eagles, as the deadly stuff moved up the food chain by way of various benthic (sea floor) organisms and bottom filter feeders such as oysters. Cronin expects that the Kepone will linger in the James for fifty to one hundred years. Tributyltin, or TBT, the lethal anti-fouling paint used to retard barnacle growth on the hulls of boats and ships, also poisoned the bay until 1987, when the Virginia and Maryland legislatures both voted severe restrictions on its use.

Many species have paid a severe price for these profound alterations in the bay's ecology. While oyster harvests have dipped before as a consequence of storms, changes in weather patterns, or disease epidemics, the drop from the peak of 17 million bushels to less than 2 million bushels a year in recent years is an unprecedented disaster caused by a combination of overharvesting and mismanagement, habitat shrinkage because of pollution and oxygen loss, and the spread of two diseases (including a particularly vicious parasitic one called MSX). The oyster crisis has in turn brought severe hardship to thousands of Chesapeake watermen. In Maryland those harvesting oysters have decreased in number from 28,000 at the turn of the century to 1,600, according to the Washington *Post*; their catch is down tenfold. Taking inflation into account, the stubborn people still trying are earning no more than they did in the mid-1970s. After Maryland's harvests of the bay's once abundant rockfish, or striped bass, dropped from 5 million pounds in the late 1960s to less than 400,000 pounds in 1984, the state banned fishing for this popular species altogether. (Though some scientists are now reporting indications of a partial recovery, others see no such trend.) Maryland's shad fishery, whose recent decline has confirmed the dire early predictions, has been closed for many years; since the 1928 damming of the Susquehanna River blocked the principal route for this anadromous species, which migrates from salt to fresh water to spawn, its numbers have dwindled precipitously.

To the dismay of birders and hunters, migrating canvasbacks, pintails, and other duck species now bypass the bay—mostly in favor of wetlands farther south—because the aquatic vegetation on which they depend has disappeared. Even the Canada goose, so plentiful only a few years back that farmers thought the bird a pest, is down to half its 1981 population around the bay. Countless other species have undergone precipitous declines. "I haven't seen an eel in ten years," mourned the World Wildlife Fund's Russell Train, who spends weekends at a farm facing the shallow, once teeming waters of Maryland's eastern shore. Only the blue crab has managed to maintain the usual fluctuations of its population in this slaughtered habitat. The reason is that it reproduces, not, as do the anadromous fishes, in the most highly polluted upper bays and headwaters, but in cleaner, more saline waters around the bay's mouth.

Near but beyond the bay, other forces contrive to undo the work of

Ocean City after Hurricane Gloria, 1985.

nature. "Ocean City gambles against the inevitable," read a headline in a special section of the Baltimore *Evening Sun* describing the drama of the town's efforts to safeguard the $1.5 billion invested in land and buildings along a vulnerable ten-mile stretch of Fenwick Island. Beach erosion continues at the rate of almost two feet a year, the article said, and the problem is aggravated by the steady rise in the global sea level and by the threat of a major hurricane which could flatten the entire settlement. Yet developers cram more and more units onto the island, often building closer to the sea than local regulations allow. Slammed hard by bad storms in the spring of 1962 and the fall of 1985, Ocean City stubbornly grows on. "Of anywhere it's the worst example of unwise coastal development," said the geologist Orrin H. Pilkey, Jr., of Duke University, an expert on beach erosion who unhesitatingly forecasts the town's early demise.

One late fall day, while on a temporary shore leave from *Sanderling*, I drove from Washington down to OC, as it's called, to get a firsthand look at this doomed community. Leaving Maryland's eastern shore, I traveled eastward through flat green farmland across the Delmarva Peninsula. "Real Estate Seminars," boomed a sign in front of the Southern Delaware Community and Technical College. It hinted at what was soon to come. First, just past the Delaware beach resort of Rehoboth, a strip of Mister Donuts and Pizza Huts along Route 1. Then onto the Coastal Highway, which, once past a protected stretch of publicly owned beach, widens to eight lanes when it enters Maryland's principal tourist attraction. On five- and ten- and twenty-story condominium buildings with names like Fanta Sea and Ocean Spray, Silver Moon and, inevitably, the Breakers, signs and banners heralded prices and deals: $79,900, $49,900, Points Paid by Developer. On TV at the place where I stopped for a crab cake: Channel 53, "The Real Estate Channel"; a free copy of the Maryland/Delaware Beaches Seaside Property Guide was easily available.

Beneath the façades the prospective damage was easily spotted. Even on a calm afternoon when wet-suited surfers lolling offshore could hardly catch a ride, waves washed under the supporting pilings of a five-story condo called the Hawaiian Village, still under construction at the end of 142nd Street. Near here the breadth of the island has been greatly reduced by dredging on the inner, or bay, side to create housefront parking for yachts. In consequence, some fear, runoff from the mainland after a heavy storm could cause a surge of sufficient power to blow a hole through the island from the *inside* and demolish the buildings in the way. Again, at 78th Street nothing separated the ocean from the buildings. At 56th I found a sliver of beach, and even a remnant of dune grass enclosed behind chain-link fencing. On lower-numbered streets broken-down groins extending outward from the shore, the remnants of futile previous efforts to "save" the beach; newly reconstructed boardwalks replaced those destroyed during the 1985 storm. At the southern end of the island, near an amusement park, I saw the pair of strong jetties installed there in 1934 after an inlet had broken through. I looked across at the undeveloped northern end of Assateague Island, a National Seashore famed for its wild ponies and known as an important habitat for nesting piping plovers. Then I drove back to the mainland across the Harry W. Kelley Memorial Bridge. It is named for Ocean City's long-term, now deceased mayor, who did more than anyone else to make the town what it is today.

Kelley was one of many OC boosters who long believed that willpower could keep the seas at bay. Left in its natural state, a barrier island like this one is molded by winds and waves and currents; gradually it will change its shape and roll shoreward, though its overall dimensions are likely to remain quite constant. The shifting dunes that face the ocean, often buttressed by grasses and shrubs that can survive high winds and salt spray, serve as stabilizing anchors in this dynamic system. Once the dunes are replaced by inflexible buildings, the sand can only pile up at their doorsteps. The beach profile steepens and waves grow higher, thus increasing the erosion rate. For many years Ocean City's usual response to this tendency was to bulldoze away the sand when views became obstructed. Later, as the beach continued to narrow, a program of groins was proposed and implementation began. But despite Mayor Kelley's messianic faith in Ocean City's future and the security that the groins would provide, others feared their mounting cost and warned that they offered no protection from a bad storm. More recently the U.S. Army Corps of Engineers proposed to replenish the beach by pumping sand onto it from offshore bars. The cost of this operation would run to $40 million or more.

As the town's year-round population rose to more than 7,000 (up to 300,000 flock there on summer weekends), taxpaying residents began to express suspicion about such expensive management schemes and opposed proposals for raising the height-limit on buildings. But Ocean City's more traditional values still usually prevail, and the effects of its continuing "progress" ripple across to adjacent rural areas and some that remain pristine. The groins and jetties have, for one thing, robbed adjacent Assateague of what was once a broad and beckoning beach along its northern end. On Chincoteague Island, inshore from Assateague at the entrance to the park's southern end, developers are trying hard to fashion a mini Ocean City. Wetlands have been badly trampled as motels and vacation homes have sprouted; the roadway to the park gates is lined with such attractions as the Wet 'n' Wild water slide.

If slurb is the trend along this section, a spirited battle on behalf of the coast has been waged by the Baltimore-based Committee to Preserve Assateague Island, Inc. More than a decade ago this group's indefatigable president, Judith Colt Johnson, recognized the position of Assateague as the only undeveloped barrier island on the Atlantic coast to which fully one-fifth of the nation's population had convenient access. She and her colleagues were also well aware of the area's importance as a habitat for several hard-pressed species, including the threatened piping plover. Over the years the Committee has been responsible for the overthrow of many damaging development proposals, and it continues to lobby for regional planning that will preserve natural values. Recently, for instance, the Committee's efforts resulted in the closure of all public access, during the nesting season, to the piping plover's principal Chincoteague habitat. The victory was accomplished against the opposition of what the Committee's newsletter called a "terrific campaign" waged by developers and ORV (off-road vehicle) interests. Extending its range, the Committee has even begun to oppose Fenwick Island's quixotic effort to turn back the seas.

Scores of similar conservation organizations had long been working to arrest the Chesapeake region's decline. But even though the lives of watermen, hunters, and many other bay residents were being directly affected, until very recently there was still no general recognition that the bay was really in trouble. Politically, the odds were often long. "Bethlehem Steel is the biggest employer, the biggest taxpayer, and the biggest polluter in the state of Maryland. No one ever really stood up to them," said Cronin. The U.S. armed forces, operators of some eighty facilities around the bay, were difficult to get at. Regional planning, even systematic thinking, were complicated by differing jurisdictions, styles, and values in the three states that share the bay's drainage area. Twenty years ago, the only environmental issue around the bay that aroused a major citizen response was Baltimore Gas & Electric's nuclear-powered generating plant at Calvert Cliffs. After a prolonged battle, the ugly plant (so large that the volume of its water discharge makes it the bay's fourth-largest "river") was built and has been operating for more than a decade without accident or, said Cronin, "demonstrated significant detrimental effects."

The awakening finally occurred about ten years ago, a time when even *National Geographic*, not then noted for its passion about environmental matters, reluctantly observed that "there's trouble brewing in our demi-Eden." More strident alarms were sounding as well. At the national level, the New Environmentalism was born and came to flourish as a reaction to the brusque indifference of such Reagan appointees as James Watt, the least sensitive Secretary of the Interior in modern times, and Anne Gorsuch, the spectacularly unqualified Environmental Protection Agency administrator. Locally the bay became a matter of political importance after Governors Charles Robb of Virginia and Harry Hughes of Maryland emerged from a closed-door meeting in 1982 and pledged themselves jointly to the task of saving it. In 1983, in response to an earlier call by Maryland's then Senator Charles McC. Mathias for a major bay study, the Environmental Protection Agency issued a comprehensive analysis of its multiple and complex problems. The $27 million EPA report included a "framework for action." Finally, said the Chesapeake Bay Foundation's Will Baker, citizens began to react: "Things had just gotten so lousy that people around the bay couldn't help noticing." His own group and scores of others paying attention to smaller units—even individual streams—grew rapidly in membership, income, and clout. Before long, Baker continued, the volume of citizen concern had become "too big for any politician to ignore."

In 1983 the governors of Maryland, Virginia, and Pennsylvania, as well as the mayor of the District of Columbia, all signed an agreement that pledged a sustained cleanup effort. Their legislatures committed more than $200 million to get the job done. Even President Reagan plugged the bay in his 1984 State of the Union address and encouraged the U.S. Congress to appropriate $10 million a year in direct support. Of local measures taken, the toughest was Maryland's "Critical Areas" program, under which all development activities affecting lands or waters within 1,000 feet of the bay are subject to stiff regulations; zoning in the most sensitive and still undeveloped areas limits construction to one housing unit per 20 acres. Since many landowners affected by the program lost the right to decide the future use of their properties, it is considered draconian in some quarters. Others, however, noting its many loopholes, felt that victory for the bay could only be achieved through even stiffer limitations on human freedom of action and that the timing was now right for them to press their case. In 1987, at the urging of the Chesapeake Bay Foundation, the political leaders renewed the bay agreement and strengthened it with specific goals and timetables for the cleanup program. Its key provision, difficult for Pennsylvania to achieve, is a pledge to reduce the nutrient flow by 40 percent by the year 2000.

"Recent progress is impressive," Cronin has written. "Further progress is imperative." Aboard *Sanderling* during the fall of 1986, and subsequently by land as well as water, I witnessed the damage and tried to evaluate the effectiveness of the reactions. We operated out of Zahniser's, a trim marina on Solomons Island at the mouth of the badly polluted Patuxent River, and watched while visible and dramatic change took place around us. Traditionally a tobacco-growing area, Calvert County still has its share of weathered barns where the leaf, hung out to dry in late summer, gradually yellows. More and more of these fields were being sold off, though, and along Maryland Route 4 from Washington the housing subdivisions were sprouting. Route 4 itself was being turned into a four-lane highway all the way to the large high bridge that spans the Patuxent from Solomons to Hollywood, a bedroom community for the nearby Naval Air Station. At Solomons a new Comfort Inn and a Holiday Inn with a convention center and its own marina were being completed and opened. Even the attractive Calvert County Museum had broken ground for a new extension. This was suddenly a region on the make, out to become a resort and yachting center to rival Annapolis, to the north on the bay's western shore, where parking a sailboat is no easier than parking a car in Manhattan.

During our wanderings we sought glimpses of how the bay might once have been, and we were not entirely disappointed. Trim white working boats—longer and lower in freeboard than New England lobster craft because they never face ocean seas—crisscrossed our bow, their after ends laden with crab pots. From time to time on the lower bay we would see one of the few surviving skipjack sailboats, required by

Maryland law for dredging on some public oyster grounds, under way and at work. One weekend we cruised the Patuxent in the good company of Kathleen and William Warner, author of the classic *Beautiful Swimmers*, a book about the blue crab and its pursuers that captures with uncanny precision the spirit of the old bay. We anchored in a snug cove off St. Leonards Creek and swam and talked and ate in undisturbed solitude. On a Sunday in May, from the terrace at Sotterley, an eighteenth-century working farm that has been lovingly preserved by the financier J. P. Morgan's granddaughter, Mabel S. Ingalls, we looked across billowing green hayfields at the Patuxent's blue waters. In Jutland Creek off the St. Marys River, not far from where the *Ark* and the *Dove* put in, Flo and I slept on deck under a star-filled sky; in the morning two bald eagles rode a brisk northwester right overhead and low. Such places as Wroten Island, a privately owned duck-hunting preserve on the remote Honga River, and several working communities on the river's western shore seemed barely to have entered the current century.

One blue fall weekend we drove with the Warners down to the quiet eastern shore of Virginia. The mediocrity that has engulfed the Maryland towns of Cambridge and Salisbury, and the honky-tonk along Highway 13 leading to the bridge-tunnel to Norfolk at the mouth of the bay, passed in a blur. At the village of Oyster, facing barrier islands and the Atlantic, we entered a quieter world. Boarding here a passenger boat that the Chesapeake Bay Foundation normally uses for its youth education program, we glided through clean milky-green water down a narrow channel. It was low tide, and shorebirds—ruddy turnstones, sandpipers, a solitary whimbrel with its splendid curved beak—scavenged the muddy banks. As we entered the shallow open water at the end of the channel, a peregrine falcon flew from a perch above the autumn-browned eelgrass. Reduced to near-extinction by DDT, this bird remains rare almost everywhere. But around Oyster some thirty nesting pairs have been identified, and it is off the local endangered list. Flocks of migrating cormorants and scoters flew overhead, along with ducks, geese, and solitary loons.

Between Oyster and Cape Charles at the very mouth of the bay, little evidence of any human presence was visible. We learned why from Barry Truitt, manager of the Nature Conservancy's Virginia Coast Reserve. Most of the barrier islands had never been developed, Truitt explained. Though one had once achieved a population of 400, most remained in private hands, used for little more than occasional hunting excursions as late as the 1960s, when development began to accelerate elsewhere around the bay. On the peninsula's mainland, farmers and fishermen remained insulated from the hurly-burly. The water was still clean. Twenty years ago the forward-looking Conservancy targeted the region as a pristine top priority for conservation. Its then president, Pat Noonan, invited representatives of a New York foundation called the Mary Flagler Cary Trust to look over the region from a low-flying airplane. "Things were on the brink," said Truitt. "Developers from New York were all over, planning to build airports, fill in the marshes, pipe fresh water over from the mainland, you name it." The Cary Trust, possessor, ironically, of the fortune that Henry M. Flagler accumulated by trampling over large sections of Florida early in the twentieth century, gave Noonan what Truitt called "a blank check" to buy land in the region. The Conservancy consequently owns all or large parts of thirteen barrier islands between Assateague and Cape Charles, and has moved ashore to acquire land on the mainland and try to persuade landowners of the virtues of applying the principles of conservation to development schemes. By means of low densities and conservation easements, the Conservancy hopes to create "buffer zones" between wild and developed areas. For the moment, though entrepreneurs with other ideas continue to look hungrily at the region, the Conservancy seems to be keeping them at bay. "We're sort of at a crossroads here," said Truitt, himself a grass-roots wildlife manager who recently had to relearn the art of tying a necktie so that he could attend a ceremony. "A lot of people are looking at us now."

From the channel we proceeded to an anchorage off Smith Island, the site of the Cape Charles lighthouse. This small windswept place, not to be confused with the Smith Island within the bay that we shall visit later in this chapter, remains devoid of human occupation. Though it is open to the public for day visits, few make the effort because the two unmarked channels to landing points are narrow and access is difficult. We were alone where we landed. Gannets, long-winged and graceful birds now migrating southward from Newfoundland and Labrador, soared and wheeled high overhead and took long smooth dives into blue water. Gulls perched along the shore, surrounded by skittering sanderlings and dunlins. Whelk and scallop and oyster shells, as well as solid-mahogany timbers discarded from passing Asian freighters, were scattered about the clean beach. Where the sand ended and a mainland of low scrub began we found red-berried holly, wild oats, bayberry, and juniper. We spent an afternoon of beachcombing under a benign mid-November sun, absorbing this last corner of the bay as it was.

More often in our wanderings we found change and gloom. At the seafood capital of Crisfield, on Maryland's eastern shore, we stood on a

Chesapeake watermen unloading catch at Crisfield.

pier and watched the action. Boats carrying oysters would swing in and make their sales directly to shippers in vans or small trucks. Twenty-two dollars a bushel was the going rate.

"When arsters are fetchin' that here, they must be gettin' a pretty dear price for 'em in New York City," said one waterman.

"Well, it's good you're finding some anyway," I said.

"Precious few," he answered glumly, watching as a frisky black Labrador crunched his way through a blue crab.

Near the town of Chance, from which a newly reconstructed bridge leads across to Deal Island, I saw a sign advertising fresh fish and crabs for sale. Inside the small wooden hut sat five older men, trading stories. I asked if I could buy a fish.

"We don't have any," said one man. "They all went away."

Later that same November weekend, Flo and I sailed to the other Smith Island. This distant place, charted by but not named for Captain John as often claimed, has been featured in *National Geographic* and elsewhere as an example of an "untouched" corner of America where handsome blond watermen, usually named Tyler or Evans, still practice their craft much as they have since 1657, when their Protestant forebears settled there. We anchored *Sanderling* at high tide in a little pool just off the narrow channel that leads into the island's principal town of Ewell. From there I set forth in the dinghy. With a loud quawk, a great blue heron rose from a mud flat. From a distance the village's white clapboard houses glistened in the late-afternoon sun. Closer up, its edges seemed frayed. Though the working boats were trim and well kept, the piers showed signs of wear. So did the cars, mostly well-rusted noisy early-1970s models. Legions of scrawny cats wandered around the yards of the small houses. At least four restaurants and a motel served the tourist trade. Towheaded kids rode the main street on bicycles or, surprisingly, new small motorbikes. The "downtown" was dominated by a crisply painted Methodist church, where, I learned, elaborate weddings and other ceremonies often take place and to which many islanders habitually tithe. A cluttered general store bore this cryptic sign:

Bills will be sent each month that are over due

—Charlie Evans
Thank You

The lady tending the store told me some of the local news. "About five hundred of us live here," she said. "Not as many as there used to be. The young ones go off to college and they never come back. Things haven't changed much. But now there's a man who wants to put in a marina, and Lord knows what all, down at the end of the town where the house burned down. I don't know—maybe it would be good for some of the boatmen. But most of us are against it. There are enough people here as it is. The new people would just come and go, and they wouldn't support the church." The project, I learned later, was being promoted by a man from Delaware who for some years had owned a 90-acre parcel on the island and had previously tried a couple of unsuccessful business ventures. Now he proposed to erect a hundred town houses on his land and install a marina with slips for eighty boats, and the unlikely scheme had received a go-ahead from a county planning board on which no Smith Islander sat. In asking around town, I heard a variety of objections to the proposal. It would create local jobs only during the busy and profitable summer crabbing season when the watermen have no time to spare. It would provoke "culture shock" and would do ecological harm.

"I don't know too many who are for it," summed up Frances Kitching, the island's doyenne and owner of a well-known, though now closed, boardinghouse and restaurant. In her living room, adjacent to the kitchen where for decades she doled out crab burgers and oyster loaf and deep-fried buckram and corn pudding to admiring guests gathered at the family-style table, she summarized the reasons for her own opposition. She worried about the requirements for roads and sewage that would accompany the project, and feared for the integrity of her 980-foot artesian well, in which she had as much capital invested as in her house itself. "Where are they going to put the spoil from the dredgin'?" she asked. As a woman, she said, she felt powerless to mobilize much support against the development, but she was hoping for help from the well-connected environmental journalist Tom Horton of the Baltimore *Sun*, then temporarily living on the island and running the Chesapeake Bay Foundation's education program there. Her wry final word on the matter: "If it ever gets built and people move in there, by the time the green flies get through with 'em in the summer, and the northwest winds in the winter, they'll be sorry they ever saw the place."

If Smith Island threatened to become a haven for affluent summer folk at the expense of the traditional local economy, the prognosis for the rest of the bay seemed depressingly clear. Even with the sort of tightening up of regulations that Maryland has imposed, developers would still be likely to win more fights than they would lose. Already, in 1987, the Critical Areas criteria were being questioned in many of Maryland's seventeen bay counties which must affirm them if the program is to become a grass-roots success. The fledgling Critical Areas Commission, moreover, found its work hampered by budget reductions. Every new marina or condominium or big new highway or hotel would be built at the cost of a remaining shellfish ground, sea-grass bed, or still unpolluted stream or byway. Each tree felled would exacerbate the bay's ill health because, scientists have found, streamside forests in the system sop up large amounts of nutrients before they reach the bay. The torment of the estuary's slide toward death would be lamented by journalists, duck hunters, and sport-fishermen, and the watermen and others who still eke a living from the bay. But the farmers would continue to profit from the sale of their land to development. Places like Frances Kitching's boardinghouse and Miz Lizzie's seafood and barbecue haven on Route 4 would give way to the relentless march of the Pizza Hut and the Burger King. Ocean City was the goal. Boaters would mill about on lifeless waters, happy as long as anchorages and marina slips remained available, concerned only about the seasonal influx of nettles that interfere with the swimming. The few remaining eagles would succumb.

Could this fate be averted? "It's going to get worse before it gets better," Will Baker said. "The rapid growth around here means that we're always swimming against a stronger current. There's no diminishing of interest, but the question is effectiveness. We've been around long enough to have solved all the easy problems—now we're up against the tough ones." For every victory—banning TBT or phosphates in household detergents, winning a court battle to compel an industrial polluter to comply with regulations, gaining a donation of a salt marsh for conservation and wildlife habitat—he and his colleagues face a hydra-headed profusion of new challenges as development and human occupation press on. In all too many instances, the Save the Bay movement must act to control damage rather than press for improvements.

Intensive farming remains a principal stumbling block throughout the bay's drainage area, and particularly so in Pennsylvania's Lancaster County, home to more livestock and poultry per acre than any other county in the United States. The Amish farmers there, without direct access to the water, still living tightly within their own culture, feel little connection to the Chesapeake's ailments. They also want to extract the highest possible yield from each increment of their land, and this means unsparing applications of manure from their livestock as well as chemicals. On the average, each acre of land in Lancaster County produces 27 tons of manure a year, and much of this ends up in the bay, where it nurtures the excess algae that soak up oxygen. Amish chickens, whose numbers have grown fast since 1960, kill the Chesapeake's vanishing oysters. Other than allowing it to drain off, researchers have identified no economic way to dispose of the manure, though patient fieldwork by environmentalists has persuaded some farmers to adopt what are known as Best Management Practices: for example, conservation tillage, a planting method that does little damage to the soil surface and thus inhibits erosion. Specifically, eight hundred steeply sloped farms located near waterways may account for much of the problem, said the EPA's Tom DeMoss, but the only effective way to control their runoff would be by means of politically unpopular regulations.

Even if the farm drainage could somehow be contained, raw or lightly treated sewage will continue to flood the bay with nutrients. Advances such as the high-tech Blue Plains treatment center on the Potomac, which according to Tom Horton is known as "the Craphouse Taj Mahal" among sewer professionals, have been helpful. Still, a major increase in sewage will accompany any future growth of the region. How it will be treated remains an open question, particularly since federal dollars will, according to current plans, contribute only a minor share of the total cost. Toxic pollution too will continue to drain into the bay regardless of tightening controls and such significant court victories as those recently achieved by the Chesapeake Bay Foundation and the Natural Resources Defense Council over such notorious point-source polluters as Bethlehem Steel and Gwaltney. Especially difficult to control is storm-water runoff carrying with it an abundance of wastes from farms and overflowing septic tanks and other poisons from factories and highways and city streets. The Potomac's sewage-treatment facility at

Blue Plains sewage treatment plant on the Potomac.

Blue Plains may be the world's most advanced, said one environmental official, but "I wouldn't go swimming in there after a storm when the runoff is really bad." If by some miracle the ongoing flow of new poisons could be halted, moreover, it would still take decades for the bay to be rid of the toxic substances that are embedded in the sediments of the hot spots.

Maryland's Critical Areas effort will forestall development along some still virgin stretches of the bay, and considerable amounts of public and private land are already consecrated to conservation. But no public entity has yet dared to place an absolute limit on the growth of human population around its edges. The numbers have already increased by 50 percent since 1950, and are expected to hit 15 million by 2000. They will double the 1980 level by 2020 or before if present trends continue. Unless governments "aggressively confront the issue of human carrying capacity and limit or prevent development of certain areas," warned the committed Maryland state senator Gerald Winegrad, "the bay's decline will continue." Said Will Baker: "We've done about as much as we can with carrots. You can only smile and talk for so long. Now we're coming closer to believing that we need some new sticks."

As of 1988, for all the worthy efforts under way, no one seemed to be staring down the developers and their eager customers effectively enough. Conservationists had ample will, not enough power. The bay's epitaph "has already been written, if not yet chiseled in stone," the well-informed Tom Horton has said in his eloquent book *Bay Country*.

Father White would not be pleased.

5

Abroad on the Banks

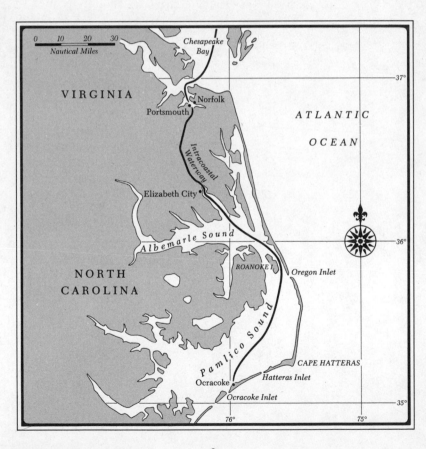

Sanderling in Carters Creek.

SNOW SHADOWED SANDERLING'S DEPARTURE FOR THE MID-ATLANTIC. On a warm sunny Sunday early in March, Peter Walsh and I cast off from our snug berth at Zahniser's and headed down the bay. Our first afternoon was windless and the bay was empty, the sunshine fading and soon replaced by a soft rain. The next day fog settled in and we used our radar to motor through shining flat black water toward Norfolk, into a little bight called Carters Creek. Here we heard talk of gales and a sharp frontal passage on the NOAA radio. By early evening, right on schedule, the westerly wind started building and our halyards rattled against the mast. Even snugly berthed in a minor tributary of the Rappahannock, we soon were rolling about. As the temperature dropped precipitously and a mixture of rain and snow began to fall, we gladly switched on our little Espar diesel-fueled cabin heater. In the morning we had a couple of inches' accumulation and flakes were still blowing almost horizontally down the deck and across the cockpit. For want of a shovel, Pete used a water hose to make *Sanderling* look like a sailboat again.

If we had not forecast snow, we had done much to prepare ourselves for this stretch of the journey. Between now and June we would cover some 2,200 miles from the Chesapeake to the Virgin Islands and much in between: the Bahamas, the northeast coast of Cuba, the north coasts of Haiti and the Dominican Republic and Puerto Rico. Not a light undertaking in terms of logistics. Peter, an enthusiastic twenty-four-year-old signed on for the whole ride to Brazil, had begun to study celestial navigation, achieved a scuba certificate, and accumulated an inventory of specialized clothing, including an elaborate foul-weather costume that looked suitable for total immersion in arctic waters. I concentrated on charts and amassed a foot-thick stack of them; in working with the yard learned something of what it takes to keep even a small sailing vessel in good shape; dealt with various bureaucracies about insurance and radio licenses and identification numbers; and tried to plan out an itinerary that would have in it some flexibility but also some firm dates for crew members' comings and goings. Now at last we were off, and the snow and associated wind held us back only for one day.

After a lay day while the storm subsided, we set off before a cold stiff northerly that whisked us the remaining fifty miles down the bay to Norfolk, yawing in short choppy seas and surfing down their faces. The water, a strange brownish gray, supported great flocks of seabirds—scoters and pintails and many loons. Averaging 6.6 knots, not bad for a boat designed strictly for cruising, we rounded Thimble Shoals by 2:30 p.m., exhilarated by the sail and warmed by the continuous exertion of energy needed to keep our rolling vessel more or less on course. Naval aircraft maneuvered overhead as we inspected the substantial fleet berthed in Norfolk, consisting now of two aircraft carriers, a battleship, and myriad smaller warships and support vessels. About a third of the entire U.S. Navy—127 vessels, five of the seven aircraft carriers that patrol the Atlantic—is home-ported here. Norfolk is the world's biggest naval base.

Once, as a guest of the Secretary of the Navy at another time, I had a chance to see something of how this outfit works. At the Norfolk base several admirals told me how far we have come from the years of World War II, when people defending the coast still manned towers on the beach and scanned the horizon with binoculars in search of enemy planes or submarines, and barbed wire was rolled out on the beaches to thwart hostile amphibious landings. Things have changed greatly even since the late 1950s, when I flew the slow but powerful old propeller-driven Skyraider off and onto various carriers. With the help of amazing new computers and radars and sonars and missiles, the modern Navy proposes to catch the enemy far out at sea; the notion of coastal defense is a thing of the past.

I flew out for a day aboard the nuclear-powered USS *Dwight D. Eisenhower*, a behemoth of a ship almost four football fields long and, at 95,000 tons, weighing half again as much as the biggest carrier I had previously experienced. I watched transfixed as young Navy and Marine pilots practiced day and night landings and catapult shots in A-6

Intruders and A-7 Corsairs, F-14 Tomcats and brand-new F-18 Hornets. Escorted by a coolly professional young aviator who looked and talked like a choirboy, I combed the ship from stem to stern, and along the way talked with many of the ship's well-schooled officers and men. On the bridge I learned that if you look straight ahead the closest thing you can see over the edge of the flight deck is 660 yards away, or more than a quarter mile, that if the *Ike* were to hit a fixed object at a speed of one knot the impact would be equivalent in force to that of a car striking the same object at 50,000 miles per hour, and that from a normal speed it requires seven miles to stop the ship without reversing the propellers. (In August 1988, embarrassingly, *Ike* collided with a tanker.) Down below were the ship's anchor chains (each link weighs 365 pounds) and its high-tech Carrier Intelligence Center and its dental clinic. I asked about the garbage produced through housing and feeding 6,000 men. There's an on-board incinerator, I was told. The biodegradable stuff is kept aboard until the ship is at least a hundred miles out, then bagged and weighted and tossed overboard "for the fishies to eat."

Back ashore at the Norfolk base I toured the line of naval vessels from the shore side, then boarded the nuclear-powered attack submarine *Hyman C. Rickover*, which is capable of patrolling almost silently, in air cleaner than what most of us breathe, for months on end without ever surfacing. Its remarkable variety of equipment ranges from deadly accurate Tomahawk cruise missiles that can be launched from below the surface, so that the sub does not reveal its position, to a downward-facing torpedo tube through which the ship's garbage is expelled when its position is fifty or more miles from shore. The *Rickover* has no incinerator.

Past this muscular array of warpower *Sanderling* now cruised on wind-ruffled water, straightforwardly muddy brown, to a marina in Portsmouth, across the Elizabeth River from downtown Norfolk. There we joined the presidential yacht *Sequoia* in negotiating a narrow entryway in the continuing stiff breeze: *Sanderling*, with but one screw and an apparent inability to be steered backward along a straight line under power, was at a disadvantage. After twenty minutes of embarrassing jockeying, we succeeded in tying up alongside a windblown dock. Thanks to a broken-down swing bridge that was closed for several days for repairs, we saw more than we intended of the Norfolk area. We spent a day in Portsmouth, a place that alternates between ghetto and "Olde Towne," with new signs announcing a shorefront historic district with old houses and brick sidewalks. The ghetto part along the old main street, now pawnshops and a blowsy young woman screaming into a pay phone, was moving and distressing. Olde Towne, though spotted with attractive eighteenth-century houses, looked unpromising as a tourist attraction. Norfolk's downtown boasts several new tall office buildings, including that of the Sovran ("sovereign" with a Virginia accent) Bank, which covers what was the red-light district fifteen years ago. Norfolk also now has Waterside, a riverfront mall echoing Boston's Quincy Market and Baltimore's Harborplace, whose booths offer cuisine from many lands presented in Styrofoam containers. When we visited, its halls were filled, not with tourists, but with young downtown professionals on their lunch break. We heard that with a good year-round climate and Virginia Beach close by, the town has become something of a magnet for such people.

Despite Norfolk's attractions, we were relieved when we learned that the bridge had reopened. Within minutes we were at the entry to the Intracoastal Waterway, the thousand-mile inner passage between Norfolk and Miami that consists in part of dredged and well-buoyed lengths of natural river or sound, in part of artificially cut canals. Soon we cleared the clutter of the Elizabeth River, lined with mothballed naval vessels and rusty tankers, and entered Deep Creek, the passage into the slave-dug Dismal Swamp Canal leading through this legendary region to Albemarle Sound in northeastern North Carolina. Avoided by many early colonials who thought it a foul and unhealthy place, this "great morass" was singled out for special attention by the Reverend Jedidiah Morse, father of Samuel F. B. Late in the eighteenth century, he wrote: "Neither beast, bird, insect, or reptile approach the heart of this horrible desert, perhaps deterred by the everlasting shade . . . nor indeed do any birds care to fly over it . . . for fear of the noisome exhalations that rise from this vast body of filth and nastiness." Later, conquering such apprehensions, settlers logged the swamp for its fine cypress and drained it for farmland.

Keen to have a look, we did not know if this would be possible. We had heard that the canal had been closed because of low water, but until we reached its first set of locks (one up eight feet, the second back down to sea level), we were not certain that it was open again. The fact was, the lockmaster told us, that we would be the very first vessel through in eight months. Since *Sanderling* draws five feet ten inches and the canal's controlling depth is six feet, we feared that we might touch bottom as a result of the lack of recent traffic along the twenty-two-mile stretch—and were not disappointed, twice striking our keel hard against what were probably sunken logs. In places the canal was so narrow that our mast brushed against overhanging boughs, at one point sprinkling the decks with tiny red leaf buds, and we took care to steer right down the center. With a warm sun and pleasant farmland along the banks, we felt lucky that the bridge delay had given us the chance to see this route, an attractive alternative to the strictly commercial Virginia Cut to Carolina that is used by most who travel the Waterway.

Late in the afternoon we emerged out into the meandering, tannic Pasquotank River, lined with swamp and gum trees and mistletoe. Boatloads of locals fished for largemouth bass, and a snake swam by in the still water. Where the river widened we anchored, all alone, in quiet water. Not even the howl of a coon hound was required to convince us that we had arrived in the South. Now, though sorry to have hurried so quickly past tidewater Virginia with its rich history, we were poised to discover the mysteries of the biologically important maze of swamps, sounds, inlets, barrier islands, rivers, salt marshes, and dunes lying between here and Florida—and the threat of Chesapeakization that this once backwater region now faces.

Once a quiet area of fishermen and small farms, eastern North Carolina is experiencing rapid change and a proportionate increase in environmental difficulties. The arrival of industries such as a Texasgulf Chemicals Company phosphate plant and large corporate farms and a quickening of residential development along the bays and estuaries have resulted in higher levels of all forms of water pollution. During the hot dry summer of 1987 the Pamlico and Pungo rivers both experienced unprecedented oxygen shortages, algal blooms, and fish die-offs. "We had eels, hog suckers, and crabs jumping out of the water and crawling up the bank," a scientist told the Washington *Post*. As further evidence of stress on the Pamlico, red sores and ulcers broke out among its finfish and even its crabs. On the outer islands, large-scale resort development activities have provoked concern about a variety of environmental issues, ranging from beach erosion to the effects of storm-water runoff on shellfishing areas in the bays between the islands and the mainland. Managing the region's rapid development is a challenging task. "You get yelled at no matter what you decide," said the legal services lawyer Dan Besse, chairman of the Governor's Coastal Resources Commission.

The history of the Albemarle, our entry point into the region, is antebellum. Refugees from the Jamestown colony settled along the Pasquotank and nearby black-water rivers during the seventeenth century, and found its climate—as we did as well—a benign contrast to Virginia's during the chilly winters. Its forests of tall, straight longleaf pine were to provide immense quantities of spars and resin for Britain's commercial and naval fleets. Trading and plantation farming quickly took hold along the Albemarle; the now vanished Currituck inlets provided easy access to the ocean. The shipping port of Edenton on the Chowan, now a backwater, throbbed with vitality during the years before what, in these parts, is still often referred to as the War of Northern Oppression. Later, when ships grew too large to traverse the shallow Albermarle and the Dismal Swamp Canal opened in 1805, the emphasis shifted to Elizabeth City at the mouth of the Pasquotank, named for the queen who in 1585 gave Sir Walter Raleigh a charter to explore and colonize this area.

It thrived until the end of slavery and until the Currituck inlets were sealed off in storms. We motored past what's left of the town on a flat blue morning, seeing little more than one sailboat anchored in the middle of the broadening river and a Fuji Film blimp maneuvering around the old Naval Air Station with huge hangars for lighter-than-air craft left over from World War II. In puffy little bursts of air we reached southeast, toward the north end of Roanoke Island, passing major benchmarks: first a single brown pelican, then a squadron of them beak to tail, first rising ten or fifteen feet above the wavelets in search of fish, then dipping down so close that their feathery wingtips seemed almost immersed. These wonderful birds—they look like pterodactyls and do controlled crashes from ten feet when they spot fish, sending great torrents of water skyward when they plop in—were all but wiped out by the DDT immolations of the 1960s. Now they are back in force, almost as common as sea gulls from here to Florida, and this first sighting of them was reassurance of the hardiness of many coastal species. We rounded the north end of Roanoke Island, looking across to the northeast at the high white dunes of Kitty Hawk with a large monument to the Wright brothers; then turned south along the shallow, narrow little channel in the sound between Roanoke Island and the town of Nags Head on Bodie, one of the principal islands of the Outer Banks. At South Nags Head, we learned later, twenty houses built too close to the water will disappear with the next major storm and another hundred are endangered; though the barrier islands farther to the south have access to fresh water from a powerful underground aquifer, continuing development around Nags Head has caused a local water shortage.

With sandy beaches in the foreground and great stands of large trees on slightly higher ground behind, Roanoke Island looked every bit as inviting as the Outer Banks region, during the summer of 1584, to Masters Philip Amadas and Arthur Barlowe. These were the two captains entrusted by Raleigh (who, preferring to keep his feet closer to the fire, never visited North America) to survey his new land grant. Historians still dispute where these mariners, piloted by the experienced Portuguese navigator Simon Ferdinando, first touched the mainland. It was somewhere along the Outer Banks and in the vicinity of Roanoke, and the landing inspired great enthusiasm in Barlowe. In his journal he spoke

The British landing on the Virginia coast, 1584.
From Theodor DeBry's *America*, first published 1590.

of the soil as being "the most plentifull, sweete, fruitfull and wholesome of all the world," of "all kind of oderiferous flowers," great profusions of wild grapes growing right down into the seawater, an "incredible aboundance" of wild animals and "cranes," and "very handsome and goodly" Indians, who seemed "as mannerly, and civill, as any of Europe." Perhaps far more so, one is tempted to add, reflecting on the minor role allocated to personal hygiene in Elizabethan England and the even scruffier condition to which the English seamen were doubtless reduced after a couple of totally unwashed months. But it must be remembered as well that Barlowe knew what Raleigh wanted him to say. If Captain John Smith was the second, Barlowe was, as the historian David Stick put it in his sprightly *Roanoke Island*, "America's first English-language publicist."

One believer was the geographer and ordained minister Richard Hakluyt, another master promoter, who had already written and spoken extensively about his "diligent inquiries of such things as might yield any light into our Western discoveries in America." Upon reading Barlowe's material, Samuel Eliot Morison stated in his *Northern Voyages*, Hakluyt developed "a vision of tidewater plantations of sugarcane, pineapple, even mulberry trees to feed silkworms; and the mountains would yield gold." Though by 1585 Queen Elizabeth was feeling Spain's hot breath

Left: Thomas Hariot. *Right:* Sir Walter Raleigh.

and had become cautious about major new North American commitments, Hakluyt's reinforcement of Barlowe's enthusiasm prompted her to knight Raleigh and take other limited steps to encourage an effort to colonize the territory. Raleigh commissioned Sir Richard Grenville to act as commander-in-chief for the expedition and appointed as governor a young adventurer named Ralph Lane. Two other notable figures were also recruited: the scientist Thomas Hariot, whose *Briefe and True Report of the New Found Land of Virginia* remains the classic analysis of the first Virginia colony, and the artist John White, whose illustrations were to govern European thinking about the New World's appearance for the better part of a century.

Commanding five ships and 108 colonists, Grenville reached Pamlico Sound in late June 1585, established Lane on Roanoke Island, and as summer ended sailed back to England. Though the colonists were not able to catch fish, they planted corn and other foodstuffs and for a while, until relations grew unfriendly, were able to trade with the Indians. Despite the usual warfare, which soon began, the colonists were able to survive the winter relatively well. Nonetheless, Lane was relieved when, in June, Sir Francis Drake happened by and took them all home. A month later Grenville returned and was surprised to find Roanoke deserted. He off-loaded a force of eighteen men to guard the colony. This force was never seen again. Either the men starved to death or they were killed by Indians. In 1587, Raleigh launched a second effort, led by the artist John White. Some hundred new colonists, of all ages and both sexes, landed on Roanoke. It was July, and crabs and fish, which by now the British could catch with hook and line, were plentiful. Virginia Dare was born. White departed for England in August, in order to act as the colony's agent at home. The Indians were quiet, food was readily available, everything seemed to be going well. What happened next has never been fully explained. But when White finally returned in 1590, after delays caused by the Spanish Armada, nobody was left. In addition to these attempts to establish a foothold on the Carolina shore, many ships had been lost, or nearly lost, in the treacherous waters around Capes Fear, Hatteras, and Lookout.

Still today, as attractive as the region appears and in many ways is, humans continue to end up as losers if they choose to battle the natural elements around the Outer Banks, rather than roll with their punches. Of this there is no clearer example than the headstrong quarter-century effort to "stabilize" Oregon Inlet, the tricky passage between Nags Head and Hatteras Island that links the broad, shallow expanse of Pamlico Sound with the open ocean. From aboard *Sanderling*, continuing southward in the narrow Roanoke Sound channel, we glimpsed, far off our port bow, the inlet and the mighty Herbert C. Bonner Bridge that spans it. Nearer were assorted Army Corps of Engineers vessels whose pumps were grinding away, creating new islands and regions of sand and muck, purposefully at work this Sunday afternoon. Abeam to starboard was the town of Wanchese (pronounced wan-CHEESE), named for one of the two Indians who went back to England with Amadas and Barlowe, and by many accounts the cause of all the fuss. Early in the 1970s, Wanchese was declared, by state and federal authorities and despite strong objections registered by many local fishermen, to be a Seafood Industrial Park. The existence of the park, in turn, was said to warrant a major effort to pump away at the inlet's shifting sands to maintain a channel for fishing vessels to have good access to the processing plants. Conversely, it was also often argued that in view of the high cost of keeping the inlet open, the park was a logical corollary. For the sake of the park or the inlet or both, politicians and some local boosters have lobbied steadily to increase the dredged depth in the inlet from fourteen to twenty feet. The Army Corps of Engineers has proposed the construction of long jetties to protect the inlet and the bridge, at a (probably underestimated) cost of $114 million, and an elaborate pumping system to enable some of the inlet's shifting sand to get where it would naturally go if the jetties were not there.

What is wrong with the scheme starts with basic beach geology. No seacoast lined with a sandy beach is static. In rhythm with waves and storms and currents, beaches and offshore bars swirl and twist and turn. Eroding at one end, an island may be growing as fast or faster at the other. Inlets between barrier islands and the mainland open in storms, then sometimes close up again. So frequently must the Coast Guard reset the buoys marking the constantly shifting channels that they are usually omitted from nautical charts. With a narrow coastal shelf that gives it the highest wave-energy level to be found anywhere along the U.S. Atlantic seaboard, Oregon Inlet is particularly dynamic. Since it first broke through in 1846, the inlet has moved southward two miles or more, and its progress continues at a rate of at least seventy-five feet a year. In such an environment, construction of any fixed object is at best hazardous. While the bridge was being built in 1962, it collapsed during the ferocious Ash Wednesday storm. Since its completion in 1963, repair bills have exceeded manyfold the bridge's original cost of $2.8 million. The best thing to do with this structure, wrote the Tulane University professor of environmental law Thomas J. Schoenbaum in his 1979 book *Islands, Capes, and Sounds,* is "let it fall into the sea." Along with Ocean City, Maryland, Orrin Pilkey has already written it off. "It *will* go in the next big storm," he said.

For fishermen the inlet's hazards are severe. During a stormy three-week stretch one recent winter, nine trawlers grounded in the inlet. Large vessels and human lives continue to be lost there; the toll has been so heavy that only a single tenant was left in the Seafood Industrial Park in 1987. Many observers cite evidence that North Carolina waters lack a single fishery of sufficient magnitude to justify an elaborately equipped home port for large million-dollar fishing boats. As the global sea level rises, said Pilkey, the channel-clogging problem will worsen. He and Dr. Stanley Riggs, a geology professor at East Carolina University who has been studying Oregon Inlet for decades, have both predicted accelerated shoreline erosion and increased storm flooding as regional consequences if the jetties are built.

Pilkey, supported by an impartial blue-ribbon panel convened by the National Park Service to look into the matter, has argued that a well-designed dredging program represents a "viable alternative" to the prospective folly of the jetties. But the pressure to build the jetties continues no matter whether Democrats or Republicans hold the power in Raleigh, and conservationists harbor dark suspicions about the reasons. One suspects Pentagon involvement, having read the exciting novel *The Hunt for Red October*, in which a renegade Russian submarine is slipped through what is apparently an Outer Banks inlet into a shallow sound. Another suggests that Machiavellian elements in Raleigh are

Left: Fisherman Willie Etheridge, Jr., passing under
Herbert C. Bonner Bridge. *Right:* Orrin Pilkey debates
the Oregon Inlet issue.

using the issue as a way to thwart the natural alliance between the
environmental community and fishermen, who know all too well the
heavy cost of exceeding the limits and capabilities of their natural
surroundings. No one quite knows who the King Canute of the game is,
though Pilkey suggests dryly that "the Army Corps of Engineers is not
the agency to lead the nation during a time of rising sea level," and offers
an arsenal of information about this agency's long history of poor planning
and low cost estimates and bad policies. Still, every conversation about
the subject seems to trail off with a sad but inconclusive reiteration of the
words "a mess . . ."

At one point we had contemplated bypassing the Dismal Swamp and
the Albemarle and making a straight sea passage from Norfolk out to
Cape Henry, then down the Virginia and Carolina coast to Oregon Inlet.
Now, having seen it after the winter's northeasters had done their work
and the channel had shifted so much that a Coast Guardsman had told us,
"I don't even advise our boats to use it now," we were glad to hurry past
on the inside. Even this was not an easy passage, for it is very shoal and
the buoys are laid out in a way that makes it hard to tell if you are
supposed to leave them to port or to starboard. Several times, creeping

along under power with no sail on, we watched in anguish as the depth indicator dropped to within inches of our draft. "Where the hell's the water?" Pete would ask in frustration as we jammed the engine into reverse and tried to back away from shoals hidden close beneath the blue-green sea, then shifted to forward when the depth got no better. We remained afloat for a while. Before long we grounded, bouncing as small waves raised us a few inches, then dropped *Sanderling* abruptly onto the hard sand.

The tide falling, a southwesterly now blowing solidly at 15 knots, the sandy beach of Dog Island but a hundred yards downwind: shipwrecked along the Outer Banks—was this to be the end of *Sanderling*'s cruise, as it had been for so many other sailing vessels? Pete started untying the dinghy so that we could lower it over the side, put the big anchor into it, row away, toss it over, and try to kedge off. Then somehow my maneuvering with the throttle and gearshift worked and we eased into deeper water—6 feet, 6.2, 6.5, our spirits lifting with each tenth of a foot on the gauge as we moved off the shoal and slipped back into the elusive channel. Once off, it was a smooth run under power and a full moon down the late-winter emptiness of broad, shallow Pamlico Sound and into the perfect protection of Ocracoke Island's Silver Lake Harbor.

Ocracoke. This legendary place, once frequented by Blackbeard (Edward Teach) and other pirates, inhabited for three hundred years by self-reliant fisherfolk who dipped fresh water from the natural aquifer for washing purposes, gathered drinking water in cisterns on the roofs of their houses, and used outhouses, not septic tanks. A plaque celebrates the feat of Naval Lieutenant Robert Maynard, who ambushed Teach, managing to dispatch him with the aid of a platoon of sailors and only after a furious struggle, and reportedly carted the rascal's head back to the state capital at the tip of his ship's bowsprit. George Woodwell's wife, Katharine, owns a house here. It belonged to her parents, who for twenty years had lived on the island and taught in its school. Woodwell had told me much of the fumbling ways of the new Ocracoke—the design shortcomings of the town's plastic-piped water system, the follies of trying to tame the island's wandering beaches and contain its sewage. "One day I'll have to make time to write it all up," he had said. Now I was here instead, with a chance to try to figure out something about Ocracoke and where it's headed.

Access to the island remains difficult. If you don't come by private boat, either you take a long ferry ride across the sound from Swan Quarter or Cedar Island or you drive down the outer islands, via the infamous Bonner Bridge and Hatteras Island, and take a short ferry ride across Hatteras Inlet. On most of Ocracoke itself, sixteen miles long, you see little but broad sandy beach and salt marsh and moor, for all but 775 acres of the island have for some years formed part of the Cape Hatteras National Seashore and are immune to development. On the remainder of the island, in housing ranging from permanently tethered mobile home to mini-condo, reside 650 assorted people. Some are 1970s retirees, some land speculators. Summer throngs crowd things on Ocracoke, but during the off-season, most of the people one encounters along the single main street, which follows the smooth round curve of Silver Lake Harbor, are from families that have been here a long time.

I asked Ocracoke's only elected official, an earnest schoolteacher named Alton Ballance who represents the island on the five-member Hyde County Commission and lives with his parents in a two-story wood-frame house, how long his family had been here. "I'm not exactly sure," he replied. "Five or six generations, I guess." Ballance and people like him have worked hard to preserve the funky diversity of the little town as it now exists—the single commercial road, the Coast Guard station, a few modest stores, even the eyesore four-story Anchorage Inn as long as it is not replicated. Those who erected this structure somehow evaded a thirty-five-foot height limit that has long applied to all buildings, and started the island on an uncertain course toward a new sort of future symbolized by two small condominium-type buildings that have recently cropped up. Visitors to Ocracoke are likely to be driving shiny campers or new Buicks. Ocracokers, more drawn to pickups or full-size 1970s sedans with rusted-out mufflers, depend in large part on the tourist trade. But, I found out, few want to be engulfed by it.

My quest for answers about Ocracoke led to David Senseney, a tall, gentle, energetic, bearded man who teaches at the school (kindergarten to twelfth grade) and also owns or co-owns several harborfront businesses, including a general store with a potbellied stove, an antique shop, a hardware store, a sportfishing dock, and a pier with slips for visiting yachtsmen. Born in a little town in South Carolina, Senseney came almost two decades ago to Ocracoke to finish a master's thesis in mental health ("It probably wouldn't have been any good anyway") and simply never left. Late in the afternoon, in weather that had once again turned cold and blustery, Senseney boarded *Sanderling* with his six-year-old daughter, Claire. David settled onto a bunk in the main cabin and Claire onto his lap, where, after a full school day, she promptly fell asleep. The most serious problem, Senseney told me, is property values. Tax assessment comes only once each eight years at Ocracoke, and the town is still reeling from the shock of the sharp upward revaluations of late 1986. One man had bought four acres for $125,000 during the 1970s; now it is assessed at $1.5 million and taxed at a far higher rate. "It's a serious situation," Senseney said. "Some blue-collar retirees who settled here in the 1970s are already pulling out. Their land is just worth too much for them to be able to stay on it. And it's gotten hard for the young people too. There's only so much room for trailers in Mom and Dad's back yard. Redevelopment has gotten to be a buzzword here, and new construction is going on all over."

Senseney suggested I talk further about real estate issues with Alton Ballance, and I did so at the well-equipped school a block in from the harborfront. Most of the pressure, he said, is coming not from within the county but from interests lying farther away, even out of state. "I'm not opposed to all new development," Ballance added. "But I think we should maintain the thirty-five-foot limit, and we ought to grow pretty slowly so that the people who are now here can make the adjustments and stay. Slow growth with more community involvement—I'd like to see that." At Senseney's invitation I remained at the school to spend an hour with a group of his high school students. All seven were keen to get off the island—to go to college, see the world. Some said they could not imagine coming back and actually living on Ocracoke (but reminded me that others among them couldn't imagine leaving). Unanimously, though, they agreed that no one among their contemporaries wanted the place to change very much. All sided with Ballance on the height limit, and none wanted big-time condos. "It's not that they *look* so bad," said one wriggly girl. "It's just the *idea*." But Ballance cautioned me about thinking that such sentiments alone would carry the day: "Where money and greed are involved, you can never be quite sure how things will come out."

Since the only meat to be had at Senseney's Community Store was either in cans or in blocks in the freezer, I set off in search of fresh fish. No dice, said the skipper of a small Wanchese trawler tied up near the Coast Guard station. He mourned the closing of Oregon Inlet due to stormy weather. How had the fishing been?

"I wish I could get out there to find out," he replied.

No, said a man in a battered Land-Rover who managed a bait dock, all the fish he had were shipped over to the mainland.

"They're not runnin' yet," said a man at Senseney's dock who alternated between commercial fishing and charter parties.

"No fish at all," said the burly proprietor of the principal fish dock. "But I do have some scallops. They're in the shell, though."

I'd heard that the scalloping around Ocracoke had been good, that these little swimmers had click-click-clicked their way clear of the mainland and the pocosin-swamp drainage projects, flapping out toward more saline water. I bought a large bagful and carried them dripping back to *Sanderling*. I put the shells into the boat's stainless-steel sink and started attacking them with a razor-sharp knife. First drive a wedge in near the heel of the shell, then twist between the two sides to open it up a little, then slide the sharp side of the knife along one side to sever the muscle. Now open the shell wide, and you have an exposed column of white muscle surrounded almost completely by the animal's slimy, inedible gray-black working anatomy. Now the trick is softly to work this ooze away from the muscle and leave the gleaming-white little cylinder standing free, sometimes after watching the rest of the creature convulse for one last time. If you are successful and avoid the temptation to down your scallop raw, before long you have a little pile and the makings of a gourmet meal: stir-fry in butter, perhaps with a touch of shallot or celery seed, sprinkle in some dry white wine at the end, and cover and simmer for an instant without committing the fatal error of overcooking. Peter and I sautéed the whole mess, thinking we would save some for the next day. We ate it all.

Out at the broad clean beach I watched as a huge school of dolphins passed by just outside the breakers. Pelicans and cormorants worked the surf line, and gulls, oystercatchers, and sandpipers patrolled the beach. On this sunny afternoon a teenage boy walked resolutely out toward where a barefoot girl was already waiting near a dune. Back near town, school was just letting out and kids on balloon-tire bikes (few ten-speeds here) headed toward home. At the Community Store, near closing time, Senseney dispensed wedges of cheddar from a large wheel. "In the summer you can sell a whole one of these in an hour," he said. He added that he was sorry not to have been able to spend more time with me, but the freezer had broken down and he had had to work hard to transfer all his frozen goods to someone else's freezer until repairs could be made.

Ocracoke, I thought as we left the Coast Guard station to starboard and headed back out into Pamlico Sound, would not be likely to change too much. The collapse of the Bonner Bridge would (will, Pilkey would say) be helpful to the people on the island who want to preserve its tranquillity. And even if the bridge stays up and the tourists keep on driving down, Ocracokers seemed far more likely than, say, Nantucketers to resist the blandishments of gentrification. High tax rates, not bad habits among the citizens, are the real threat here.

6

Southern Discomfort

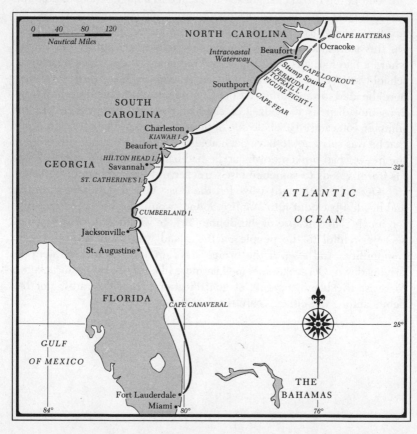

PUFFS OF SMOKE OR SPRAY ON THE PORT BOW, FAR AWAY. WE LOOKED through the binoculars. Then we saw the Phantoms and Intruders from the nearby Cherry Point Marine air base, bombing and strafing targets within a restricted area clearly noted on the chart. Mergansers and canvasbacks and a great many pelicans were also about, unruffled by the circling, roaring, diving fighters and bombers. Under mainsail and the pretty blue-and-white lightweight sail that we could fly when sailing downwind, *Sanderling* plowed southward along Pamlico Sound, bound now for a reentry point back into the Intracoastal Waterway, which would lead us to the important twin ports of Morehead City and Beaufort, North Carolina.

These towns, which form the southern gateway to the Outer Banks, face south; the beaches run east and west. At Beaufort, before an oak fire in the living room of his carefully restored 1812 house, Dr. John Costlow awaited me. A Beaufort resident since 1951, director of the nearby Duke marine lab, a former mayor even though he bears the double stigma of being a Republican and a Yankee, a former chairman of the state's Marine Fisheries Commission and an indefatigable participant in many other coastal management activities, Costlow knows the territory.

I asked him about the chances that, through a more careful conservation approach, the Pamlico-Albemarle area might be able to avoid sinking to a Chesapeake-like level of deterioration. Costlow's reply, delivered slowly in a mellow bass between long puffs on a pipe, opened with a short recitation of the state's legislative history, starting with the passage in 1969 of a benchmark Dredge and Fill Act that effectively closed the door to salt-marsh drainage (although it did not preclude the drainage of freshwater areas). Next came federal (1972) and state (1974) coastal zone management laws and the involvement of new federal agencies such as the EPA as well as an upswing in land clearing and forest removal for logging and to make way for large-scale corporate farms. Despite these pressures, the latest initiative, supported by elements in the state capital as well as by Walter Jones, the powerful local congressman, is a comprehensive program to bring about the region's "balanced development."

A regional study commissioned in 1984 had been completed, Costlow said, and its implementation was beginning. The program, as usual, faces opposition—from corporations and real estate speculators and some politicians. As in the instance of the Oregon Inlet fiasco, beach and inlet "control" programs are "not yet uniform" in their sensitivity. A recent call from the governor for "coastal initiatives" could provide support for the concentration of marinas and other development projects in areas already built up or at least closed to shellfishing; or it could open

A sadly typical scene of overdevelopment
on the North Carolina coast.

the door to random and capricious bulldozing of areas that remain pristine. But many diverse groups appreciate the importance of careful development, young people are insisting upon it, and above all there is the simple truth that the lightly populated and virtually industry-free region has not yet suffered much degradation. Can the overall effort, in which Costlow himself was deeply immersed, finally succeed? "I think we can do it," said Costlow. "I wouldn't be in this if I didn't."

Gene Huntsman, a marine biologist at the National Marine Fisheries Service lab in Beaufort, agreed with this assessment. "Maybe I'm just an optimist," he said. "But the level of development around here is still far behind that of places like the Chesapeake. We have their experience to learn from, and we have EPA, and we have a lot of local coastal zone management legislation, and we have the Clean Water Act, and we have a lot of people down here whose livelihoods depend on keeping things more or less the way they are. We've tended to put too much emphasis on the beach issues and to have neglected the sound side. We've put housing in some bogs where the septic tanks are almost sure not to work, and by letting people get away with bulkheading in the estuaries we're abandoning the shallows near shore, a part of the system that's very important biologically. Overall, though, my feeling is that in spite of all the obstacles and pressures we've got it under pretty good control and have a good chance of keeping it that way."

Aboard *Sanderling* on a warm sunny afternoon at Beaufort's well-appointed public docking facility, I heard more detail from Todd Miller, the founder and director of a lively coalition called the North Carolina Coastal Federation. This agency, established in 1982, acts as a useful medium of public education and as a link between people living and working along the shore and the authorities in the state capital. An amiable man in his thirties who wears thick eyeglasses and has a curly dark beard, Miller operates out of a long one-story house on his family's property, which faces on Bogue Sound and the Intracoastal Waterway. He and his wife, Julie, administrator for the little town of Swansboro down the road, live in one end of the house; the Federation office occupies its other end. The peripatetic Miller is not always to be found in these pleasant spaces; often he is in his small truck on the way to or from meetings. His hope, he said during a two-hour conversation, is primarily based on the weight of numbers: 25,000 fishermen, along with many others still using the North Carolina waters in traditional ways, have a stake in their remaining more or less as they are. When a company with only a few local employees attempts to obtain a permit for large-scale farming or "peat mining" (which, Miller said, is often a euphemism for draining marshes and stripping peat just to get at the rich soil underneath), strong local opposition is likely to pop up.

In this environment, the little guy often wins if his pocket carries more votes. People count more than dollars. After repeated efforts to develop a 120,000-acre parcel met community resistance, Prudential gave up and donated the land as a wildlife refuge. For years aggressive lobbying by local interests has kept the peat miners at bay, though the threat never quite vanishes. The local media have been attentive to the coastal issues, and coverage has tended to be sympathetic. But the opposition is powerful and insensitive. Land and beach developer pressures are strong; much of Miller's time is spent trying to counter proposals to build houses between water and primary dunes. North Carolina has more than five hundred almost surely doomed houses that are located within twenty feet of the ocean, Miller said, lamenting that most of these have been constructed within the past decade. Large condominiums have appeared on some of the Outer Banks islands, notably Topsail, where a notorious developer named Marlo Bostic has concentrated his attack on the beach.

Miller had recently lost a round in a long-running battle to maintain stiff storm-water runoff regulations that would help to protect shellfisheries from pollution during flood periods. The composition of two state commissions had shifted away from professionals and toward political cronies of the governor and the state's Secretary of Natural Resources, the latter an appointee not universally admired by the coalition of conservationists. Still, Miller echoed others' optimism. "We're better off than many other areas, that's for sure," he said. But before running off to a Saturday-night community meeting in Hatteras, this determined planner, a native of the region that concerns him, added a final defiant note: "For me, that's not good enough."

(More than a year later I checked back with Miller on how things were going. The 1987 brown or red tides had not returned, he said; the current algae problem was an apparently harmless purple variety— "ocean vomit"—that had been flooding onto the region's ocean beaches. On the positive side, Miller's colleague James Kennedy had unearthed 1970s federal Clean Water Act discharge requirements that Texasgulf and state authorities had both long ignored. Alerted by the public, the state ordered compliance and Texasgulf agreed to cooperate. The resulting anti-pollution program, to be implemented by the company over four years, would reduce the entire flow of phosphates into the Pamlico by 90 percent. The company, which had previously been heavily fined for air-quality violations, had changed local staff and was being more agreeable.)

As we sailed down the narrow channel of the waterway the next day, with the wind at our backs and a strong sun overhead, the great beauty of this coast, just west of Morehead City, clearly revealed itself. To seaward lay salt marshes in the foreground, still brown from the winter but already showing the first sprigs of new green. Beyond were brilliant white stretches of dunes along the barrier islands; overhead and in the marshes a profusion of bird life, including now large flocks of white ibis and great egrets. Dolphins surfaced within the narrow confines of the channel. Now we were approaching the Marines' Camp Lejeune, widely heralded as a buggy, snake-infested hellhole. Our conclusion, though, was that the region would be a yachtsman's paradise were it not for the extreme shallowness of the bays and sounds. And when we reached Thomas' Landing, just beyond Swan Point, we found others who agreed about the quality and value of what we were seeing: Lena and Graham Ritter, both fishermen, he also a custom cabinetmaker, she until recently a factory worker.

Todd Miller had suggested we try to meet with the Ritters to ask them about their battle to save Stump Sound, and more particularly a 50-acre sliver called Permuda Island, from the sort of real estate development that would kill their oyster beds. They arrived for a late supper aboard the boat—both in their fifties, she tall and slender with short black hair slightly gray at the edges, he chunky with reddish-sandy hair. First the Ritters talked of how it was when Lena was a child

Lena Ritter.

(representing the sixth generation of her family around here), how it was when the Ritters were first married. You never locked your door, you could easily scoop up twenty-five bushels of oysters (each bushel worth $22 in the Chesapeake market of 1987) in a single day, no one needed money since fishing and farming covered all needs. Until the early 1950s there were no electric bills in much of Onslow County, for there was no electricity.

Lena's most beloved recreation was clamming, "to get in the water and get my fingers wrigglin' around with them. When I'm doing that I don't even want anyone talking to me." The idyll endured until developers arrived in the 1970s, each with a scheme to put condos or groups of houses along the beaches in sufficient quantities to pollute adjacent shellfish breeding grounds and deprive the fishermen of their principal means of livelihood. For a while the Ritters and other fishermen were unable to lobby effectively. "Ninety-five percent of the state's population isn't here," said Graham. "They didn't use to care at all. As a plain fisherman I couldn't go up there and persuade them. They wouldn't listen to us or believe us."

A particularly searing issue surfaced when a developer named Marshall Thomas applied to the county planning board for a zoning change on 50-acre Permuda Island in Stump Sound, a treasured piece of landscape for the fishermen and an archaeological site strewn with Indian

★ ★SPECIAL STORMWATER EDITION★ ★

COASTAL REVIEW

IV NO. 1 SPRING 1986   NEWSLETTER OF THE N.C. COASTAL FEDERATION   PRICE - $5.00 A YEAR

IF YOU'RE WORRIED THAT THE COASTAL BUILDING BOOM WILL DESTROY YOUR CLEAN WATER AND SHELLFISH...

REPRINTED FROM THE NEWS AND OBSERVER JULY 13, 1983

NOT IF YOU PARTICIPATE!

PARTICIPATE IN THE RUNOFF HEARINGS!

NC Coastal Federation, Inc.
Rt. 5, Box 603 (Ocean)
Newport, N.C. 28570

Bulk Mailing
Permit No. 12
POSTAGE PAID
Swansboro, N.C.

PUBLIC HEARINGS TO BE HELD:
MAY 5 - MANTEO
MAY 6 - MOREHEAD CITY
MAY 7 - WILMINGTON
MAY 8 - RALEIGH

Front page from *Coastal Review*, the lively quarterly
newsletter published by the North Carolina Coastal Federation.

tools and potsherds. "We had a rude awakening come in fast," Lena said. "I knew that if they developed Permuda we were sunk, and that if that water is not polluted we can survive. The sound is as much a part of our lives as our hearts are part of our bodies." The Ritters and their neighbors rallied as never before, holding raffles and bake sales to raise money for legal defense. They started a fishermen's association; Graham and a few others built a 16-foot wooden skiff at a total cost of $45 in materials, and auctioned it off for $1,700. Signatures were collected on petitions. Todd Miller's group and another statewide organization got wind of the effort. After a struggle that lasted almost six years, during which little support for the project was voiced except from real estate interests, Thomas's application was turned down. In 1987, the state finally purchased the island for $1.7 million. Graham credits the victory largely to the outside help he was getting. "Now we have the Federation with us, and some scientists, and they get attention even if they say exactly the same things that we were saying. Now we have a much better chance than before."

The experience turned the Ritters into activists on a variety of issues all over the state and beyond its borders. After our visit Lena was elected president of Miller's organization, where in 1988 she was working full-time. She was also appointed to the state's Marine Fisheries Commission, but she denied that she could be co-opted: "If the governor did that to shut me up, he made a big mistake. My husband can tell you that." (Lena resigned from the commission soon after her appointment, but not for political reasons: she simply felt unable to take the required time away from work.) Her strong philosophy remains unchanged. "If nature don't want you to do it," said Lena, "nature won't let you. And if you try to defy it, it'll jump up and bite you." Lena continues as a guardian of the North Carolina coast, neglecting her housekeeping, hurtling from meeting to meeting in a battered 1973 sedan. She knows she can't win them all, but remains determined to keep on trying to win some of them.

On the mainland, opposite Permuda, live Bill and Bernice Rice. Married in 1940, this sturdy couple have owned and worked their waterfront farm for almost as long. On its sandy soil they grow peanuts and corn and collards. They raise hogs. Out on the water, they carefully tend 135 acres of "oyster gardens" leased from the state. In the summer they dig for clams. They used to net shrimp, but have given up this practice. "I quit my shrimpin' for several reasons," said Bill, a solidly built handsome man with strong hands. "One of them was that when I pulled up my net I'd get a pound of shrimp but along with that I'd get twenty pounds of little tiny fish from the nurseries in the sea grasses in the sound. I couldn't stand killing those little fish anymore." On the modest income they derive from farming and fishing, Bill and Bernice have put seven children through college; one daughter has a Ph.D. Used to living close to the edge of poverty, Bill said that not everything was wonderful in the old days. During and after World War II, liberal use of DDT poisoned the local waters and ruined many fishermen, and there were earlier times when he found that "there was somebody else helpin' me harvest my resource." But he took such blows more or less in stride. "When hard times come, the cars just set up and rotted away," he recalled.

Nothing, though, fully prepared Bill and Bernice for the current wave of development around Stump Sound. "That size of an oyster garden is more than we need," he said. "But we had our dreams for a long time. We even wanted to open a seafood restaurant along here, and our children got the education they needed to make this happen. But then they grew up and got married and moved away, as far as New Mexico, and then these developers come in, and they have their dreams too, and they tell us to take our dreams and get out of the way, and gradually they've been poisoning us out. And now we've got people from all over the country comin' down and bringin' their freezers and settin' a few nets. When you bring in new people they start harvestin' too tight, and strippin' that resource, and then they'll move on and go somewhere else. Even the clams are down now from overharvestin', and we never thought they would give out. We're not against progress or development; we think that the productivity of these waters should be everyone's concern. But the sound is worthless without the marsh that is being destroyed."

The bind in which Bill and Bernice, Graham and Lena, and two hundred other Stump Sound families are caught extends beyond development and overharvesting to overtaxation, with skyrocketing assessments leading to huge real estate tax increases on land that in some instances has never been sold. Higher taxes can only be avoided through selling off some land ("I don't want to sell our land," said Lena. "Where would we go?"), or by continuing to farm, as the Rices are doing despite their advancing age. There was no apparent way to surmount this problem. At least, Stump Sound seemed on its way to being classified by authorities as among the state's "outstanding resource waters." The special status would slow but hardly stop the sound's gradual degradation: at the end of 1987 the first red tide in its history swept in, thanks, it was said, to an aberration in the Gulf Stream. The red tide rendered local clams and oysters inedible and caused the closing of the Rices' and Ritters' gardens.

Moving beyond Stump Sound on a sunny, windy, warm Sunday, *Sanderling* continued down the waterway in the company of many small pleasure boats. Along the banks were small frame houses, each with a separate rickety wooden pier and at the end of it a bench to sit on and look out at the marshes. Willows were beginning to turn green now, and the woods showed red from just-opening leaves. On the lawns girls sunbathed in bikinis—a new sight for *Sanderling*'s still chilly crew. Soon after midday we reached an island called Figure Eight, much like Permuda in configuration but said to be developed in a carefully planned way. Todd Miller had urged us to visit here in the company of Paul Foster, a retired State Department official who was living there year-round and serving as vice president of the North Carolina Coastal Federation. Foster was on the dock, waving, when we arrived. We tied up, jumped into his little car, and set forth on a tour of this little (four and a half miles long) island. It was all but empty back in the late 1960s when Foster found it, paid $12,000 for a small beach lot that would now fetch $200,000, and built a modest house for himself and his wife. Even if he had been able to, Foster would not have built a more elaborate house, because of the hurricanes. "You've got to figure that a house out here will last about a generation," he said.

The lesson seems to have been lost on some of the Fosters' neighbors. We saw English imitations, Nantucket clones, elaborate contemporary houses, determined efforts to create lawns where beach grass belongs. Since no bad storm has hit the island in recent years, people have gotten bolder, Paul said, and begun to build well within the three hundred feet of the beach where 90 percent of storm damage occurs. Houses right *on* the beach were being built, so low they seemed likely to vanish in the first sturdy northeaster; the foundation of one such, not yet completed upstairs, was already under attack from the ocean and buttressed with sandbags. "The people out there have more money than they have sense," Todd Miller had told me. Sprinkled about the island too were more commendable construction efforts, including some houses almost completely hidden, in the surprisingly lush climax maritime forest, among oak and red cedar trees and bay bushes. Foster showed us the results of his own efforts as chairman of the environmental committee of the island's controlling association: beach grass plantings, appropriately scaled dune-control measures. He also noted the island's unblemished record at beating back condo development proposals. "It's always been five to nothing in our favor at the county commission," Paul said. "These developers come in here with all kinds of promises from the capital. But down here it's just a question of votes. We islanders represent more of them than they do."

Overall, it looked nice out there, the ocean water a crisp sea green and the well-washed beaches clear and the salt marshes and shellfish areas protected by the island people. We wanted to linger, but needed to shove off in time to catch a strong push from the current in the Cape Fear River, which whistled us by sundown to the pleasant town of Southport. Here we stayed overnight and into the morning only long enough for a trip to the food market. The film *Crimes of the Heart* was made here, the red-haired young helper told me. "I got to fill Diane Keaton's shoppin' bag when they were filmin' in the store. They paid me $362, but they left me on the cuttin'-room floor." Before noon, with sunny weather and benign northerly winds easing the way, we set forth for what would be an overnight sail to Charleston, bypassing Myrtle Beach, South Carolina's Ocean City and a reminder that this is a state still lacking effective coastal development control mechanisms. Many porpoises visited and played around our bow, and we also saw a number of northern gannets on their spring northward migration. Two or four of these large seabirds would fly together close to the water, occasionally climbing to ten feet or so, then dropping very close to sea level in what seemed an almost formal ritual. After midnight I spent some anxious hours making sure that we had properly rounded Cape Romain, a shoal-ridden point marked only by a small unlighted buoy. This accomplished, we were off the Charleston jetties soon after daybreak and by ten o'clock were asleep at the municipal marina.

Charleston seemed gratifyingly well preserved. Its blocks of eighteenth-century houses, most of them white and shining beside brick sidewalks, are models for faithful historic preservation; even the downtown remains devoid of modern glitz, except for one section whose storefronts have such familiar names that you forget where you are. Out at nearby Kiawah Island, a Kuwaiti-financed resort development said to have been organized with great ecological sensitivity on the basis of a six-hundred-page "environmental impact study," I was thrust abruptly back into the teeth-grinding 1980s. In this immaculately kept place, the condos ("We call 'em villas," said Kiawah Island Resorts' PR director, Leonotia Miller) are discreetly tucked back among the live oaks. The several golf courses are said to be landscaped with native plants and designed with respect for the land's natural contours: "When they build a water hole here, they don't chop off the end of the pond," Miller said. Housing design is so carefully controlled that just removing a tree requires permission from an architectural review panel. One hundred and fifty bird species continue to use the island, a program to protect nesting beaches for loggerhead turtles is in place, and in fact the only "unnatural" thing going on that Miller could think of was that the company replenishes the beaches from time to time. Nature's gift, Miller called it.

As Miller talked I began to wonder about how the great amounts of water and fertilizer required to maintain the three golf courses are affecting the surrounding salt marshes, and about sewage and other forms of pollution as the number of housing units grows. She suggested I talk with a person familiar with these matters, and I phoned him. He said that he would require "clearance" (from whom? how could I be traced or labeled or run through a computer check?) to talk to me. I said I would call back. When I did, I reached a secretary who told me that the "clearance" had not been obtained.

"I wasn't so suspicious before," I said. "But what makes me suspicious now is that you're so suspicious. It makes me think you have something to hide."

"No, that's not it at all," the secretary said. "We treat everybody the same way. We've been burned so many times, we try to be careful."

So much for my efforts to plumb the truth at spotless Kiawah. To find it at nearby Folly Beach required no special help. The road from Charleston dead-ends at a spanking-new Holiday Inn completed, as a large billboard on Highway 26 to the airport loudly attests, when it faced a broad beach. Now, thanks to winter storms and misbegotten "beach control" measures, the ocean waves were lapping right up to its foundation; a solitary ladder led right into the water from its ocean terrace. Groins had not worked. Nor had a heavy rock seawall done much beyond offering a measure of protection for the hotel's foundation. "Nothin' seems to work," said a waitress at a restaurant down the street. "Up and down a ways, there is some beach. Last year we had plenty of beach right here too. But not now. Seems like the Inn took up all the space." At the county beach a mile away, white sand sloped gradually into muddy-looking brown water. The only car in the parking lot had Iowa plates. Along the beach road almost every house had a sign. Half said "Summer Rental." The other half said "For Sale."

Away from Charleston we cruised on down the waterway, wider now and featuring our first groups of black skimmers, the graceful shorebirds celebrated in Rachel Carson's *Under the Sea Wind*. At the celebrated Hilton Head Island resort and retirement haven, I was surprised to see a commercial port and a shrimp fleet as well as the condos and marinas. In lowering, foggy weather we powered through greenish-brown water, dipping into ever smaller creeks in search of solitude. We found it in Bull Creek, where only a dock with a mercury-vapor light marred the calm of the marshes. In the morning we heard warbler choruses over on the high ground; a sandy beach in a cove was host to many shorebird species, including whimbrels and dowitchers. Aboard came less welcome guests—gnats, our first insects, and they seemed immune to screens and Muskol. This did not seem to bother our weekend guests, the Fessendens, who feasted as hungrily on the scenery as the gnats did on us. Later in the morning we motored out of the serpentine river system and into a confused ocean with choppy seas like those of Buzzards Bay, and shouldered our way down to our next destination, a unique island called St. Catherines.

One of the few barrier islands anywhere along the East Coast that remain intact as one single private holding, St. Catherines boasts a rich history. It was originally home to a group of Indians called Guales, who there maintained a placid life based largely on the bountiful supplies of oysters around the island's shores: middens scattered across the island attest to the oyster's importance in Guale life. In 1556 Spanish churchmen, probing northward from the mission at St. Augustine, made contact with the Guales at St. Catherines, and soon thereafter a Franciscan mission called Santa Catalina de Guale was founded at the southern end of the island. For more than a century the Indians supplied corn and other foodstuffs for consumption as far away as St. Augustine, and in return were awarded the benefits of conversion to Catholicism. While some would think this not an equitable quid pro quo, it appears to have worked rather well, with the exception of at least one major revolt, up until the time the British decided to consolidate their power along the Georgia coast. After several attacks in the 1670s, the end came in 1680. In a scene right out of *The Mission*, a film about Catholic activism in South America, mass was said before priests and Indians went out to die in the final battle. Others fled, and the mission, not to be rediscovered until the 1970s, was burned.

The island later passed through several incarnations. In colonial times its tall straight longleaf and slash pine trees supplied spars for the British fleet, and the logging was merciless. During the slavery era cotton was king at St. Catherines, and even today the old fields, mostly now being turned back into forest, are scattered with big gnarled live oaks, called "slave trees," where the laborers could seek shelter from the midday sun. Because of the deep water that still today brought *Sanderling* right up to the shore of the island, the German merchant who then owned the island—and for whom Wahlberg Creek remains named— could ship his cotton directly to the market without having to pass it through the hands of middlemen in Charleston or Savannah. After emancipation a succession of owners struggled with St. Catherines. None did much with it, except for one man who in the 1920s restored and added a wing to a 1780 structure made of tabby (a combination of mud, oyster shells, and lime made from burning oyster shells) that is now known as the Button Gwinnett House and ranks as St. Catherines' only "mansion." In 1943 the businessman Edward John Noble purchased the island and ran Black Angus cattle there; currently the foundation that runs it is managed by Noble's daughter June and her husband, Frank Y. Larkin.

Under the Larkins' guidance, St. Catherines, an island the size and shape of Manhattan, has become an oddly fascinating place. For one thing, their foundation has long encouraged archaeological research there: initial surveys they commissioned from Dr. David Hurst Thomas, of the American Museum of Natural History in New York City, led to the rediscovery and careful excavation of the mission. A trustee of the American Museum and the New York Zoological Society, Larkin has also set aside a large portion of the island for captive breeding of endangered species, maintenance of some rare species for which there is no need in zoos, and—most recently—pioneer efforts to acquaint zoo-bred animals with the real world. Thus it was that, soon after we had tied up and were greeted by Royce Hayes, the island's affable and deeply knowledgeable manager, Flo said out of the blue: "A special prize for the first one who sees a lemur."

"No one will have to look very hard," said Hayes, explaining that Kate and Falstaff, two ring-tailed lemurs who had been rejected from a larger group loose on the island, often hang around the barn close to the dock where the maintenance vehicles are parked. Sure enough, they were up in the rafters, stacked lemur-style one atop the other, four shoe-button eyes peering down at us. At Hayes's coaxing they shinnied down a pole to the ground and, grunting, approached us with little catlike steps. Kate's tail flew high in a question mark; since Falstaff is an older and bedraggled male, his drooped. Later we strolled on the island with Tim and Lisa Keith-Lucas of Duke University, Tennesseans who regularly visited the island to study the released lemurs' adaptations from small cages in the Bronx to the wild. "They have to learn it all," said Lisa. "When they start, they have no vocalizations. They can't climb a tree. They don't know what's good to eat. But they catch on remarkably quickly, and when it comes to tree-climbing the young ones really put their parents to shame."

Later we were to see several clumps of ex-captive lemurs settled high in the trees; and be taken on a tour of the NYZS facilities and their occupants. These included hoofed animals such as Grévy's zebra and several unusual species of gazelle; red-fronted macaws and sandhill cranes and large nimble birds called hornbills from India and Indonesia; and two very rare kinds of large tortoise from Madagascar, where all lemurs also originated. All but the lemurs are kept fenced off from the rest of the island, and I wondered what would happen if more were allowed to commingle with its existing populations of wild turkeys, deer, and feral pigs. Since any exotic species introduced into an ecosystem brings change, I wondered what might be the result of such radical juxtapositions.

More interesting than the exotics, I found, was the way in which the natural ecosystem has already been used and abused over time. It isn't much to start with—poor sandy soil with only a thin layer of topsoil, the sort of stuff that nutrients leach through quickly. Despite this drawback, the island boasts great stands of virgin magnolia, a different-looking tree from the ornamental back-yard variety, and very old oaks and pines, and smaller bushes like the red bay and the toxic Florida soapberry. Little of the island is in its original condition, though, because of all the logging and farming and ranching, and a large portion is now allocated to pine seedlings that have recently been planted. Like a tropical forest, St. Catherines is quite clear and open at ground level; the walking is easy unless you hit low swampy parts. The island's many feral pigs have done heavy damage to the ground nests of resident wild turkeys. Hayes and his crew of five assistants have ambushed and killed many of the pigs, but a stubborn residue remains. Thanks to this work, as well as the reforestation program and the very limited use of island resources for any of the projects on it, the island is getting closer to its natural state than it has been since the Franciscans arrived. This gives Hayes, a veteran of a decade and a half on the island, great satisfaction.

The breeze was building as we motored out of Wahlberg Creek and back into the waterway, passing many undeveloped Georgia islands, including Wolf, a wildlife refuge, and Sapelo, a state park. By noon it was gray and sullen, with the wind clocking close to 30 knots. We bucked out to a buoy to round a long shoal, then scampered downwind to a marina at St. Simons, where, having learned a thing or two about maneuvering *Sanderling* in strong currents and breezes, we rounded up smartly into a slip and tossed neatly coiled lines to men standing ashore. "Nice dockin'," one said. That night the wind continued strong and record low temperatures descended all over the Southeast. We laid over in this region for a day, looking mournfully across at large paper mills sucking vast amounts of water out of the deep aquifers. At St. Catherines, Royce Hayes had told us, so strong was the natural water pressure that, before a small mill started up in the 1960s, powerful streams would burst forth at the turn of a second-floor faucet that now provides only a trickle. The next day, April Fools' Day, the northerly moderated, and in clear weather we continued southward toward the splendor of Cumberland Island.

This large land mass, once a private playground for Andrew Carnegie's brother Thomas and his many descendants, is now almost entirely a National Seashore; some inholdings are still by contract in private hands. The Park Service maintains the island with great care, limiting public access by ferryboat to three hundred people per day ("a number we just sort of picked," park superintendent Don Hooker admitted) and maintaining a wild appearance outside of a few attractive campsites, for which the competition (reserve by phone a year in advance) is fierce. Relations between the rangers and the private owners seem excellent. Hooker noted that it was they who led the long fight to get the island declared a seashore rather than be turned, by the developer Charles Fraser, into a super Hilton Head with gondolas in the lagoon. "If it weren't for them, you wouldn't be here," he said. For their part, the inholders seem satisfied as well. I found one packing his fishing gear into the back of an old car. "We get along real well," he told me. "Every time a problem comes up, I stop and count my blessings that we don't have condos and golf courses out here."

We wandered down Cumberland's hard sandy roads and trails, seeing all manner of life in the woods and along the broad white ocean beach, where 200–300-pound loggerhead turtles come ashore to lay their eggs. Northern parula and yellow-throated warblers were evident here, and a great horned owl sat fiercely upon eggs in a nest. Alligators in the ponds, deer in the forest, where the foliage is that special and beautiful combination of palmetto, live oak, pine, and Spanish moss which characterizes the Georgia islands. Again, introduced ferals: some two hundred wild ponies, a herd that Hooker calls "out of control"; tame scuffling armadillos; wild pigs doing obvious great damage. For all its great charm and beauty, in fact, Hooker wryly called Cumberland "a manager's paradise" because of all the conflicting pressures upon it. Since animal-welfare opposition rules out drastic measures to curb the excess populations, the rangers must settle for less effective steps such as trapping, temporary sterilization, and very brief controlled deer-hunting seasons. The deer in particular were worrisome to Hooker: their consumption of acorns is so high that the natural succession of the oak forest is in jeopardy, and no natural controls on the deer population are present. The pigs tear up the forest floor; plenty are still around, though more than 1,500 have already been trapped. The island cannot supply sufficient natural food for the ponies, which totter about weakly late in the winter. Yet the public wants to see these creatures, and campers and birdwalkers and hikers and wilderness people and those interested in historic aspects all have different needs and priorities. Hooker was doing his best to balance it all out, and keep the island as it is.

After winning a frosty reception from a humorless thin-lipped young woman at the Greyfields Inn, located on some of Cumberland's scant supply of private land (the place looked musty, very turn-of-the-century; the original owner's books in the library), I returned to *Sanderling*. We had dinner, then identified many stars. In the morning we heard talk of yet another frontal passage on the weather radio, but since winds were forecast not to exceed 30 knots we opted for the twenty-mile outside passage to Jacksonville. It began pleasantly enough, but in midafternoon the skies blackened to the west and the wind rose. We shortened sail and began to yearn for the aircraft carrier tied up at Mayport to grow larger. When the squall reached us we were ready. Still, nothing quite prepared us for the full effect of icy spray and an air temperature that dropped some fifteen degrees from one moment to the next. The water boiled white. Since we were near shore and the wind was from the west, the sea was calm, and in the cabin it seemed quiet. A Navy helicopter flew low overhead, apparently making sure we were all right as things snapped and crackled. We waved. At the height of it, Flo, who had been quietly reading and napping below, poked her head out of the companionway. Looking glum, she said, "Hey, Rog, the radio is forecasting winds of fifty knots."

"I know," I replied. "We're in 'em."

The squall passed and the wind settled back to a steady northwest as we crept up the St. Johns River against a five-knot current. Dolphins jumped clear out of the water at the end of the jetties. By sundown we made it to a marina in Sisters Creek, from where Flo could catch the last plane back to Washington and her job. Peter and I summoned the "courtesy car" provided by the nearby Captain's Table restaurant and eventually it arrived, driven by an older man with a blond year-old child on his lap, clutching tightly to the wheel. The parking lot was full and we had to wait in line for a table. But the reward was a "free" raw bar included in the price of the meal. Peter went for it like a homing pigeon and asked the waitress if he could have seconds on oysters. "I don't mind," she said. We ate well and were amused by the crowd: lots of families with children in high chairs and daddies wearing their baseball caps, one table of teenage girls, several of boaters from the marina. It turned out to be one of those places that started out as a bait shop and then just grew. "Puzzles me how they fit 'em all in," said Grandpa as we returned to the boat. "All I can do to feed myself these days." His daughter, it turned out, minds the register and her husband runs the show. It's all they've ever done. Bless them, I thought, as I had several times before along the coast. All it takes to realize that America is not yet entirely homogenized is to enter one of these wonderful places.

Detail from a seventeenth-century Portuguese map
illustrating the abundance of Florida wildlife.

KER-BLOM, BLOB-BLOB-BLOOM. BLOM! The dawn sound, as loud as an explosion, sent us hurtling out of our sleeping bags to see nothing more ominous than the crew of the *Sunray*, a substantial motor yacht that had been tied up just ahead of us, making ready for their day's northward run. We followed soon after, arriving lickety-split, with the current, at the Jacksonville jetties shortly after seven in the morning. We found there a sprightly northwesterly wind and set off on a direct course to round Cape Canaveral and then continue southward to Fort Lauderdale. We would thus bypass all the Florida coast, already much destroyed, and do so under the finest conditions of furrows following free, as Coleridge put it in *The Rime of the Ancient Mariner*'s one happy passage. With our loran in top form, the navigation was simple, even though we did the tricky part around the cape in the dead of night. Peter and I managed to spell each other on watches so that one crew member could snatch some sleep.

At night we wrapped ourselves in sweaters and parkas and gloves as the temperature again reached record lows. During the first evening we spotted two flares and duly reported to the Coast Guard, which responded with a surface and helicopter search (we heard no results, but were glad at least that we made an initial report later confirmed elsewhere). During the day it was warm and the water a clear soft blue-green, with occasional flying fish skittering by and large turtles swimming ponderously along and dolphins often around the bow. Few birds, though, and practically no boats or people. Was everybody ashore playing canasta? The second evening we began to sight the lights and condos of southeastern Florida; our only challenge here was to keep them close aboard to starboard, so that our progress would not be slowed by the northward-rushing Gulf Stream, which passes close to the coast along here and hits four knots. Exhilarated, we hit the Fort Lauderdale jetties forty-seven hours after we began, having hardly adjusted the sails the whole way and having seldom dipped below six knots.

Flori*da*, strewn with flowers, the Spaniards had called the peninsula. Now it is more commonly known as *Floor*da, a lazy pronunciation with no special significance in English. Etymological change echoes a shift from natural paradise to plastic desert. The remorseless twinkling strand of high rises that *Sanderling* passed along the state's southeast coast made me fear the worst. Somehow living treasures still flourish, even beyond its few parks and nature reserves, on this shrinking sandbar. Stalwart people living here try with courage to protect the Everglades and other hard-pressed natural wonders. But I had left no time to study these struggles. Perhaps wrongly, we had positioned ourselves in Florida only for our own getaway into a sharply contrasting environment.

Part II

CARIBBEAN
MÉLANGE

7

Governing the Bahamas

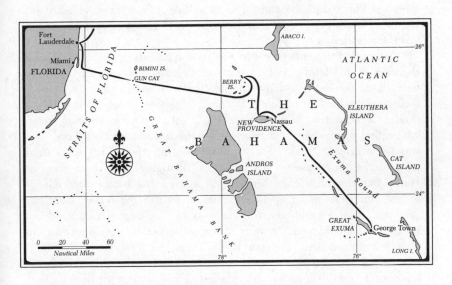

"TAKE A WEAPON," SAID A YACHT-DELIVERY SKIPPER WHEN HE HEARD that we were going to the Bahamas. "You'll be glad when you're out of there and into the Caribbean," another informant added. I recalled articles about a small cruising sailboat that pirates boarded in the Bahamas a few years ago; the vessel was found adrift a few days later, containing the bullet-ridden bodies of its husband-and-wife crew. Bahamians would be rude and uncooperative, we feared, driven by easy money to the drug trade and to stripping their reefs and coastal waters bare of conch and crawfish. We would be surrounded by droves of cruise-ship tourists. Up on the banks in shallow water, the navigation would be tricky. Entering an anchorage, I read, one often had to navigate through the reef by water color for want of buoys to follow.

Bahamian history since Columbus' discovery supports this unpromising view. The 360-mile-long archipelago, stretching from the Florida banks to the open Atlantic and from a latitude well north of Fort Lauderdale almost to Cuba and Hispaniola, contains some 3,000 islands, cays, and rocks. Most remain uninhabited and few are fertile. Between 1492 and the mid-seventeenth century, the European presence in the region was limited to occasional visits by Spaniards who braved the risky, reef-clad coasts in search of food, water, gold, or slaves. They found no treasure, but did manage to carry off all but a handful of the 20,000 Lucayans, peaceful Arawak Indian migrants from the South American mainland who had occupied the previously uninhabited Bahamas since about 1000. Early European explorers who cruised the archipelago included Ponce de León and Sir Walter Raleigh's captains Amadas and Barlowe, who were to continue on to North Carolina and advocate it as a site for settlement.

Sporadic European efforts to occupy the islands began in 1648, with the arrival on Eleuthera of a colony of British "adventurers." Twenty years later the entire colony's population still barely exceeded 1,000, including slaves. Subsequently Bahamian life was largely controlled by pirates. Freebooting in the region began with a wild international clan who called themselves *boucaniers*, after the *boucan*, or beef jerky, that was their principal food. Early in the century these "brethren" had marauded from a base on the island of Tortuga off the north coast of Haiti. Later, with Henry Morgan as a principal leader, buccaneers scored conquests as far afield as Panama. In the 1690s they began to originate their expeditions from various of the ungoverned southern Bahamas. Emboldened for want of opposition, they then moved onto New Providence Island (Nassau) itself. There, for some years, they held more sway than the ill-equipped governors sent by the Crown on futile missions to establish order. Blackbeard, along with most of the other best-known pirates of the time, including two notorious women, operated principally out of Nassau. Plundering Spanish galleons, and other passing or wrecked ships, was far more profitable than trade in the salt that had become the basis of the islands' official economy. Frequent harassment by Spanish invaders further strengthened the pirates' domination of weak British authorities.

In 1718, the year of Blackbeard's death at Ocracoke, an especially

Left: Sir Henry Morgan. *Right:* Christopher Columbus.

determined and incorruptible governor named Woodes Rogers arrived
at Nassau with a Royal Navy escort. His most visible reception came from
the pirate Charles Vane, who launched a fire ship against the official
flotilla, then slipped into open water and, defiantly flying the Jolly Roger,
vowed to return. Ashore a thousand brawling freebooters awaited the
new regime amid tawdry surroundings. "Nassau's harbor was a wreck,
unkempt and neglected, in keeping with the shantytown nature of the
town itself," wrote Frank Sherry in his *Raiders and Rebels: The Golden
Age of Piracy.* "There were no roads, no agriculture, no wells or
sanitation." Rogers managed against long odds to expel many of the least
lawful, and far greater order was finally restored early in the nineteenth
century.

Never in recent times have the Bahamas been totally free of pirates,
who gravitate there "as surely as spiders abound where there are nooks
and crannies," according to a sea captain quoted in Michael Craton's *A
History of the Bahamas.* One way or another, many there have
continued to operate beyond the conventions of law or power. During
the U.S. Civil War, the islands served as launch points for many of the
high-risk blockade-running vessels that slipped past Federal lines to
keep commerce open between Europe and the Confederacy. Rum-
running was a staple of the islands' economy during the U.S. Prohibition
era. More recently famous citizens of the Bahamas were the Canadian tax
dodger Sir Harry Oakes, victim of a bizarre murder one night in 1943,

and the Colombian drug czar Carlos Lehder, who ran his empire from Norman Cay in the Exumas before he finally got busted and jailed late in the 1980s. After he won his sixth term in 1987, the islands' Prime Minister, Sir Lynden O. Pindling, continued to face local and international accusations of being a patsy for drug traffickers.

The islands' legitimate economy has, meanwhile, hardly flourished. Various forms of agriculture, as well as salt-drying and a sponge industry that collapsed because of a fungal disease, rose and fell under the British rule that lasted until 1968. Today the islands' economic base rests on the willowy pillars of U.S. tourism; often overharvested marine resources, including the conch, a large aquatic snail whose meat is popular at home and abroad; and money laundering by means of storefront bank branches. Proximity to the United States, and its vast drug market, is doubtless the principal source of income for many among the 100,000 or so Bahamians.

Early April 1987 found *Sanderling* tied up along Fort Lauderdale's New River, adjacent to the local jail and the county courthouse. We had lain over in Lauderdale for minor repairs; rest and recreation for the crew; and a major stock-up of food and drink for the next legs of our trip, which we thought would involve ports where supplies would be scarce and expensive. We had installed satellite navigation gear to supplement our loran, whose reliability would dwindle as we moved ever farther away from waters where the U.S.-generated signal could be distinctly received, as well as a new single-sideband radio to replace the one that came with the boat. That one, we were told, was "a piece of junk" for which no spare parts could be found, since the manufacturer had long since left the field to more effective competitors. During the changeover, I tried to pass ashore a cardboard box containing the old radio and one of my notebooks. The box collapsed and fell into the water. Both the radio and the notebook remained afloat. While I was instinctively reaching for the notebook, the radio sank and was lost. Finally, and unexpectedly, we had been compelled to acquire an eight-and-a-half-foot Achilles inflatable dinghy—after a power cruiser, maneuvering while awaiting the opening of a lift bridge near our berth, caught a sudden crosscurrent and crunched our elegant little Dyer between the two vessels, bending it dangerously far out of shape. Peter and I bellowed in indignation. "Catch you on the way back in," the offending yacht's helmsman yelled back from a high perch. Then he gunned his mighty engines and thundered off. We never saw him again. The experience made us feel as powerless as Henry M. Plummer, a salty mariner who in 1912 sailed his 24-foot catboat *Mascot* from Massachusetts to Florida and back. Not equipped with an engine and therefore often compelled to anchor well clear of the shore, *Mascot* was frequently rammed by passing tugboats, barges, and log booms. Plummer was lucky to survive to tell his tale, a classic narrative called *The Boy, Me, and the Cat.*

Now, ready at last to be gone from plastic Florida and to test ourselves among the unruly Bahamas, we slipped down the New River just before sunset. Soon we were past the stacks and towers that guard the Port Everglades harbor entrance and out in open water. For several hours we sailed southward on this balmy night, keeping the coast's bright lights close aboard to starboard so that we would stay inside the Gulf Stream. This powerful ocean river, flowing northward from the Caribbean to New England and the Canadian Maritimes and then across the North Atlantic, reaches a maximum velocity of up to four knots as it sweeps around Florida's southern cape. We planned to enter it from off Miami on a slant that, even with the strong set, would carry us smoothly across forty-five miles of deep blue water to the islands. In a restless sea we rattled through the night, dead before a dying breeze, and fetched up off Bimini early in the morning. Still in cobalt water, the bottom so far below that our depth sounder could not achieve an echo, we motored toward Gun Cay light, where we could climb up onto the shallow Bahama Bank, duck into nearby Cat Cay to clear into the Bahamas, then continue eastward toward Nassau.

Nothing had quite prepared us for the drama of the transition from the navy blue of the deep water to the brilliant shades of green and turquoise that abruptly began to prevail as we approached the bank. I stopped believing in our electronics as the bottom came into view, apparently just under the keel although the depth sounder still gave us sixty feet. That far below we could see the beige of sandy patches, the black of coral heads or an occasional rock, the brownish green where sea grass grew. Ahead lay a new and vastly different world from what had dropped astern: cays formed of barren limestone, with poor soil and scrubby vegetation and beaches of the purest white. The cays are frequently bunched tightly together, forming fine natural anchorages. Because the archipelago has no rivers or streams to deposit sediment in the sea, the Bahamian water is "gin-clear," to use the adjective that often appears in yachting-magazine articles, and below its surface are edible pink conch and fleshy groupers, Technicolor fish, ten-pound spiny lobsters (locally called crawfish), and great stretches of coral reef. The question to be examined was that of how the islands' unruly history and their inhabitants' current practices had affected this oddly beautiful part of the world.

Once we were inside Gun Cay and rounding up into the little Cat Cay basin, our depth went down, down, down—to thirty feet, twenty, fifteen, twelve, even ten, or just four feet below our keel. We all but drifted at bare steerageway into the tidy little marina. On this Easter Sunday morning, in air as clear as the water, we made fast to the dock. I jumped ashore and began looking for customs officials. "They said they'd be back in an hour," said an occupant of a nearby boat also awaiting clearance. "Someone said they ran out of forms," a bystander outside the empty office informed me with a shrug. "You'll probably have to go up to Bimini to clear." With no official in sight, no assurance that one would turn up soon, facing the likelihood that we would have to sail nine miles back over the ground we had just covered, I decided to forge on eastward. We would not venture ashore while flying our yellow Q, or quarantine, flag, but instead would try to clear at Chub Cay, at the southern end of the Berry Islands chain north and a bit west of Nassau. It was an easy coast across the bank, its sandy bottom only a few feet under our keel. En route we spent a night near Russell Buoy, in smooth water but with no land in sight: a strange sensation for one accustomed to the protected harbors of New England. A second fine day, with a following wind, brought us into the Chub Cay marina by early afternoon. A beleaguered but dedicated customs official managed to clear us in quickly enough for us to make it back out the narrow shallow entrance minutes before a falling tide would have imprisoned us within the marina. We swam in crystal water and charcoaled chicken, feeling far away indeed from the driving Chesapeake snows.

For a week we then ambled among the small, low islands in the center of this long, wide chain, spending lazy stretches at anchor so that we could swim and snorkel and explore. First we visited the fine anchorage and beaches of Frozen and Alder cays, and were surprised at the large number of yachts also there. Offshore we sailed through clumps of garbage littering the clear waters—much of it from large ships whose crews simply heaved it over the side. Separated from their contents by waves and the swirl of currents, the plastic bags often end up wrapped around coral heads, killing them. Briefly we dipped into crowded, casino-dominated Nassau to provision and to meet Flo, who had come to rejoin the boat. Then it was south and east to the ninety-mile Exumas chain of small cays and tight little harbors of coral and limestone, each often crowded with other yachts but also offering its own special qualities.

Near Allan's Cay, which we shared with thirteen other sailboats, we visited two islands that boast remnant colonies of the now largely vanished Bahamian iguana. These overfed animals are so tame that they move swiftly *toward* you when you ground your dinghy and step out onto the beach. Under clear skies and enjoying light northerly air, we continued southward at leisure, gradually learning how to tell depth and distinguish channels by the fast-changing water colors. Norman's Cay, where the drug king Carlos Lehder had established an island fortress-cum-international-airport, passed well to starboard. From an anchorage between the allegedly haunted Warderick Wells Cay and Hog Cay we rode the dinghy a mile across to Hall's Corner Cay, where the remains of a defunct resort now serve as the headquarters of the Exuma Cays Land & Sea Park, crown jewel among the protected areas managed by the Bahamas National Trust. Ashore we found an old, unapproachable dock, rusty machinery, and abandoned buildings—and also a well-worn but useful collection of conservation messages drawn from a Sierra Club handbook:

TAKE . . . only pictures.

LEAVE . . . only footprints.

KILL . . . only time.

Wandering here on a dry, hot afternoon, we learned that the Exuma Park's warden and presiding conscience was Miss Peggy Hall. She patrolled the region aboard her boat, the *Moby*, and evidence of her presence was ubiquitous. On the beach near our anchorage was a mailbox containing correspondence: a letter from a young boy from Quebec who had been awed by barracudas; a note from a cruising yacht crew that had planted eleven coconut palms and requested help in keeping them watered; and several billets-doux from Miss Hall commending passing yachtsmen for having provided help and specifying planting and cleanup tasks remaining to be done. We tried to find Miss Hall via our VHF radio, but could not raise her; later I heard from Gary Larson, executive director of the Bahamas National Trust, about the great importance of her visible presence in such a lightly governed place.

From Hog Cay we continued southward to the aptly named Paradise Bay at the foot of Cambridge Cay, where, snorkeling, we squealed at the sight of great forests of elkhorn coral and large groupers, deep in the shadows, to supplement the customary rainbow of bright-colored squirrelfish, angelfish, parrotfish, and other reef species that we found everywhere. Familiar as these fish had become, nothing could lessen the beauty of seeing them grazing and twisting—sometimes alone, sometimes in thick schools—close at hand. "At last I have found my sport," Flo had said years before, when we first experienced the underwater wonders of the Red Sea. Here we reconfirmed the thrill of it.

Here, too, our honeymoon with *Sanderling* ended. In Fort Lauderdale, sitting at the feet of the Australian yacht captain Lindsay English, Peter had learned that if our engine's rpm's began to fluctuate a little, it was probably time to change the air filter. Peter had accordingly bought a couple of spare filters and begun to watch for a surge. Now it had begun to happen.

After breakfast I said, "Pete, are you going to try to put in that filter?"

"No," said Peter. "I am *going* to put it in."

He then removed the companionway stairs, revealing the sky-blue majesty of our Perkins diesel and its mysterious complexities: pumps, hoses, injectors, alternators, belts. I have always been hopeless on engines. Even during my days as a naval aviator, when I had to depend on a powerful but cranky piston radial to get me off and back onto the carrier, I learned little more about it than how to read the gauges in the cockpit. Pete, having owned and carefully maintained a motorcycle, could claim greater rapport. Up went his tail and down went his head, the Perkins instruction manual close at hand along with the spare part. Our idea was to complete the filter installation quickly, then set forth on this clear, calm morning for a thirty-mile run under power to Lee Stocking Island, where scientists at a branch of the Caribbean Marine Research Laboratory were expecting our arrival. While Peter worked below, I bustled about the deck, stowing the dinghy and cleaning up in anticipation of weighing anchor. I finished and waited. No sign of Peter except for legs and an occasional muffled expletive. After more waiting, I felt the need to take action. If I asked Peter if he wanted help, his answer, I knew, would be no. So I tried another tack.

"Everything O.K. down there?" I asked.

"No." A growl.

The problem, it turned out, was not the filter itself. That had long since been changed. But, Peter added, showing me what had suddenly become a greasy oil-stained page from the manual, there was more to it than that. Once the fuel system, of which the filter was a part, had been opened up, the engine would not start until all air had been "bled" back out of it. This procedure involved a set of steps described as comprehensibly in the manual as the installation instructions that arrive in the carton along with your new Japanese stereo: consecutively loosen a number of venting points along the line between the fuel tank and where combustion occurs; use the manual fuel-priming pump to make sure all the air pockets are out and fuel is flowing freely; then tighten everything up again. Trouble was, Peter found, the engine fit so snugly into its space that he could barely reach several critical nuts, and could not open them without the 5/16" wrench that fit them exactly. Such a wrench we did not have aboard. For some time Peter tried to improvise, and we made several unsuccessful efforts to restart the engine. Then we began to worry that we would exhaust the power of our starting battery, and decided to sail out of our anchorage, bypass Lee Stocking in favor of the yachting center at George Town on Great Exuma Island, and there seek the proper wrench, if not professional help.

After one final swim and snorkel, we hauled up the anchor and, taking advantage of a favorable current flowing eastward through the cut between the cays, crept in light air out into deep blue water. We crawled southward as Peter, now fuming, persisted in his bleeding efforts. We borrowed the right wrench from the passing yacht *Interlude*. But even with this improvement the Perkins refused to turn over, and on we drifted into the evening. We had no time left now to anchor for the night for fear, I calculated, that with no power we would miss our rendezvous with three new crew members: Mauricio, Lita, and Javier Obregón, who had long planned to meet us in George Town at midday the next day and cruise with us for ten days in the southern Bahamas. So we sailed on as the relentless sun gave way to a black starry night in which shooting stars sent sudden shafts of white across the sky. In the morning Peter gave the bleeding one last try. Not a cough. "There's nothing more I can do," he sighed.

Early in the afternoon we began to negotiate the tricky, shallow, reef-flecked entrance to George Town, meticulously following the sailing directions since we were without power to back ourselves off if we grounded. Once inside, we shortened sail almost down to bare poles to reduce our speed, and crept across the wide bay with as little as six inches of water between our keel and the sandy, coral-free bottom. We stayed to the seaward side along Stocking Island and its various bowls and bights, passing a large anchored fleet of cruising vessels. Every one of those engines works, I thought to myself as we ghosted past, then turned ninety degrees toward Kidd Cove and our rendezvous point, the Exuma Docking Services marina.

I reviewed our approach with Peter. "We'll sail in on the starboard tack, round up, and catch the dock," I said. "If I undershoot and we lose way before we get there, drop the anchor. If I come in too hot, I'll take it around and try again." Once more I thought of the intrepid Henry Plummer. Pete readied anchor and lines and awaited the chance to make his grab. None of these preparations proved necessary. No more than a hundred yards short of the dock, having cut the point of the cove a shade close, we settled softly aground. Without a motor to help us off, we could not break out, and we remained where we were until the rising tide finally freed us later in the afternoon. Tied up at last to the dock, we made contact with a veteran local mechanic named Ken Symonette. With not even a glance at the now battered manual, crackly new only days before, he gave the Perkins' innards a jolt with raw diesel fuel poured right into the air intake (some, we discovered later, use lighter fluid) as we cranked the starter with the throttle halfway open. The Perkins wheezed, gasped unevenly, then roared into life before I could ease back to a slower idle.

We cheered. Peter, who had been watching closely, shook his head in disbelief and anxiety, having concluded that there must be something dangerous about what Ken had done. Ken then regaled us with island stories, told with a lilt in his voice, before he whacked me with a whopping bill. At least we were whole again and our spirits high after we had plugged into the marina, used shore power to bring our refrigeration unit up to full strength, gotten *Sanderling* well tidied up and all systems running, and gathered full strength for the expedition's next leg. We had seen some of the islands' natural beauty, starkly juxtaposed against their scruffy history and uneven contemporary values. Now, while continuing to explore these relationships, we would also turn to the question, ever more hotly debated as the 1992 quincentenary drew closer, of where among the Bahamas Columbus first alighted.

8

Retracing 1492

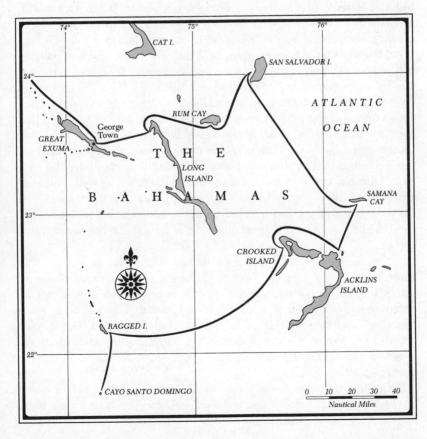

LONG A SUMMER FIXTURE ON MOUNT DESERT ISLAND IN MAINE, Professor Samuel Eliot Morison was also the nation's doyen on the subject of Christopher Columbus. In his deft biography *Admiral of the Ocean Sea* and in several other works, this prickly Harvard Brahmin and yachtsman reaffirmed the long-standing notion that Columbus' first Western Hemisphere landfall was indeed San Salvador Island in the southeastern Bahamas, and not one of several other islands that are from time to time suggested as alternatives. No theory about the landfall and the Admiral's subsequent cruise through the southern Bahamas provides a perfect match between what is written in Columbus' journal and the actual geography. Morison and others have favored the San Salvador route on the grounds that it has the fewest discrepancies.

For many years the San Salvador scenario remained unchallenged, in large part because of Morison's towering reputation. But in 1986, several years after Morison's death, *National Geographic* fearlessly ran a well-publicized article by one of its top editors, Joseph Judge, that makes a persuasive computer-based case for Samana Cay, an outpost island even farther afield than San Salvador, as the real McCoy.

Mauricio Obregón, who along with his wife, Lita, and son, Javier, had arrived in George Town just in time to greet us from the marina as we drifted aground, had worked closely with Morison. A Colombian diplomat, aviator, executive, and raconteur, Obregón is also a historian with a deep interest in the European discoveries of Africa, Asia, and the Western Hemisphere. During the 1960s he flew Morison around the Caribbean in an old Catalina seaplane to take notes and photographs of the Columbus routes; the result was a book written jointly by the two men. Obregón had previously overflown the Bahamas as well, and had visited San Salvador many times. But having never seen the region from the water and equipped with a challenging reason to gather new data, he welcomed my invitation to come aboard *Sanderling* and conduct a fresh survey.

Now here he was, fresh from a debate with Judge in Nassau, his white beard newly trimmed, wearing a jaunty yachting cap, brimming with jokes and stories (often at the expense of the British he first met at boarding school), along with the striking Castilian Lita and their son, Javier, an architect who lives in Bogotá. Tall and gaunt, the black-bearded Javi looked the very model of a Spanish conquistador. He bore a sackful of motorized cameras and would serve as the expedition's photographer.

Our first destination was Calabash Bay at the northern end of Long Island, a region that, according to Morison, Columbus visited soon after his departure from San Salvador. We left George Town late in the

Samuel Eliot Morison and Mauricio Obregón, 1949.

morning, first motoring out of the tricky eastern entrance to the harbor, past many anchored yachts, including two with European crews swarming about jay naked. Once clear, we set out a little jib to steady the boat and reinforce the engine, now running smoothly with a deep growl, and, close-hauled, made rapid progress toward Cape Santa Maria. A few miles short of the bay, the engine began surging anew. Then it quit entirely, and once again refused to restart despite Peter's passionate efforts. We sailed in, across a wide gap in the reef that surrounds the bay, and anchored in limpid, swimming-pool-colored water. Then, over tasty if costly fresh grouper that the mechanic Ken Symonette had made available to us just before we left George Town, we considered our options. Should we return to George Town and let Ken have a full go at the Perkins? Should we get him on the radiotelephone and ask him to fly out? Might there be a helpful mechanic somewhere on the island?

We would do nothing until morning, we concluded. Then we would go ashore to see what help we might be able to rustle up. Early the next day, a Sunday, Mauricio, Javi, and I set forth in the dinghy. I found no local mechanic and could not get through to George Town, or anywhere else, on the one party-line telephone in the little village of Seymours, even with the kind assistance of the amply proportioned lady whose home I had invaded. A second communications effort by means of the town's only VHF radio, which was suffering from weak batteries, fared no better; and without a walkie-talkie I had no way to relay the news of my failure back to Peter aboard. Mauricio, searching not for a mechanic but for Columbus clues, had better luck. He set off on foot toward Newton Cay, which well matched Columbus' description of a "harbor with two entrances" separated by a rock, and nearby found wells where the Admiral might have watered.

Back aboard *Sanderling*, Peter continued to wrestle with the Perkins. Javier talked him into replicating Symonette's shock-start technique.

It worked. Peter shook his head and said, "I don't know what I did."

Overnight it cleared and the following morning we set forth around Cape Santa Maria to examine the Newton Cay harbor from the outside. Once again, Mauricio was pleased to note, our observations agreed with what Columbus reported: the anchorage clearly had two entrances when seen from the outside, and could easily be approached by taking a longboat across the reef. Later in the day, which turned sparkly clear between small rainsqualls, we agreed with Mauricio that as it receded Long Island's low points dropped beneath the horizon, causing several high places to resemble the "many islands" that Columbus had been able to sight after moving on from his initial landfall. By early evening we had reached a good anchorage inside the reef that guards the southern shore of Rum Cay, Columbus' second stop, according to Morison and Obregón.

Few people live on Rum Cay, and little seemed to be happening there other than the activity generated by a U.S.-owned hotel and diving club on the south beach. Earlier attempts to raise pineapple and cattle on the island had faltered, and even the large trees that Columbus reported had long since been felled—by British and American loyalist settlers, to make way for sugarcane plantations. Here was a clear reminder of the harshness of these islands. Though their soil is fertile, it occurs in thin layers and is arable only in limestone "pockets" scattered among the islands. Not even the Lucayans were able to produce many crops other than maize and cassava. Early British settlers relied chiefly on imported goods paid for with proceeds from sales of ambergris (used in perfume manufacture) and other whale products; materials scavenged from shipwrecks; and a dyewood from the braziletto tree. The only meat to be found on land was that of the now endangered hutia, an endemic rodent; but the animal was always scarce and highly prized. Today one can find in the Bahamas excellent deep-red tomatoes, which flourish in the salty pockets, and lettuce and a few other vegetables. Almost everything else is imported, as part of the price the Lucayans themselves paid for their move to the islands. For them as for us, it is an irony that the names of so many of our foods— avocado, guava, maize, potato—are derived from the unwritten Arawak language (the Arawaks also gave us hurricane, canoe, cannibal, hammock, and barbecue).

Farming has disappeared almost entirely from San Salvador, which we reached after a smooth sail-and-power run from Rum Cay. Few here can afford fertilizer, and nutrients leach quickly through the porous soil. In earlier times tree falls helped the nutrient supply, but this source dwindled as the British stripped the forests. The soil is too salty for many crops. Chickens suffer badly from the island's mosquito swarms. In large measure, the 700 San Salvadorans depend on the sea and foods brought in from elsewhere. Tourism, such as it is in this remote place, has become an important source of income. We tied up at the cozy marina that forms part of the Riding Rock Inn. Forewarned that Colombia's ambassador-at-large to the Caribbean and delegate to the international Columbus Quincentenary Commission was aboard *Sanderling*, an impressive delegation was assembled to greet us: the prospering owner of the hotel and marina, along with half a dozen other business leaders and politicians. With most of this group we repaired to the hotel's well-screened bar and were there joined by Philip Smith, a thoughtful if mournfully pontifical local politician who wanted to serve as Obregón's counterpart on the commission. During a long evening, we inconclusively discussed the question of how, in the light of the new landfall controversy, the Bahamas might best plan to celebrate 1992. With San Salvador already designated by the government as the official landfall site, Judge's contentions were troublesome to the Bahamians.

The next day we toured the island, twelve miles long and five wide, in the company of Don Gerace, a voluble academic who has been there for almost two decades. Piloting a well-worn VW bus with carefree panache along the island's indifferent roads, Gerace showed us several Columbus monuments along Fernandez Bay, the protected western shore of the island where Columbus is said to have crossed the reef and come ashore. A cross erected by Morison and Obregón remains much in evidence, along with a smaller rock placed by the founder of the company that makes Tappan stoves, and a garish Mexican structure

Obregón, the author, and Donald Gerace at the monument
on the beach along San Salvador Island's Fernandez Bay.

featuring a large bronze sculpture. The short and rotund Gerace also
showed us a moribund real estate development called Columbus Landings; introduced us to an American Catholic priest who lives in comfort
upstairs from his chapel and spends much time educating the island's
teenagers; arranged a visit to the one-room New World Museum created
by a Columbus aficionado and longtime island resident named Ruth
Wolper; and drove us by the hand-operated lighthouse on the island's
north point. Fueled by kerosene, it features a lens that floats on mercury,
and as we were soon to discover, it flashes vividly at night. Finally,
Gerace gave us lunch at his headquarters, a former U.S. Navy missile-
tracking station which he bought for one dollar in 1971 and converted
into a field research unit serving a consortium of U.S. colleges with
undergraduate and graduate programs in archaeology, biology, and
carbonate geology. Now Gerace was skillfully operating the place by the
seat of his pants, with the capable help of his wife, Kathy, and one other
permanent staff member.

In the evening, agreeing that Obregón needed to have a firsthand
look at the infamous Samana, we set sail. A moonlit beam reach brought
us to Samana by early the following morning. We stopped at the
anchorage off the reef, on the island's southern shore, where Judge and
National Geographic have Columbus making ready to land. Late in the

The Saint at Samana Cay.

morning, we saw a handsome Bermuda 40 sailboat slowly approach the
small cay off the eastern end of the harbor and later reappear snugly
anchored inside the reef. Emboldened, we decided to give it a try
ourselves. We crept toward the cay, looking for a break in the coral. The
anchored boat came up on the radio to help, telling us to look for three
tiny buoys (placed there by the *Geographic*, I learned later) that mark
the passage over no less than twelve feet of water. At the helm I failed
to hear, over the noise of the running engine, the other key part of the
instructions: *line up* the three buoys before you get close to them. We
approached at a small angle, the slant of the sunlight inhibiting our view
of the bottom. Fifty yards from the three buoys, moving at a crawl, we
felt a sudden jolt and then heard the crunch of coral heads grinding
against our fiberglass hull, an interaction that can destroy a boat in fifteen
minutes during a storm. With light wind and a calm sea, we were able to
back off quickly and try again. A successful second attempt brought us
smoothly into the well-protected anchorage. We exchanged greetings
with the crew of our neighbor boat, donned bathing suits and face masks
to assess the damage (minimum) to our keel, then swam off to view huge
branches of elkhorn coral and swarms of attendant fish just twenty yards
away.

   A small outboard containing two crew members materialized alongside. Its skipper identified himself as Levenson Rolfe or, more precisely,
the Saint. He lived over on Acklins Island, he said, but every year he
would come to Samana to catch conch and fish. We asked him if he could
get us a grouper.

   "You want grouper?" he asked. "I get you grouper, mon. We be
back in one hour."

He and his mate cranked up their balky fifteen-horsepower motor and sputtered off in the boat, aboard which, we learned later, they habitually negotiate the more-than-twenty-mile crossing to Acklins. An hour later they returned, not with a grouper but instead a ten-pound crawfish that, said the Saint, he had caught free-diving. We paid him with rum ("I like half a bottle before breakfast," he told us with a broad smile). Javi blanched, then charcoal-grilled the huge crustacean; it was delicious. The next day the Saint returned with several conch, still plentiful at remote Samana. Javi hammered open the hard shells and I sawed the rubbery meat into pieces. They made good seviche, though we learned that conch, like abalone, becomes more tender and more palatable after it has been hammered.

If conch and lobster remain plentiful at remote Samana, I later heard sad tales about the general condition of these fisheries. "A generation ago around these islands," said Gary Larson of the Bahamas National Trust, "you could go into the water up to your knees and get as many conch as you wanted." Now, added Oris P. Russell, a former national fisheries director, "even though they are low on the totem pole economically, they are being seriously overharvested anywhere that's within two or three days' voyage from New Providence. Now you have to go further and further away to get any." It is newly illegal to take young conch without a well-formed lip. Nevertheless, both men fear that the disappearance of this basic foodstuff will continue inexorably. They found the situation even worse with regard to crawfish, whose tails were commanding prices of $11 to $12 a pound on the international market. During the early 1980s, fast-growing numbers of Bahamian skin divers (including perhaps even the Saint) learned that the easiest way to catch a crawfish was to squirt full-strength household chloride bleach into reef crannies; the irritated crustacean emerges into the open and is easily speared. Thanks to such practices, large areas of the Bahamas have already lost their entire crawfish populations as the annual catch has soared; wide-ranging U.S. fishermen as well as Bahamians are responsible for the damage.

The use of bleach not only leads to the death of adult crawfish but also kills larvae, many other members of the reef community, and in fact the reef itself. "The coral heads become infected and, as the infection spreads, white patches appear over the coral heads," Russell has written. "These dead white areas are later overgrown by algae or green moss. The fish population of a bleached reef also changes. Most fish leave the area and those remaining often show signs of disease. In many cases, sea eggs take over the reef." The continued use of bleach, Russell warned, could lead to scarcities of crawfish and of "grouper, mutton fish and other fish species loved by Bahamians." As of 1987, Larson told me, resident fishermen had reached an agreement to stop using bleach; a new ordinance prohibiting all noxious substances aboard fishing vessels replaced a softer one requiring that, to be found guilty, offenders had to be caught actually using the poison. The future seems a little brighter, but much damage has already been done. "There's hardly a reef around New Providence that hasn't been bleached," said Larson. "The bleaching may be slowing down now, but it surely hasn't stopped."

Beyond the overharvesting of conch and crawfish and the unconscionable bleaching, Larson mentioned other, equally serious problems with the fisheries. Many areas, particularly the shallow Abacos, he said, are "literally fished out." Big mechanized rigs now sweep the great Andros barrier reef, one of the world's largest such areas, which still lacks protection of any sort. "They're even still allowing green turtles to be taken," he said. A decade of vigorous lobbying has resulted in some stiffening of the fishing rules, but no limits whatever have been set on the size of the catch and authorities continue to express confidence since the annual figures continue to rise. In reaction, Larson has altogether banned fishing in marine parks and protected areas, hoping that these will serve as nurseries to replenish the stocks. Educational efforts have brought about some results, particularly in the attitudes of younger Bahamians. Still, Larson lamented, overfishing and mismanagement remain almost as prevalent as ever. "The annual poundage caught goes up and up," he said. "One of these days there's going to be a great awakening, but it surely hasn't happened yet."

At Samana's anchorage, still spared most of these ravages, we snorkeled and Flo and I took the dinghy and explored the little outlying cay. It brimmed with nesting brown noddies and Zenaida doves, and an occasional bright-yellow-and-greenish bird that we could not identify. The Saint took Mauricio and Javier ashore to reconnoiter and make comparisons between what they saw and Columbus' journal entries. Back aboard, we all agreed that Samana was well worth a visit even if the approach, to an anchorage that Columbus may never have seen, was difficult. Mauricio now even had additional evidence to support his side. The spit extending from one jaw of the harbor mouth did not "look like an island," as Columbus had written of a rock at the mouth of Cut Cay at the northern end of San Salvador; nor did it appear that you could "cut it in two in three days."

Over the next several days, Mauricio accumulated further data to counter the *National Geographic*'s assertions. Halfway across from Samana to Acklins, at a point where Columbus reported seeing "many islands," we remained totally out of sight of land even in clear weather with no haze. Sailing westward from Acklins to Crooked Island, we passed the entrance to the Bight of Acklins, a large shallow bay containing several harbors, including one that is fetchingly called Lovely Bay. Passing the entrance close aboard, we could easily distinguish between Acklins and Crooked islands and, even though the land is very low on all sides, agree unanimously on the location of the bight lying between. So much, said Obregón, for Judge's statement that, when you sail along their northern coasts, Acklins and Crooked appear to be one single island. In all, sporting a red woolen cap to protect himself from the fierce sun as he viewed the terrain, Mauricio amassed sixteen major reasons to counter Judge's contention that after his landfall at Samana, Columbus visited Acklins and then Crooked Island before continuing to Long Island, and to uphold the San Salvador–Long–Crooked route that Morison had reaffirmed. (Judge, for his part, advances as many arguments to support the Samana landfall.)

At Crooked's northwestern corner, rounding the splendid 1884 lighthouse on Bird Rock, we turned on our VHF radio to hail Marina Gibson, proprietor of a nearby restaurant and guesthouse. She coached us in through the reef and to the anchorage off the Seventh-Day Adventist settlement at Landrail Point. The only store in town was locked up tight in honor of Saturday, the Adventists' Sabbath. Fresh food was in short supply anyway, for farming has dwindled here as well. "When I was young," an old man told me, "everyone grew sweet corn and yams and cane. But not now. The soil's the same, but people are doing different things." We found Marina, who volunteered her son Robbie to drive us to the airstrip and diving club at Pittston Point two miles northward. From Robbie's shiny red Toyota he showed us his new and powerful outboard. At the airstrip Robbie inspected a plane parked there. He surprised us by saying he was thinking of buying it. For Flo's return to Washington we then sought an alternative to the multi-stop itinerary for which she was ticketed: the twice-weekly one-stop flight from Crooked Island to Nassau, Nassau to Miami, Miami to Washington. At the club's bar we met Larry Edwards, a laconic Arkansan, who, we learned, planned to leave for Orlando early the next morning. Aboard his fast, new six-passenger Aerostar would be Larry and his wife. I asked if Flo could hitch a ride.

"I don't have any problem with that," Larry replied.

We hastened back to *Sanderling* for a quick conch-stew dinner, accompanied by champagne to celebrate our twenty-fifth wedding anniversary, since the date would fall a few days later, before I could return to Washington. After dinner, under a sky crackling with stars, Mauricio recited the plot of the opera he was writing, an elaborate epic involving love, war, and the deities of Greek mythology. Then he asked us to summarize what we thought it was about.

"Time," said Flo.

"You're right," said Mauricio.

Flo packed. We retired early in preparation for her dawn getaway. Robbie had promised to fetch us in his fast outboard at 5:45 and whisk us the two and a half miles up to the airstrip. But he did not show up and Flo and I boarded the dinghy. As we set forth, three flamingos, looking black in the dawn light, flew low overhead. Three-quarters of the way along, our motor began sputtering. In an effort to keep it going I jerked the gearshift out of "forward" and into "neutral" without throttling back. The sudden action sheared the pin on the drive shaft and left us powerless. Now, running late to meet Larry's strict schedule, which called for a takeoff at no later than 6:30, we rowed ashore and stumbled barefoot up the beach, laden with Flo's weighty luggage. The burden reminded me of the bejeweled lady who once, at a party, told Flo and me, "I travel heavy." Clouds of mosquitoes pursued us. We arrived panting at the airstrip and were relieved to see the gleaming Aerostar still parked. A few minutes later Larry and his wife ambled up, and soon after the appointed time, they taxied past me to the near end of the runway. Swatting mosquitoes, I watched wanly as Flo's face, framed in the plane's elliptical rear window, grew smaller and then disappeared into the soft morning sky.

FROM LANDRAIL POINT, *Sanderling* took off on a gentle reach down to French Wells, where Columbus, along with many pirates, had paused to take on water. Passing through shifting channels of varying depth, of an assortment of greens and browns and blues, we (the three Obregóns still aboard along with me and Peter) made our way ashore in the dinghy, whose drive shaft was now equipped with a new pin, and identified the watering spot. From French Wells we continued southward to the place where Crooked Island and Long Cay meet at the southern entrance to the Bight of Acklins. We entered the bight, passing a nondescript Bahamian fishing boat at the entrance. Finding little comfort inside because of swells rolling across the shallow bay, we doubled back out past Windsor Point, a low promontory that Columbus had inexplicably named Punta Hermosa, and anchored near the cliffs in only somewhat calmer water. At dawn the next morning we started off for Ragged Island in the southwestern Bahamas, the last port Columbus visited before departing for Cuba. We expected to enter its unlit harbor before dark. I had erred in measuring the distance, though, and soon after departing

realized that it was a good eighty-five miles away. If we averaged a brisk
six knots, we would still arrive well after sundown. To get to Ragged,
moreover, we would have to sail almost due downwind and under the
constant threat of a sudden jibe and with much banging and crashing and
chafing of gear in the moderate northeasterly breeze. Under the
circumstances we were pleased when Mauricio found an uninhabited dot
on the chart called Cay Verde, closer and on a more favorable heading,
and offering the possibility of an exposed but viable anchorage.

Pursued by squadrons of brown boobies, which would bravely
approach the boat and then veer off with strange squeals and little shrugs
of their wings, we arrived off Cay Verde by midafternoon. The birding
was wonderful. Pretty black-and-white Audubon's shearwaters moved
gracefully near the surface of the sea, and magnificent frigate birds,
tropic birds, and small terns of several species soared and swooped
overhead. On the lee side of the island we found plenty of water for
anchoring, and yearned to get ashore to a fine-looking beach. But we
found no shelter from a relentless swell coming around both ends of the
small rock.

Figuring that we would be just as comfortable under way as at
anchor here, we decided to soldier on toward the seldom visited group
of islands that includes Ragged. We could reach a harbor just north of
Raccoon Cut before midnight, and use the full moonlight available at that
time to pick our way in through the reef. On the way across I produced
a decent hot dinner in spite of long high seas, and we arrived at the entry
point at ten o'clock. I turned on the engine-room blower and then the
starter. After days of faithful operation, the Perkins chose this moment to
refuse to start. That morning, I recalled, we had experienced a slight
surge and Peter had said prophetically, "We'd better cut it off now, so
we'll have it when we really need it." Now, not even the shock-treatment
restart method worked. Two tries produced no result, and a third evoked
only a few turns and then a flameout. We could not cross the reef without
power, particularly with a moderate onshore breeze still blowing, and
could find no handy alternative on the chart. Other than simply bypassing the Ragged chain and continuing southward toward Cuba, our only
logical option was to lie to for the night, moving slowly back and forth
offshore. The time passed uneventfully, but few of the crew slept well
as *Sanderling* pitched and bucked, even while hove to, in open water.

In the morning we sailed into the harbor near Duncan Town. Our
anchorage was in a wide expanse of turquoise so brilliant that the water's
reflection turned the undersides of passing clouds and seabirds from
white or gray to a vivid blue-green. Ashore on Ragged Island proper, we
could see a road leading across the peak of a high hill toward the village,

which oddly faces into the prevailing easterly wind. Closer by were a few buildings on the beach, dominated by the wingless remains of a four-engined DC-6 air transport. A speedboat made out toward us from this quarter, which we learned was called Sweetwater Farm. At the skiff's helm was Charles Wilson, brother of the farm's full-time inhabitant and great-grandson of a man who a century ago had emigrated from England to this remote place and purchased much of it. Charles made fast and came aboard. He told us that he had come down from Eleuthera, where he lives, to spend some time working and fishing around the family property. We asked him about the plane. Its Colombian pilots had come in too hot and skidded off the end of the runway, totaling the plane. One project on which Charles was intermittently working was its conversion into a double-decker restaurant.

"What happened to the drugs?" I asked.

"They all just disappeared," purred Charles, a tall and muscular man of about thirty. "And I wasn't even on the island."

Thus began a visit that provided us with a keen sense of contemporary life in a distant corner of the Bahamas, a place occupied by but seventy people, of whom forty are children, infrequently visited by anybody but drug runners, often-corrupt law-enforcement authorities, and the weekly mail boat that also brings supplies. Charles ferried Mauricio, Javi, and Peter ashore to Sweetwater Farm, where some twenty people, including several with dreadlocks, were assembled to give them what turned out to be a friendly reception. One man provided a ride into town on the back of his truck. In the village, which has no food market, Mauricio supervised a door-to-door canvassing operation in which the supplies we needed—eggs, canned milk, meat, vegetables, canned juice—were pieced together by barter or purchase from several households. Peter found a mechanic who would later alarm him, once again, by casually restarting the engine with lighter fluid. I meantime skirmished with a beefy police corporal who boarded *Sanderling* in search of passports (I could find only mine), conducted a cursory inspection in the main cabin, expressed curiosity about why we had made the effort to get here, and seemed interested in a payoff.

Charles later took me ashore and drove me into town aboard a little three-wheeled motorbike. Along the way he showed me his family's extensive landholdings and a salt pond that is worked only upon occasion these days. We saw many feral goats, no agriculture, and few signs of work being done. One young man, a relative of Charles's, did not stir from a supine position when we approached his small house. I learned that the population of the village is gradually declining as more and more families move to larger islands so that their children can continue their education beyond the primary level. Though I was not able to find ice as I had hoped—without an engine we could not work our refrigeration system except at marinas with AC power—I did manage to obtain some additional supplies. On the way back to the boat, Charles kindly tossed into my bag many extras from Sweetwater Farm's ample reserves. We also took aboard half a dozen gallon jugs of the fine pure well water for which the farm is named.

Charles and his fellow Ragged Islanders left me saddened about Bahamians more generally. Many of these gentle and generous people seemed compelled, more by the depletion of the resources around them than because of inertia on their own part, to become peripheral adjuncts to the drug world and its instant riches. Some, such as the staunch Marina Gibson of Crooked Island or the touching group of old men we had seen at church at Seymours on Long Island, wearing coats and ties and singing hymns in cracking voices, find ways to resist the devil. But for younger people the temptations are everywhere at hand, and television, beaming in via dish antennas, imposes radically new material standards and forms of behavior. To bring the illusions alive one need only take a short plane or boat ride to the Bahamian Mecca of Miami. For no other people in the Western Hemisphere does the United States represent more of a burden and a blessing than for the quasi-Americans of the Bahamas.

Columbus did not tarry in the Raggeds. Nor could we. With unanimous determination, despite our lack of sleep, we sailed off across the shallow bank to the south and west of Ragged Island at seven knots on a broad reach. Now our destination was Cayo Santo Domingo, a small rock which by all accounts was Columbus' last landfall before he reached Cuba. Again escorted by curious brown boobies, we arrived toward evening at what turned out to be a dismal and almost totally unprotected anchorage under what the sailing directions, stretching a point, called its lee. Here we rolled about remorselessly in confused seas. Peter puttered about trying to fix several things that were broken, including the flushing mechanism on the toilet. At one moment of exquisite frustration, he peered down the length of the main cabin and, to no one special, shouted a rhetorical question: "Why does everything on this boat have to be so goddamned unreliable?"

Slipping and sliding around the galley, I produced a dinner that was no match for the excellent Spanish tortilla (eggs, potatoes, onions) that Lita had somehow gotten together for lunch. Then, since we had only forty-two miles to go before we would reach the Cuban coast and did not want to get there until after dawn, we tried to sleep aboard our bucking steed.

9

Cuban Interlude

"Gibara, Puerto Gibara, el yate Sanderling, *Whiskey Tango Sierra 9734, Canal 16. Adelante."*

IT WAS NEARLY DAWN. WITH AN AUTHORITATIVE VOICE MAURICIO WAS trying to make VHF radio contact with officials at our destination. I sat at *Sanderling's* helm, trying to make the lights and landmarks of Cuba's northern coast match the information on our chart, as a gentle northeast breeze eased us southward from Cayo Santo Domingo toward the port where Columbus made his first major Cuban stop. No response after several efforts. Mauricio widened the net, asking any station in Cuba to come up. Again, nothing from anybody except a curt voice from the military base at Antilla stating that he was "on maneuvers" and could not talk. Since we were unable to communicate with the Cubans, our only choice was to continue tracking toward the high mountains flanking Gibara's large bay. As the moon set and the loom of daylight began to brighten the sky off our port quarter, the outlines of these distinctive ranges gradually sharpened. One lighthouse had been switched off and replaced by another in a very different location. Still, we had no trouble finding the way in.

At the mouth of the bay we dropped our sails and continued under power into the little port on its northern flank. A fishing boat passed us, its occupants apparently uninterested. Next came a ferry of sorts, full of boisterous *compañeros* on their way to work across the bay. "*Son de Batista, carajo,*" one man wisecracked to another, and the sound rolled across the water to us. Then we saw a vessel containing a uniformed man who motioned to us to follow him. We did so and were soon at a mooring amid the fishing fleet.

Thanks to his title of Colombian ambassador-at-large to all the nations of the Caribbean, Mauricio had been able to arrange our visit through Cuba's Ministry of Foreign Relations. In his proposal to them, he had stressed that the quincentenary celebration of Columbus' first voyage, in which Cuba too would participate, would be greatly enhanced if he had an opportunity to look firsthand at the Gibara area, doubtless the Admiral's Cuban landfall. At Gibara, after completing this portion of his research, Mauricio would, along with Lita and Javier, leave us to return to commitments at home. My idea, still pending approval from the Cubans, was to take *Sanderling* along the north coast from Gibara to Punta Maisí, at the island's extreme east end, and jump from there across the sixty-mile Windward Passage to Haiti. I would be accompanied only by another American: Peter.

In following the route I planned, *Sanderling* would revisit several other Cuban ports that Columbus mentioned in his journal. Perhaps also we would be able to gather impressions of how the island had been faring ecologically in the Castro era. At the very least, we would be among the very few U.S. yachtsmen in three decades to undertake such a cruise with the blessing of the Cuban authorities. Since 1959, when Fidel Castro and his Marxist guerrilla force brought down the seemingly well-entrenched regime of General Fulgencio Batista, both sides have maintained tight controls on visits to Cuba by U.S. citizens. Even during the brief period of relative warmth between the two nations that flickered during the mid-1970s, when I was serving in a position that should have given me access—the presidency of a well-intentioned and nonpartisan U.S. organization that sought better understanding among the nations of the Americas—I was unable to arrange a personal trip. Some U.S. yachts have entered Cuban ports under emergency conditions, and received assistance. Others have simply blundered in. An officially sanctioned passage there is just about unheard of. So I was eager to convince the Cubans of my good intentions and persuade them to allow *Sanderling* to proceed.

Now, at our mooring, I started to cook breakfast while awaiting further developments. Just as the eggs hit the frying pan a rowboat approached. It contained several men, principally a Frontier Guard captain in well-pressed fatigues and black boots, a small pistol holstered at his hip. I turned off the stove while he carefully inspected all our passports and documents, including copies of the exchange of telexes with the officials in Havana that Mauricio had prudently brought along. Once satisfied, the captain leaned back, smiled, bid us *bienvenidos*, and asked us what we needed. Mauricio requested a small boat to take him and Javier, as his photographer, on a short cruise around the bay where Columbus spent two weeks. With *Sanderling* short of supplies I asked for ice, water, fuel, and perhaps a little food.

Within minutes a frenzy of activity commenced. Fifty pounds of free ice landed on our deck, and we were instructed to move immediately to a nearby pier to take on water. Here, amid rolling swells and shouts from twenty-odd men all tending our lines, we barely managed to do so and get away with *Sanderling*'s toe rail and topsides unscathed. Back at our mooring, the captain apologized for the delay in producing fuel. He had sent his men to borrow a jerry can from a fisherman, and it would be coming soon. As I cast a longing eye at our half-cooked eggs, I was told that we would all have breakfast ashore, at an incongruous gingerbread house on the waterfront that was once owned by the Portuguese consul and is now called the Restaurante Miramar. Here we were joined by several other Cubans, including the hefty José Antonio Pellerín Hernández, a local Communist Party leader, and Pedro Pérez Hernández, historian and representative of the Ministry of Culture.

After breakfast, while the Obregóns went off on their boat trip, Peter and I were given a tour of the small, quiet town (population about 60,000). We visited the Museum of Natural History, which consisted mostly of bird skins, an art museum, and a metropolitan museum. We were told much about local progress since the revolution. Not only are health and education services much improved, it was said; Gibara now has three museums as compared with only one before. On the streets, asphalt over the old cobblestones, cars were far fewer in number than bicycles, motorbikes, and donkey carts. Inside old colonial residences and shops, people made cigars and fixed furniture and cared for children. At the Casa de la Cultura someone was practicing for a piano recital. We walked past the church and were told that it continues to function ("It has priests and everything") and that the congregation tends to consist of older people. Along the shorefront, members of the fishermen's cooperative seemed active, and teenagers ran speed trials in racing kayaks from the sports club across the harbor. Overall, the pace seemed languid at Gibara, and its appearance little changed from the placid images in the 1930s color postcards that we had seen on display at one of the museums.

At the government's guesthouse, where we rejoined the Obregóns at lunchtime, two smartly uniformed immigration officers arrived, aboard a trim motorcycle with sidecar, from the nearby city of Holguín (where Columbus' advance men, looking in vain for Asia's Grand Khan, had first seen tobacco—smoked by Taino Indians). The senior official took a seat behind a desk. We sat like schoolchildren in a quiet circle around him and his colleague. After disposing handily of the Obregóns, they inspected the two gringo passports and then, without stamping them, completed landing cards that, for Cuban use only, showed that we had both entered and departed. Then Mauricio dropped the major question. "I must leave here," he said. "But the boat is headed for Haiti and needs permission to travel along your coast in order to get there." The presiding immigration man, who had the sharp features and flashing white teeth of a star flamenco dancer, smiled and reached into his briefcase. "For that you'll need one of these," he said, holding up an Inward Clearance form for the boat. It had already been filled out and stamped. I had only to sign, and did so with alacrity. The official countersigned, then silently handed me the precious document.

After a sumptuous lunch featuring excellent small cultivated oysters in a peppery tomato sauce, we returned to *Sanderling*, with Pedro and José Antonio in tow, for an afternoon sail eastward to Bahía Bariay. Here, in a tight little anchorage below a mountain that he said resembled a

Cubans on board *Sanderling*.

"pretty little mosque," Columbus made his first stop on Cuban soil. The swells were big as we approached and the 20-knot wind blew dead against us. *Sanderling* commenced to pitch. José Antonio, who wore black dress shoes and a well-pressed blue sports shirt, hung on grimly as spray flew past the dodger into the cockpit where we all sat; before long Pedro, mumbling apologies, had his head over the rail. We nosed our way into the entrance to the bay, marked by a small fishing village. Javier photographed the distinctive mountain range that Columbus had admired. Then we turned downwind for the quick run back to Gibara. En route, now chilled, José Antonio toasted our mission with an unrevolutionary glass of neat bourbon. At Gibara we tied up to a rickety pier, now being rebuilt, that had long consisted of rusty old rails attached to each other like jackstraws. From a skiff a redheaded man, past his prime and already well into his daily rum ration, bobbed about supervising the operation and shouting instructions. A swell hit while he was attaching our stern to a mooring buoy, and his head cracked hard against our topsides (later he was reported to have been looking woozy, but by the next morning he was back in full form). Once secure, we clambered ashore, and returned to the guesthouse for a shower (lots of water, bring your own soap) and a round of *abrazos* for the Obregóns as they departed in a taxi for Holguín.

It was calm and grayish the next morning. Early on, the captain appeared to tell us that the food we had ordered was ready and I should go ashore to the restaurant to pick it up. Assembled there I found about two kilos each of smoked pork, fresh chicken, and ham; a big slab of good Russian cheese; a case of Cuban beer in half-liter bottles; a bushel of tomatoes, ten small watermelons, and two bottles of aged Havana Club rum. There also appeared a bill covering eighteen gallons of diesel fuel as well as the food. It was for an astonishing $165. Things aren't that expensive in Cuba, I was told. The problem was the absence of an official exchange rate between the U.S. dollar and the Cuban peso: for fear of being criticized by higher-ups, the local authorities felt compelled to scalp me. Besides, said one man helpfully, "the rum is the most expensive thing. If you want to save thirty dollars, just take one bottle less." I paid. Pete and I tried to make phone calls to the States, but were told to expect a waiting period of up to fourteen hours. We walked back to the harbor, passing a school class of uniformed ten-year-old girls dancing to old rock music. Pedro, revived, helped us ferry our things aboard, and then came aboard himself. I gave him a Coke ("I haven't had one of these in a year") and, wrapped inside a brown paper bag, copies of some fairly current U.S. magazines. He and the captain warmly bid us goodbye and we were off.

Out in the open ocean, once again battling a vigorous easterly, we tacked past Bariay and Puerto Vita with its prominent white lighthouse. Inland were mountains and sudden soaring stretches of bare rock echoing the drama of the Brazilian coast near Rio de Janeiro. By midafternoon we were off Puerto Naranjo's entrance, unmarked on the chart except by a lighthouse on one of the flanking points, and decided to give it a try. At the mouth of the long, narrow bay, which splits into several smaller sections, we found a pair of large flashing buoys, one red and one green, and could see that the entire channel was equally well marked. The reason soon came clear: though on one side we could see little but mangroves along an unpopulated shore, a large modern deep-water port facility suddenly emerged to starboard. We motored on, intending to pass the port and find a snug anchorage beyond. A launch came out from the wharf and headed toward us. Aboard was a young man carrying a rifle at parade rest. I told him that we had permission to cruise these waters. "To enter here you need special permission," he said. Then he ordered us to anchor across from the port, near the mangroves, while he returned ashore to radio his superiors for further instructions. Later he reappeared and said it was all right. We swam in clean greenish water, photographed *Sanderling* from the dinghy, and began to wonder what sort of place we had wandered into. Was this where they unloaded Russian weapons or missiles? Or a covert submarine base? A distant explosion added to the mystery. From here, I decided, it might not be wise to use the radiotelephone to call Flo in Washington.

We ate a peaceful dinner, went to bed, and were just dozing off when horn blasts and blinding lights emanated from what seemed to be a large vessel that, when we stumbled up on deck, we found lying close aboard. An authoritative female voice announced that we could not stay here but would have to come into the port.

"The big-ship port?" I asked.

"No, there's another port."

"We'd rather stay here. We're all settled and we're very tired."

"So are we."

"Our engine may not work."

"We'll tow you in and then find a mechanic."

No excuse would do. Soon we were groggily following our captors up the little bay, around a big bend, and into a little facility where several other small boats (expropriated during the revolution?) were already tied up. A uniformed soldier, barely able to control a furiously barking German shepherd at his side, patrolled the end of a small pier. I turned off the engine. The woman to whom we had talked emerged out of the gloom, a small poodle prancing at her side. Was the dog expropriated as well? A uniformed Frontier Guardsman came aboard and explained. "Fidel likes all his guests to feel very secure," he said without a hint of sarcasm. "We could not protect you well enough without being able to see you, so we had to bring you in here." He, the woman, and the poodle all then departed, leaving us under the gaze of the frantic shepherd, hardly a modern version of the mute hound belonging to the Tainos that Columbus had discovered at Bariay and that his crew members had zestfully eaten. Some protection, I thought as I finally dozed off, vaguely wondering when the interrogation would begin.

Morning came. Mercifully, the attack dog had been withdrawn and its barks were muffled by distance. The woman returned, wearing a dark blue striped jersey and with Musi (the poodle) still trailing along, to ask if we needed help. Ice would have to be ordered from the nearby village of Cuernavaca and would take a *momentito*. But it could be arranged. I strolled on the pier and there found the boat that had hailed us at midnight. It no longer seemed so menacing: the principal feature of its main deck was a bar and stools. Other sportfishing boats tied up there, I was told, were for the use of the mostly Canadian and East German vacationers who frequent several nearby resorts. It was for the sake of this tourist trade and not the ceaseless struggle against the Norteamericanos, I finally figured out, that the channel was so carefully buoyed all the way in to where we now were. We had been brought in from our anchorage not for reasons of national security but simply because the little port was where pleasure craft "belonged." My apprehensions were groundless.

Eventually the ice arrived, a great slab of it lonely on the back of a midsize flatbed truck. We stowed it, said farewell to the Frontier Guardsmen, and made our way back out to the ocean. The lush coast seemed all but untouched, much as Columbus would have seen it, with little evidence of people or activity of any sort. Close at hand now was Sama, another picture-book port with a narrow entrance opening into a wider, light blue basin tucked under high green hills, a little beach on the port side, a small fishing village to starboard. As I ventured inshore for a good look, a snappy-looking gray vessel with shiny maroon trim charged us. From its bridge a man pointed toward the harbor. Then the boat sped off. Peter took down the sails and we motored in. At the village landing stood a cluster of Frontier Guardsmen, including one I recognized from Naranjo. They waved us closer despite my protests about drawing almost six feet and not wishing to end up on the rocks. I stopped short of the landing and asked what they wanted. Were we all right? they asked. Yes, everything's just fine, I yelled back. O.K., that's all they wanted to know, they said. They had seen us approaching and thought that we were in trouble, so if there were no problems, we could proceed. After a couple of brief thumping groundings we eased out into deeper water and made sail.

Soon we were rounding Cabo Lucrecia, the prominent landmark that Columbus called the Cabo de Cuba, now decorated with a tall lighthouse attached to a large rectangular stone building. Here the coast at last turns to the southeast, giving an eastbound sailor a welcome chance to free sheets and bear off from the prevailing wind. For us on this day, the easterly had a touch of north in it, and our ride down into the large Bahía de Nipe turned into a hull-speed reach. We enjoyed a spectacular sunset and as darkness fell were pleased to find that all the lights and buoys were as charted. We crept into an anchorage near where we had been told we would find the Frontier Guard station, and received a visit from three motley-looking guardsmen who alarmed us by insisting on making off with our Inward Clearance form. "If we lose this we'll be burned at the stake," I said. They laughed and said we could have it back first thing in the morning.

They were almost as good as their word. At eight-thirty, half an hour after they said it would reappear, I set forth in the dinghy in search of it. At the dock stood several men. I asked the one in uniform if he knew about our paper. With something of a snarl—this was the first surly person we had encountered—he dug into his pocket and handed it over.

Later we motored out of the spacious landlocked bay, noting large Russian tankers at anchor and listening on the VHF as they communicated in English with local pilots and port officials. A small Cuban naval vessel, sort of a PT boat, escorted us along part of the short fifteen-mile run to the Bahía de Sagua de Tánamo. Quickly again we reverted from the bustle of modern shipping to the more tranquil green of a virtually unpeopled shore. After negotiating a break in the reef, we headed *Sanderling* toward a small, well-marked cut in the coast, then turned ninety degrees to the right and continued down the narrow channel past a Frontier Guard observation post. Agitated guardsmen waved us in and we started to comply. Then one, having conferred with superiors on the radio, shrugged his shoulders and, with a gesture like that of a headwaiter ushering guests to a table, waved us into his splendid harbor. It was almost starfish-shaped, with long, narrow bays under brilliant rolling hills extending in several directions. A high mountain range lay to the south. No town was visible except a small village at the harbor mouth, and though we heard a tractor wheezing in the distance, we saw no people. We picked an anchorage on the windward side, nestling as close under the lee as we could, for the breeze was still blowing strong, and dropped our anchor. For the first time we were alone in Cuba.

I found it hard, as Columbus had, to forsake the charm of this place. In *Admiral of the Ocean Sea*, Morison wrote of Columbus' reluctance:

> There was no gold in this lovely bay, no hint of Asia . . . no large village of natives, nothing of profit to the Spaniards. Only Columbus's love of natural beauty, a trait unusual in that era and still uncommon among navigators, kept him there five days. He even excused himself for not departing on the fourth day because it was Sunday. But mere scenery was not getting him anywhere. . . .

As for ourselves, after only an afternoon and an evening, we felt compelled to keep slogging eastward. For our next day's run we had planned a relatively long hop across to Cayo Moa, an open anchorage inside a series of reefs whose shore consists, as best I could piece it together on the chart, of steep mountains tumbling down into the ocean. In the book that Obregón wrote with Morison and published in 1964, *The Caribbean As Columbus Saw It*, the authors allege that the Admiral "went into ecstasies over the peculiar beauty of this great harbor, so placid between the austere mountains and the hissing barrier reef." The authors also note the mountain stream that descends into the harbor and is clearly marked on the chart, and recall that when Morison visited in 1940, aboard the ketch *Mary Otis*, the place was still "clean of human touch." As we approached, our enthusiasm for the anchorage was dimmed first by the sight of a large open-pit mine that made an ugly reddish-brown slash across the brow of one of the high green mountains. Then, as dark fell, the lights of what was obviously a major smelting and refining complex began to glow ominously bright. It was almost a relief when, unable to make the flashing entry buoys conform to what was on our chart, or find the range also noted there, we decided that it would be unwise to try it. Better, we thought, to push along overnight to Baracoa, the last major harbor on the northeast coast.

We proceeded uneventfully along this magic shoreline, missing many of its boldly shouldered harbors in the darkness. After dawn we caught the flavor of the region by sighting just such a place a few miles short of Baracoa: a narrow river flowing gently into the sea, soft mounds of striking green on either side, mountains behind. Training biplanes from the town's airstrip, taking off from under fluffy gray clouds, heralded our arrival; by midmorning, sweating in humid air as the wind turned light, we were there. Clouds already shrouded the anvil-shaped mountain, called El Yunque, that dominates the little town. A guardsman guided us to a mooring and was soon followed aboard by a sincere gray-haired captain. Ice came without delay. We were asked to pay $4.40 for two *quintales*. The captain apologized for not being able to give us change for five U.S. dollars. I said we would contribute the sixty cents to the further progress of the revolution. Then the captain delivered his ultimatum.

"This is a very dangerous coast," he said. "Sometimes we get high winds and rainsqualls, and when this happens, it is our duty to close the port. The weather forecast for later today and tomorrow is not good. If we have to close the port, you may have to spend three or four days without leaving. What you do is, of course, your choice. But if you want to be sure, you might want to leave by early this afternoon."

Tired as we were after having already spent a night at sea, we agreed that we should not risk the threatened impoundment. So on this still, slow day, we paused only long enough for a quick look around the harbor. Lumber—many of the hills had looked deforested—was being loaded aboard a barge. Uniformed schoolchildren walked about on the quay. A shantytown, much like what one would see almost anywhere in Latin America, festered along one stretch of the muddy shore. We heard the tinkling of a distant ice-cream truck. Like Gibara, Baracoa seemed to boast a quiet faded charm but lacked bustle. Is this good or bad? "Keeping yourself busy?" Americans ask each other all the time; the answer is always affirmative. Such a question would not occur to many Latins, and Baracoans, under Fidel or otherwise, are probably happiest when they are not busy at all. At the very least, the guardsman assigned to us, sitting motionless in a rocking chair at the head of yet another spindly dock, seemed a model of contentment. No time now for such musings if we were to get out of town before becoming embargoed by the threatened bad weather. Having heard of our intention to leave—he was doubtless immensely relieved to be unburdened of us—the captain came aboard to complete the departure formalities.

Solemnly, this gray-haired, well-starched man wished us all the best for our work, and for our families, and for our lives.

"Igualmente para usted," I replied, and we shook hands, the little ceremony heightening my frustration about the parlous state of U.S.-Cuban relations. If the United States can trade and exchange tourists with all sorts of Communist nations that are our deadly political enemies, I wondered, why should it be that difficult for us to communicate with the Cubans on a basic people-to-people level? Surely we have more in common than the ivory-billed woodpecker, a large North American species long thought to have gone extinct but recently rediscovered in a remote corner of Cuba and of great interest to U.S. ornithologists. I pondered the question as we dropped our mooring and, with half the town's population silently watching, motored out into the ocean swells. By sundown we were celebrating my twenty-fifth wedding anniversary just off the entrance to yet another breathtaking river entrance, a little west of the prominent Punta Silencio. I raised Flo on the SSB and we agreed that we missed each other. Then night fell and the moon rose, feathery clouds for an instant holding it in a delicate embrace between an outstretched thumb and a curved forefinger. The powerful beacon at Punta Maisí, at the easternmost end of Cuba, flashed us a final goodbye as we sailed eastward toward Haiti.

10

Warmth and Squalor
in the Greater Antilles

THE WIND COOPERATED FOR OUR RUN ACROSS THE WINDWARD PASSAGE from Cuba to Haiti, veering north a little so that we could sail, close-hauled on the port tack, encouragingly near our rhumb line of 095 degrees magnetic. On this point of sailing, with seas tossing the boat about, our autopilot was no use at all. Peter and I alternated at the helm, two hours on and two hours off, finding it surprisingly possible to sleep off-watch on the lee bunk, with the boat heeling steeply, wedged in between the mattress and soft pillows. By eight in the morning we caught our first glimpse of Haiti, steep gray hills that seemed almost cloudlike in the haze of the early hour. As we approached, this coast grew higher and more imposing. The cliffs, triple the height of the Hudson River's Palisades, say, turned a soft greenish color and mountaintops soared above and behind them. The seas flattened and, later in the morning, the breeze moved even further to the north. For a while we were making good a heading that would carry us straight up the channel between the Haitian mainland and the towering bluffs of Tortuga Island.

Just as it had for Columbus, who made almost exactly the same passage in December 1492, our luck failed to hold. In the afternoon the breeze turned eastward again, and the seas made up high around Tortuga's western end. Our progress slowed to a crawl as we punched into the chop. Along this coast there are few buoys or lighthouses, and we began to worry about where we could safely spend the night. Under Tortuga's heights, we had supposed, there might be a snug berth for us, as there had been for the *boucaniers* who early in the seventeenth century used the island as home base. But with the wind now whistling right down the channel, this shore seemed very exposed. On the mainland we poked our nose into Moustique Bay, where Columbus had raised the Spanish flag for Ferdinand and Isabella, but it too offered little protection.

Just as the sun lowered behind us, setting the sky ablaze with red and gold, we calculated that we could squeak in to the little fishing village of Port-de-Paix before we lost the last remnants of daylight. The entry looked simple on the chart and so it proved to be. As we drew closer, we even had the anchor light of a small coastal freighter to use as a beacon. By soon after nightfall we were in what turned out to be a crowded little harbor, full of rusty fishing and commercial vessels. Two boys in a skiff guided us to *une belle place*, and we gladly settled in, watching with admiration as a little gaff-rigged Haitian sailboat, lightless and powerless, entered the harbor at full speed, rounded up near the high town dock and simultaneously anchored and dropped sails, then tidily drifted back just far enough to be able to cast a line to the shore astern. Shadowy figures moved about ashore, and from somewhere in the gloom came scratchy music from an old record player.

On our starboard spreader we flew our yellow Q, or quarantine, flag, indicating that we had not officially entered Haiti and were requesting what is called *pratique*—clearance for *Sanderling* to move freely along its coast. Not knowing whether Port-de-Paix was a port of entry, we intended to spend the night, then proceed to Cap-Haïtien, an easy day's run with the weather cooperating, and clear there. We awoke

Greater Antilles as plotted in 1592.

to clear skies and a beckoning breeze, and were keen to get away early and take advantage of it. At the town dock an olive-colored powerboat was tied up, with uniformed men moving about aboard. I suspected trouble if we simply pulled up anchor and steamed out of there, but the gamble seemed worth it. Ten minutes later, just as we were setting sail, we saw the vessel bearing down on us, lights flashing and a siren screaming. We dropped our sails and waited while the police, or whoever they were, approached and tied up alongside. In soft polite English, the skipper informed us that we should have come ashore to check in but that, as long as we were already under way, he could complete the formalities on the spot.

He asked where we had come from. The Bahamas, I replied, not knowing the status of Haiti-Cuba relations but assuming them to be bad. We produced passports and ship's documents. No, we had no weapons aboard. Then we were told that we would have to undergo "a small search," and a corporal wielding a pistol, trailed by another soldier with a rifle, swung over the rail. They went through the main and forward cabins with considerable care; I wondered what would happen if they ran across our Cuban beer or our precious Havana Club rum. But all went well and before long, almost apologizing for holding us up, the captain waved us on our way. Later we discovered the extent of our luck. Port-de-Paix, once a thriving station, had recently become something of a pirate's cove where, especially during the period of weak governance that followed "Baby Doc" Duvalier's abdication, law and order was fragmentary. At best, we were told, we might have expected a shake-down; we might even have been robbed at gunpoint. In this instance, our innocence was rewarded with the gentle courtesy that, we were to find, is commonplace in Haiti.

After our liberation, things improved quickly. All morning we tacked up the Tortuga channel, four to five miles wide, the deepest blue to the north shifting abruptly to a brilliant turquoise up to the end of the bank extending from the mountainous Haitian shore. Small sailboats, their passengers waving as we passed, flecked the channel. On the Tortuga side, densely populated villages dotted the shore, and little paths reached up the precipitous slopes to cottages and cultivated tracts of steep land. Under Baby Doc, U.S. investors had successfully evicted many of these people and brought in heavy earth-moving equipment to make way for a resort. But, in a heartening and unusual reversal, the refugees later were allowed to return to their homes; the bulldozers were abandoned and left to rust as the developers' political fortunes waned. The sun turned the calm water to gold as we tacked along. When the morning breeze faded, we even successfully ran our delicate engine for a while before the usual heart-stopping surging inevitably began and we were forced back to our sails. But the breeze filled in and we enjoyed a fine afternoon sail past Acul Bay, a fully protected anchorage so enchanting to Columbus that he lacked the words to describe it, and around the imposing heights of Cap-Haïtien into the harbor.

"American sailboat entering Cap-Haïtien, American sailboat enter-ing Cap-Haïtien. This is the mechanic. Over."

The soft Virginia-accented voice wafted in to us on Channel 16 of our VHF radio. But what mechanic? And what authority did this person have? Was he somehow an official of the port? Or just trying to be helpful? From where was he calling? How did he know we were there? Imperturbably, he continued after we had identified ourselves. "You just come on around the back side of the big-ship pier that you're looking at. Then you'll see me tied up at another place behind. You can't come in here with me if you haven't cleared, and now it's too late to clear unless you pay a forty-five-dollar extra charge, so you'll want to anchor just outboard of me, and stay aboard tonight, and then enter tomorrow."

We followed our instructions to the letter and were soon resting at anchor, in a little artificial harbor between two wharves, a few yards from a large U.S.-flag sloop bearing the name *Mechanic*. Before long her owner, a trim middle-aged American, was alongside *Sanderling* aboard his tender, a rakish shark-fishing skiff from Mexico. We introduced ourselves. He said his name was Moe, and continued his monologue.

"I've been in and out of here for fifteen years," he went on. "I know it pretty well and they know me. You may have heard bad things about the Haitians, but they're not true. Stealing is not common here. You'll have to get yourselves a boat boy, someone to be aboard when you're not. Then that boat will be safer than a church. Even in Port-au-Prince, the most beautiful blonde in the world could walk down the center of the street in the middle of the night, take her clothes off, and lie down. In the morning there would probably be about four people around her taking care of her. They'll want more, but about five dollars a day is about right for the boat boy. Lots of other people will want money, but try to ignore them. See that newspaper I have pasted across the side of my cockpit? That's so I can sit in there and they can't see me. Don't believe what you hear about poverty here. Right now their cruise-ship business is down—this fancy port they built is a colossal failure—but there's a boom on in broken-end rice they're bringing in from Louisiana and selling at a far lower price than the local rice. Everybody's fat and shining here now. Rice is what's separating this country from a revolution. I'm a mechanic. That's what I do. I make a living off that boat, fixing things and buying and selling. I move around—here, some places in the Bahamas, Belize. My boat is part pleasure, part commercial. I carry motorcycles in there, in the hold. My girlfriend, Robin, she works on them with me. You'll meet Jacques and you'll want to make friends with him. He does everything here and he can help you a lot."

Moe's lively harangue continued as another boarding party, led by Antoine, a crisp young man with a walkie-talkie who said he was the assistant pilot for the harbor, approached. "I'll let you take care of this alone," said Moe, casting off. Antoine clambered aboard along with a uniformed sergeant and two older, unidentified civilians, and asked our intentions. I said we planned to spend several days here, and would present our papers at the office first thing in the morning. But, said Antoine, we could complete the formalities right here and now; anyway, we could not stay here at anchor but would have to go in and tie up behind the *Mechanic*. Shades of Puerto Naranjo. Couldn't we just stay here? I asked. No. Why? Because I say so, and I am the pilot, I am the official authority here. But would we not have to pay to enter now? Oh yes, it will cost forty-five dollars. Oh my, that comes as a shock, I'm not prepared. Well, then, whatever you feel is right. I offered twenty dollars, for the four men to divide as they saw fit, and they accepted with no hesitation.

In we went to tie up, now in darkness, throwing our docking lines to dozens of pairs of waiting hands, then completing a customs declaration on our own blank paper. Lacking carbon paper, I made two copies and

Antoine made two others. The sergeant looked briefly into the forward cabin, then grunted approval. With the ceremonies complete, he and Antoine and one of the older men withdrew. The other, tall with an erect posture and a quiet lilting voice and fringes of short curly white hair, remained aboard.

This was, it turned out, Moe's all-purpose Jacques. He asked for beer and we complied. He told us that all the men along the dockside would like to be our boat boy, and the selection could be tricky and lead to bad squabbling. I said I would leave it to him and Moe. They quickly came up with Nelson, a mild-mannered young father of three whose wife had left him and who was desperately seeking a way to support his family. Nelson asked us whether he could ride with us to wherever we were going. I said I regretted we just could not do that, we had other people coming aboard. "I won't take up much room," he said. "I'll work hard and I can sleep anywhere." He pointed to the cabin floor at the foot of the companionway. "That place would be fine." I insisted that it would not be possible, and Nelson accepted this, abjectly bowing his head. Once Nelson had been selected and had come aboard, most of the other men on the dock drifted away, except for one who requested a fee for services rendered when he caught one of our docking lines.

Thus commenced a respite of several days at Cap-Haïtien. There we ate very well, often in the company of Jacques, who would drive us to a restaurant in his balky old Valiant, then walk in and sit down with us. He ate lustily, pouring volumes of ketchup onto whatever he ordered—even already well-seasoned Creole specialties such as *lambi* (conch) in a fiery sauce. We discovered that during Papa Doc's time Jacques was a *tonton macoute*, or gun-wielding civilian law enforcer. In the U.S. press, "dreaded" is the conventional accompaniment to any mention of these men. Many of them were killed, and for good reason, in the wave of reprisals that followed Duvalier's fall; many were held responsible for the bloodshed that occurred, six months after *Sanderling*'s visit, during the military government's halfhearted effort to conduct elections. But some *macoutes* had more compassion, and Jacques was clearly one of these; only because he was universally popular, I was told, had he survived. He came to the open-air fresh fruit and vegetable market with me, and made the ladies selling their produce laugh out loud at his joshing bargaining style, and handled all our paperwork.

Jacques also found a four-wheel-drive vehicle to take us to the base of La Citadelle, the impressive mountaintop fort that Haiti's black king, Henri Christophe, used 200,000 workers to build, over thirteen years ending in 1820, as protection against local enemies as well as Napoleon. Led by Philemon, a young guide, we walked up a steep path in a light drizzle, our destination obscured by clouds. "You must ox me anything," said Philemon. "It is my job to know the onswer." The sky cleared as we neared the top, and suddenly the clouds parted and we could see the huge sheer walls of the oblong structure. We strolled its parapets and cannon galleries and inhaled the splendid view extending across billows of green all the way back to Cap-Haïtien. From Philemon we learned that no cannon was ever fired in warfare from La Citadelle, that it was abandoned in 1820 after Christophe committed suicide there, and that efforts to restore the fortress—as well as the elaborate Sans Souci palace at the bottom of the hill—date back to 1932. As of 1987, though there was much to be done, the latest round of restoration work seemed well under way at this world-class historic site.

Moe too became a frequent companion. The black sheep of an old U.S. naval family, many of whose members had been graduated from Annapolis, Moe lasted only three months there and even now claimed that one of his hardest jobs was "avoiding work." Moe regaled us with tales of shipwreck and adventure: the *Mechanic* hung up on a coral reef for six weeks; little Robin, barely out of her teens, standing in firing position in the *Mechanic*'s main cabin, keeping a swarm of Miskito Indian pirates at bay by brandishing a machine gun in their direction; Moe himself imprisoned in Fort Lauderdale after a tiff with a "nasty" DEA man. Then there was Moe the romantic. "You get on your bike and drive out of this town to the first big river that flows down from the mountains," he told me with moist eyes one evening. "It's about eleven in the morning. You turn off onto a little footpath and you drive your bike a little ways up. Then you get off and walk a little ways further to the river's edge. Then you look out and you see about one thousand girls all in the water, and they're all naked, and it's the most beautiful sight you've ever seen."

Beyond the immediate area of the port and the vanished cruising ships, the town was a Haitian painting unframed and brought to life, with balconied two-story buildings, vibrant street life, the strong colors, the poverty. Little was wasted here and resources were obviously scarce. For want of offal, few gulls frequented even the fishing fleet. Every evening, students, without electricity or even candles at home, would sit under the mercury-vapor lights of our pleasure-craft port to do their homework; the intensity of one girl, memorizing a poem, was especially vivid. Soon after daybreak men would come to our dock to bathe, using hoses meant to transfer water from dockside pipes into yachts' water tanks.

Near *Sanderling* a violent squabble burst out one morning over the ownership of a bucket of sludgy old diesel fuel that we had drained from

Haitian all-purpose vessel coasts offshore.

the bottom of our tank and had casually asked Nelson to dump. In a sudden evening downpour we huddled in a doorway with two women whose work was to sell sticks of chewing gum from little sidewalk carts. We visited the Roi Christophe Hotel, once the governor's palace and later home for one of Bonaparte's sisters, now carefully restored and handsomely redecorated. The pool was full and clean, and men in red coats swept fallen leaves from the circular driveway. This hotel was without guests. An art gallery far from the center of town was closed; a man snoring on an adjacent table under a tree awoke with a start and opened up the place for us.

Our last morning Jacques took me to a pig farm owned by a rangy American named Starle. It was Sunday morning at eight o'clock. At the farm two men stood in pens, from whose floor one might eat, hosing down pigs that already looked immaculately clean. Apologizing for not having any center-cut chops on the premises—missionaries had picked the freezer clean the previous day—Starle sold us some newly frozen "pork steaks" and told us to hurry back. Aboard we paid off the mournful Nelson and bade farewell to Moe and Robin, who was assertively test-driving a motorcycle around the parking lot. Then we cast off and made our way past the reef, past the nearby coral shelf onto which the *Santa María* ran and quietly met her end, past a little place called Limonade Port-de-Mer, where Columbus' men subsequently paused in January 1493 to build a fort. Gradually the heights of Cap-Haïtien grew smaller as we drifted in the light air that Columbus too had encountered here. The cliff called El Morro grew higher off our starboard bow, and we crossed from Haiti into the Dominican Republic. We lacked the large-scale charts to enter Isabela, where Columbus founded his first real colony in 1494, just at the end of his second voyage, but Morison's description persuaded us that we had not missed much:

> The maps of Central America are studded with sites of settlements made by the conquistadors and abandoned by their more practical successors. Isabela was the first of these unfortunate choices and the most excusable since nobody aboard the Castilian fleet had any experience in colonization. . . . Fishing is good anywhere along that coast, but [in the] harbor at Isabela there was none. . . . Good drinking water could be had only from the Rio Bajabonico about a mile to the southward, and that river was not navigable.

Within a week of landing at Isabela, Morison continues, "discontent was rife . . . and worse," with illness prevalent:

> The history of American colonization proves that you cannot land a body of men after a long ocean voyage, subject them to hard labor with inadequate housing in torrential rains, expose them to mosquitoes full of germs with which their systems are unprepared to cope, and feed them on fish, maize, yams and cassava instead of beef, pork, wheat bread and wine, without excessive sickness and great mortality.

In all, we did not regret bypassing this gap in the rugged Dominican shore, which seems little different from when Columbus and his men first explored it, and riding an unexpected westerly wind, overnight, into the commercial hub of Puerto Plata. Here, near the commercial fishing dock, we found a line of sailboats and power yachts lying stern-to at a small pier, anchor cables stretched Mediterranean-style from their bows, and crashing about in a mounting harbor swell. I decided not to tackle the task of squeezing into this row, and we anchored off. Soon three immigration officials appeared in a skiff, came aboard, and requested and received cold beers. We completed the formalities swiftly.

Puerto Plata, which Moe had characterized as "a good liberty town," seemed sharply oriented toward the cruise-ship trade. Close to the port facility lies a part of town that consists mostly of shops offering amber and black-coral jewelry, clothing, and knickknacks (what do cruise-ship passengers do besides shop and lie about?). Farther in from the water is a central plaza, with trees, a gazebo, and street vendors, around the edges of which swarms of snarling motorbikes cruise and flock. Here, at last, is a real town: a big church, restaurants, municipal buildings, a market. All this, we discovered, is set upon a low coast planted heavily in sugarcane and sprinkled with beachfront resort hotels. One, the Playa Dorado, is not far out of town; we drove past its golf course, intensely green, but saw nobody on it, with the weather humid and very hot. Nearby too is a smaller resort town called Sosua set along a curving golden beach, where small hotels and guesthouses and restaurants cater to an international clientele and the well-off from Santo Domingo. Passing yachts, we heard from a crew member aboard *Cat Sass*, a Florida-based catamaran that we ran into several times, are not allowed to anchor off Sosua even though the town is but ten easy miles east of Puerto Plata.

At the teeming Puerto Plata International Airport, itself a surprise, I met Flo. She had managed to get the last seat aboard a raucous charter flight full of Dominicans returning from New York; in the seat next to her was a lively man dressed, down to the shoes, in canary yellow. She arrived with visions of resuming the swimming and snorkeling she had done with us in the Bahamas. Peter's father, John, arrived too, bruised, stiff, and aching from a bicycle accident but keen to board *Sanderling* and get going. This took some doing, with visits to several offices scattered around town. As I made the rounds I verified what I'd heard rumored about cruising the Dominican coast. Our *Cat Sass* acquaintances and others had told stories of pleasure yachts being driven away from small harbors at gunpoint. One skipper who attempted to buck it had been jailed for a week in Santo Domingo, and his wife was compelled to fly in to bail him out. I was asked what my next port would be.

"Puerto Escondido," I said, referring to a remote little harbor mentioned in the cruising guide that looked snug on the chart and closer by twenty miles than the next major harbor at Samaná Bay, more than one hundred miles away—a long nonstop journey with the trade wind dead against, aboard a slow sailboat with a balky engine.

"You can only go there in an emergency," said the port official. "I can only clear you to Samaná."

"Then what can we do?"

"I cannot tell you. This you must negotiate with the authorities at Samaná."

Discouraging news. I awaited the arrival of the captain of the port to sign our Outward Clearance form. A car stopped in front of the building. A whistle sounded and everyone around, however dressed, snapped to attention and saluted. The captain, a tall, broad-shouldered man with flowing waves of shiny black hair, exuded confidence as he strode into his domain. Soon after, the integrity of my wallet intact, I was in possession of the completed document and en route back to *Sanderling* in the company of a young sailor, who gave the boat a cursory inspection, lingered for a moment hoping for a tip, then went ashore with a smile.

The afternoon breeze gave us a good lift eastward toward Cabo Francés Viejo, then dropped almost to a dead calm for much of the night. We slatted about in slick swells. On my first two-hour watch (Peter and I were alternating, leaving John on the reserve list until he had limbered up and Flo on "standby") I gingerly started the engine. After running well for about an hour, it again began its peculiar surging—voluntarily increasing its rpm's by as much as three or four hundred, then receding with a sigh and threatening to give out altogether, as it had in the Bahamas. I began to think that the surging related to a flaw in the fuel-supply system that became evident when the boat rolled about in the open water.

Rrrroooaagh. A pronounced surge evoked a muffled worried "Rog" from Peter below, trying vainly to sleep while his engine spluttered. With little enthusiasm for going through the long and smelly restart procedure in the dead of night, he was eager for me to switch off the monster before it gave out entirely. As he called, I had my hand on the button, and soon again we were back to bare steerageway. A gray dawn revealed rainsqualls on all sides. For some time we got a good eastward lift out of one, but by midday we were back in doldrums and moving so slowly that we could dive over the side and swim in the salty warm cobalt water. We tried the engine; it surged again and this time quit altogether. Peter's restart procedure failed to work. He looked crestfallen.

In the afternoon the craggy heights of the two great Dominican capes, Cabrón and then Samaná, gradually grew closer. For a while we had visions of being able to round them in the last of the daylight and continue up the bay to find an anchorage amid unmarked reefs and small islands too hazardous to approach at night. By about five in the afternoon it was clear that we would not make it, and we began to look for an alternative to another rolly night out in the open water. On the chart we found a little hole near Cabo Cabrón. Called the Ensenada la Posa, it looked uninhabited and seemed to offer some protection from wind and sea. Were Dominican gunboats to happen upon us there, we figured, we could claim an emergency in the form of our dead engine and allege that we had to stop in relatively calm water in order to fix it and proceed safely. Towering red-and-gray cliffs loomed above us as we drifted closer to the Ensenada, their sheer sides plunging into a restless sea, and on one side of the bight the near-perfect arch of a natural bridge came into view. On our depth sounder we anxiously sought signs of water shallow enough to anchor in, but none materialized. We began to wonder if, in a light breeze, we would be able to get back out of there in the event that we could not find bottom with two hundred feet of anchor chain.

At this moment, with the Ensenada's twin jaws beginning to encircle us, a little flotilla of three outboard skiffs, two men aboard each, came into view at the eastern point and began to head our way. One came straight at us, and the others steered toward positions on our port and starboard sides. Were we being surrounded by fishermen, or by soldiers, or by thieves? As they drew closer, we began to lower our inflatable dinghy into the water and attach its little outboard. With this rig we could tow *Sanderling* further in toward the cliffs, and back out if we could still not reach bottom with our anchor, and suggest departure aboard this small craft as an alternative to walking the plank.

The three little boats stopped. No guns in sight.

"*¿Que pasa?*" asked one of the men.

"We are trying to reach Samaná, but it's late and our motor is broken and we have to stop and fix it," I replied, summarizing all our excuses in case we were confronting a posse sent out by the authorities.

"You cannot anchor here, because it is too deep," the man replied. "Throw us a rope and we will tow you to a better place where the sea is smoother and the bottom closer."

Whew. Fishermen happening by at a critical moment. We stowed our dinghy, tossed them a line, and set off in an odd linked convoy, with *Sanderling* attached to one skiff and it to a second in the lead. We proceeded back westward, away from Cabo Cabrón, past several little bays shown on the chart, and into none other than the Puerto Escondido that had been our original destination. Here we found a little beach, tall cliffs, a green forest climbing high from a tiny protected inner harbor behind a large isolated rock—and bottom at thirty-five feet—amid confused seas. The fishermen let us go and wished us luck. We gave them Haitian rum and U.S. dollars. They gave us newly harvested mangoes. We settled in for what turned out to be a wave-tossed squally Shakespearean night of thunder echoing in the cliffs, lightning sheets, williwaws.

In the morning we looked shoreward. In a scene little different from when Taino Indians inhabited these parts, except that they wore clothes, three people hand-lined from the rock. We saw one small shack near the tiny beach. Otherwise there was no sign of life in this isolated place. We set sail and once more coasted near the towering cliff of Samaná, intending to round up into the bay. Now the wind veered steadily toward the south, which meant more wet and slow windward work if we were to continue toward Samaná Bay, but a direct shot on a single tack across the

Mona Passage to Puerto Rico. "I think," said John, by now reviving, "you are just fated never to get to Samaná." We agreed and slanted off for Puerto Rico even though, too soon, we were pushed northward as the wind shifted back to its usual due easterly direction.

Midafternoon. I was at the helm, others dozing below. Lately we had seen little life of any sort: few birds but the occasional shearwater or red-footed booby, not even very many little flying fish, to whose graceful skims and sudden dives we had become accustomed. Now to starboard came a splash larger than a normal whitecap, leaving a green streak in the blue water. A big ray? No, here it came again, a sudden opening in the water, a large projectile lifting like a missile out of the water, then collapsing back into the sea amid foaming clouds of white water. Holy Toledo, this was a breaching humpback whale. In Alaska, in Baja California, in New England, I had been close to many whales basking or swimming along, but this was something else. Now again one broke through the surface. Oooooo, I yelled and all hands scrambled up from below, Peter with his camera and telephoto lens. It was hard to tell how far away or how large this projectile was, but I guessed that it was a fairly small calf, for now larger whales were visibly browsing at the surface, only perhaps a hundred yards away, so close that we could hear their little exhalations and see little clouds of spume emerging from the blowholes. More breaches and several whales now performing: some launching straight up, some twisting into rolls or quarter or half turns.

The sea around us became frothing white. For five minutes or so it was rare not to have an airborne whale in view, or the disappearing flukes of one of them sounding. Oooo, wooooo, wow. We hollered in wonder and exhilaration, contemplating the vast animal energy required to blast so many tons through the surface of the sea. Then the last splash faded behind us. The water grew calm again, leaving us to recall that we were not far from the banks north of the Dominican Republic where the humpbacks congregate to breed in early spring.

To celebrate the whales and bolster the spirits of a tiring crew, I worked hard that night to cook a good dinner. This is no easy task under way, in capricious waves, where a sudden steep heel usually comes just as you're trying to return a hot cooking dish to the oven or pour boiling water over something. You have to hang on yourself, and sometimes it gets slippery around the galley, from previous spills or flying waste that missed the garbage can adjacent to the Shipmate stove. Sometimes you feel as if you are cooking at a 45-degree angle, your feet on one side of the main cabin and your head and arms hanging over the three-burner stove on the other. Somehow that night I managed an ersatz tetrazzini with the smoked chicken that Peter had purchased in Puerto Plata

Whales frolic off the Greater Antilles.

thinking it was fresh-frozen, reconstituted dried mushrooms and condensed milk, good Dominican pasta and lots of Maggi. Alongside were broiled fresh tomatoes, some remaining from the bushel we had been given by the Cubans, and a salad with dressing built around the extra-virgin olive oil that John had brought with him. We ate in the cockpit balancing our plates and forks. Between my knees I tried to protect from spillage one of the few bottles of good California chardonnay remaining from the major wine investment I had made in Florida.

For most of the night we continued northeast. Early in the morning, figuring that if we tacked and headed back on a southeasterly course we could at least fetch the port of Mayagüez on the Puerto Rican west coast, we brought *Sanderling* around. Brooding dark gray clouds were building, and sheet lightning flickered to the north. For a while it looked as though we might escape a direct hit from a big squall, for the sky ahead looked broken and harmless. But we were being ambushed from behind: to the west, the still blackness thickened and crept around either side of us, fronted with greenish vapor streamlets. The water beneath began to look white. Soon we were in it—only wind at first, the puffs fast growing from almost a flat calm to forty miles per hour and more and erratic machine-gun bursts of rain, then steadying. We were ready, with the jib completely rolled in and the mainsail pared down to G-string size, and were pleasantly surprised when the squall began to push us with great speed, up to 8.5 knots surfing down the sudden waves, right in the easterly direction we wanted to make good. John, now at full strength, sat at the helm peering into the murk through rain-spattered round metal-framed eyeglasses. "I could do this all day," he said.

Others of the crew, now manifesting the frustrations of sustained life aboard a small boat with few amenities, were muttering with increasing frequency about how good it would be to get "there." Hot humid weather returned after the squall passed, and a real shower with controllable water temperature became a high priority. Little things—that the morning cornflakes and the luncheon lettuce would fly overboard in little wind gusts if you ate on deck and were not careful—suddenly became bothersome. Late in the afternoon half a dozen dolphins, small and nimble, pink and white below and yellow-gray above, glowed in the clear water as they danced around our bow. But even I could not face cooking and produced a cold dinner, then cussed like a drill sergeant when, as we tacked abruptly in the night to avoid a converging ship, the windward jib sheet got caught under the forward hatch and ripped it cleanly off its hinges.

The miles clicked off ever more slowly until, once past several protected beaches where turtles come ashore to lay their eggs, we fetched up outside San Juan's El Morro Castle in brilliant late-afternoon sunlight. We motored into the city's fine protected harbor. The engine gasped as we passed through a narrow channel with fishing boats on one side and docks on the other, but mercifully kept going until after we had completed our approach and made fast at a marina. Tired, we stumbled on foot across six-lane freeways to the Caribe Hilton and were soon immersed in air conditioning, showers, and rum.

Two nights there allowed us a glimpse of San Juan, which seemed not provincial, as it must to many visitors from Stateside, but coolly modern and sophisticated in contrast to the cities on neighboring islands. Flo and John both departed as the local weather turned dark and squally. The radio bristled with reports of flooding, waterspouts, tornadoes, hail in the mountains, and other manifestations of the "tropical wave" that was said to be passing through. Nothing to be out sailing in, Peter and I said to each other as we crunched through yet another fine dinner ashore.

Out sailing the next day, we were caught by the tail end of the wave. It brought heavy squalls and rain and high seas all afternoon; it was not until the sky broke into a dismal pale yellow sunset that we finally cleared the island's eastern end at Cabo San Juan and, wet and cranky, picked our way through gathering darkness southward toward an anchorage near the town of Fajardo, which lies below Puerto Rico's 4,000-foot El Yunque. Another day's sail eastward, this time with less taxing weather, brought us to the Ensenada Honda, the superb large bay ("a cruising ground in itself," says the guidebook) forming the heart of the island of Culebra.

Here we awoke unscathed by naval gunfire from nearby Roosevelt Roads that has occasionally bothered the two thousand islanders. We saw soft hillsides and lowing Holsteins and evidence of a growing population, learning later that the U.S. Navy had recently sold the island to Puerto Rico and that it is currently enjoying a resort development boom. Peter went ashore to take a look at the new hotel at the head of our bay. It was occupied, he later reported, mostly by its managers, staff, and voracious mosquitoes. I remained aboard, where the trade wind kept the insects at bay, but not visitors of another sort: the curious crews of other sailboats anchored nearby. Since we had left the Exumas we had encountered few pleasure-yacht people, for we were off the beaten track and out of season. Now we were rejoining the fleet, and one particular squadron of it: the live-aboard boats belonging to the legions of retired moms and pops that drift for years on end about the Bahamas and the Caribbean.

First to come to chat were Warren, deeply tanned with white hair, and his wife, Jane, a sandy blonde with a hesitant voice. Warren invited us to "happy hour" at the hotel, told us of Jane's health problems ("She reached Condition Blue twice. You know what that is? That's when you stop breathing"), helped us get our balky outboard motor started, and talked of their many years of cruising the Caribbean. Next came Doug and another Jane from their ketch, *Blue Eagle*, aboard which they had spent fifteen years commuting between the Bahamas, the Caribbean, and "Venzuela," as they called it. Doug, a retired Air Force pilot and Pentagon official with Latin American experience, looked fit. Jane, small and thin, had frizzy hair. Doug frequently reached into his pocket, extracted two king-size menthol cigarettes, put both into his mouth and lit them consecutively, then passed one to Jane. She told us that, although frozen chicken is plentiful "down-island," we could not expect to find much in the way of canned pork and beans or corned-beef hash. Doug advised us to lock up our belongings, especially our dinghy and its outboard, since theft is commonplace in the region; for this he particularly blamed "uppity niggers" and, simply, "French."

"French?" I asked.

"Yes, French," Doug replied. "They're famous. Young French hippies who come over with nothing, and then you'll see their boats with four or five dinghies, four or five motors all aboard. At the marina in

Venzuela, anytime they saw a boat flying a French flag, why, they'd drive it away with rifles."

I asked Doug about what sorts of retired Americans he had most frequently encountered aboard boats around the islands. Many of them are former pilots and submariners, he said, agreeing with me that part of the appeal of the life is a sense of control and command, even if the island is small.

Peter returned from a trip to Dewey, Culebra's principal little town, with two handsome chunks of fish that he had found glistening on the dock, the exception proving the rule that fresh fish is the hardest thing to find when on a cruise such as ours. Having eaten and enjoyed this, he promptly came down with a bad case of the *turista* and was immobile for most of the next day. I do not know what rule that proves. Maybe what he got was a mild case of *ciguatera*, the fish poisoning that affects even the freshest fish of several commonly eaten Caribbean species.

Before Peter succumbed, we both boarded the dinghy and motored out toward the buoys marking the narrow entrance to the Ensenada Honda. A long coral reef separated the shore from the interior of the reef. Many boats anchored here to stay away from the mosquitoes. Along the shore, on a little point marked by a large mangrove tree, was a small sign marked "Souvenirs" whitewashed on a wooden plank. We approached this place, as directed by Warren, and soon found ourselves being welcomed to Fantasy Island by two barking dogs and its sole human occupant, a fiftyish woman named Johana Taylor. Under the big mangrove, a few decorated seashells and pieces of bleached coral were laid out for sale on weathered pieces of wood. Numerous small and large boards, all personally salvaged or collected, Johana told us, constituted a floor of sorts, and loosely covered bits of foam rubber served as chairs.

"This is our favorite part of the island," said Johana, speaking for the dogs as well as for herself. "We like the breeze out here, and the view. There's St. Thomas in the haze over there, and straight ahead, at night, you can see the loom of St. Croix's lights. I've been here for six years. Before, I was on the beach over at St. John, and before that, on a boat in St. Maarten—I was lucky to get off that island alive, after I'd tried to turn in some drug dealers and found they were in cahoots with the government—and before that, on the Greek islands. But this is my favorite place. Angels brought me here. You believe in angels? Well, you better, for I am only here because of them."

Johana, who wore tidy white shorts and a blouse, led us across a sort of gangplank to terra firma. She showed us the inside living room—bedroom to which she and the dogs repaired in poor weather—a round well-kept space that had originally been fashioned after a native *bohío*, or fishing hut, and had a thatched roof, but because of leakage was now covered by a sail given Johana by a passing French (French!) yachtsman. She showed us her well-appointed kitchen, with a propane-gas stove and shelves for staples and spices, and a small, well-stocked ice chest; her "meditation area," or privy, cantilevered over the water; her chicken house; and the steep path up from the mangroves that she had to climb the one time that rising water in a storm forced "us" to evacuate the camp.

"Love each other—we are the endangered species," said one of many such signs sprinkled about the sprawling premises. Johana could ascribe no special purpose to her being on her island, she said. She was just "lucky" to have landed here at a time when the real estate situation was in flux and she was able to assert more or less permanent squatter's rights. Not only do the islanders not bother her; they help her in many respects, Johana said, and so do the sailors who anchor nearby. From her sales she earns enough money to go to Dewey from time to time, in a rowboat with a two-horsepower outboard, to buy rum and food for her animals and to fulfill her "personal needs," but she hates to make the trip to town and only goes when she must.

Mosquitoes came at dusk. Peter, who hates them, began to thrash about. "Rog," he said, "I've got to get out of here." We mumbled excuses and headed toward the dinghy and open water. Johana, looking well, invited us back our next time through. I said I did not know when that would be. "It doesn't matter," said Johana. "I'll never leave here."

A day later we were at anchor in St. Thomas, far indeed from the unusual attractions of Culebra, and poised to discover a different sort of Caribbean.

11

Storms Brewing Down-Island

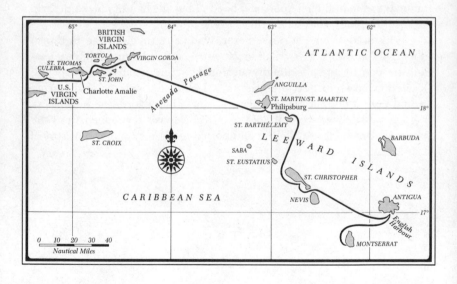

No part of the New World has suffered more brutal environmental change than the Lesser Antilles. From the three Virgins at the chain's northern end to Barbados four hundred miles to the southeast, the complex and tormented history of human incursions and nature's own cataclysms have combined to inflict major alterations and obliterations upon these small points of land. Dramatic shifts in how people on them have tried to get along have consequently often taken place in this badly abused paradise. Yet conservation has gained a few footholds, and the future may hold more promise than history would suggest.

Long before Columbus the region's little-known aboriginal people, called Siboneys, had given way to gentle Arawak migrants from the South American continent. On some of the islands these people, in turn, ended up in the pepper pots of cannibalistic Caribs—Amerindians from the same stock but with fiercer habits. Not even these aggressive occupants of the region, however, did much to mar its pristine and verdant beauty. They harvested most of their food from the bountiful seas around them. Except where scattered villages bordered the shore, forests tumbled unimpeded from mountain heights down into crystalline waters lapping against silky white coral beach or volcanic lava. A limited but little-disturbed fauna, consisting largely of birds and reptiles and bats, inhabited the dense forest.

Change had started with the Arawaks, who brought from the mainland small animals (the agouti, a large rodent) and exotic plants (the pineapple, the pawpaw, the guava) to cultivate. But their alterations paled beside those of the Europeans. Within a century of the first transatlantic arrivals, 90 percent of the pre-Hispanic people had vanished. By early in the seventeenth century settlers from Holland and England and France, many of whom had come to prey on richly laden Spanish cargo vessels bound eastward, had found European markets for agricultural goods that could be grown on the islands. They clear-cut the woods to plant fields of cotton and tobacco and, somewhat later, almighty sugarcane that reached high up even on the steepest hillsides. The European domestic animals they introduced—cattle, goats, dogs, and cats—quickly became dominant on the islands. Newly introduced plants pushed aside the indigenous vegetation.

Slavery brought another great wave of change. Many of the earliest British and French settlers were a sorry lot of "adventurers and persons of low character," as one historian called them, who had during the early seventeenth century "poured like flies upon the rotting carcase of Spain's empire in the Caribbean." These people overstressed the soils they cultivated, were beset by disease and poor diets, and had difficulty competing with the economics of large plantations containing large numbers of slaves. Most of the small settlers moved on, often to North America, leaving the islands to the mercy of the usually absentee plantation owners and the environment in disarray. The planters did little to improve things. They continued the clear-cutting and stripping. Even around the great houses built during the height of the slave-based sugar prosperity, native trees and plants were ripped out to make way for European-style gardens.

The effects of these changes were magnified by ceaseless rounds of warfare that plagued the islands. Early on, pirates (who, after the Spanish finally swept the buccaneers out of Tortuga, established new beachheads from the Bahamas to Jamaica) often pillaged and burned the little settlements. From the mid-eighteenth century through the Napoleonic era, the islands frequently suffered from being expendable pawns in far wider wars, though the War of Jenkins's Ear of 1739 was in fact provoked by a West Indian incident. For one reason or another—far more died of malnutrition or malaria or yellow fever than from battle wounds—few of the soldiers sent from Europe to the Caribbean ever returned. Of 19,676 men sent by the British in 1796, 17,173 died within five years. Throughout, there boomed and echoed the understandable if deadly instability of the slave rebellions. The earliest of these took place on the Virgin Island of St. John in 1733. It caused the death of every resident European on the island. Eventually it was put down by *macoute* mercenaries imported from Martinique, who killed all the former slaves.

Modern times have brought new forms of devastation. While sugarcane cultivation remains a major factor in the economies of only a few islands, such as Barbados and St. Kitts, banana growers elsewhere have capitalized on boom times in the market by chewing ever more deeply into the forest to make room for more crop. In St. Lucia and Dominica, the blue plastic envelope that protects the fruit from insects is as much the state flower as is the fifty-five-gallon oil drum in John McPhee's Alaska. Deforestation has done severe damage to some watershed areas and threatened water-supply systems. The effect of tourism, which has galloped forward throughout the region since the 1950s, has been every bit as jolting.

Some resort managers have shown sensitivity. While planning his project, a hotelier in a quiet place called Maho Bay, on St. John, voluntarily called a community meeting to discuss it with future neighbors. Most are less polite. They chop away at native plants, often replacing them with coconut palms, which, whether they belong there or not, have become as prevalent on tropical beaches as plastic pink flamingos on front lawns in North American suburban towns. With thirsty golf courses to maintain, they tax limited water supplies; runoff containing chemicals needed to keep the greens green has done little good to mangroves and coral reefs. Even more harmful to these important but vulnerable ecosystems has been the siltation of surrounding waters simply because of indiscriminate bulldozing that, for the sake of views or the removal of vegetation that thieves might hide in, exposes large areas of unprotected topsoil.

Loosely controlled fishermen, responding to demand from hotel kitchens, have caused severe reductions in populations of conch, lobster, and other significant marine species; for local people seafood has become so scarce and expensive that chicken consumption has risen rapidly. Careless fishing and yachting practices have done grave damage to many of the very reefs that the tourists have flocked to see. One study shows that, although the yachting boom has not done great harm overall, it can produce devastating local results. In one harbor on the north shore of St. John, the persistent clawing of yacht anchors reduced once highly productive sea-grass beds to less than one-twentieth of their original size.

The central question, endlessly debated in the Caribbean, is that of how jobs can be provided in sufficient quantity, basic needs met, and equality between races achieved without sacrificing in the name of "progress" the very pristine qualities that keep the tourists—now the islands' principal source of income—wanting to spend vacations on them. Intellectuals express concern about how traditional cultural values might withstand the U.S. media blitz and the onslaught of vacationers expecting little more from them than sun and sand: only 4 percent of visitors to sophisticated Barbados actually go to its attractive museum or the historic site alongside. Here as everywhere, developers seek ways around the sharpening rules.

Sanderling cruised among the islands for some months in 1987 and early 1988. In mid-1987, Peter, skipper for the first time with his lanky younger brother Frederick, a University of Colorado sophomore, as crew, pointed her nose out of boat-choked Red Hook Bay on St. Thomas. With her engine now purring—an intuitive mechanic named Desmond had found that a mangled washer allowed air to enter the fuel line and diagnosed this as the source of our previous grief—*Sanderling* bucked strong head winds along most of the 350-mile route between there and St. Lucia. Peter proudly brought her in unscathed; six hours after their arrival, Leslie Stone (back from her college junior year in China for another round of crew duty) and I, having flown in to meet them, found them happily addressing rum punches at the Hurricane Hole Hotel bar on idyllic Marigot Bay. From there the four of us began a leisurely sail, mostly down or across the wind, back to the Virgins. There *Sanderling* rode out the hurricane season at a strong mooring kindly provided by Dr. Edward Towle and his Island Resources Foundation, a deeply knowledgeable private organization dedicated to the balanced and ecologically sound development of the islands. We returned to the region on several occasions, once to attend the Caribbean Conservation Association's annual general meeting in Tortola, later to cruise again southward from St. Thomas to Barbados, *Sanderling*'s jumping-off point for South America. Along the way we gathered impressions.

U.S. Virgin Islands

As many as nine cruise ships at a time enter the spacious harbor of Charlotte Amalie, the bustling principal city on St. Thomas, and disgorge mobs of vacationers to exercise their credit cards at the myriad duty-free shops. Even during the off-season, Red Hook Bay, headquarters for yacht charter operations in the U.S. Virgins, is so cluttered with sailboats that the mere act of anchoring is often difficult; one evening we watched as a large handsome sailing yacht, with no room to turn around in the shallow and congested inner harbor, backed all the way out of it. On a stormy New Year's Eve at our Red Hook mooring, we watched helplessly as anchors dragged and yachts broke away from their moorings in the high winds and three-foot swells; though several boats washed ashore and we ourselves stood ready to cut ourselves free as an unattended 65-foot ketch bore down on us, serious damage was miraculously avoided.

Already St. Thomas' narrow, twisting roadways, along which you drive on the left-hand side for reasons no longer clear, seem perilously overcrowded. Yet the population soars upward. In 1987 applications for permits to build new hotels and resorts and condominiums reached an all-time high. Help-wanted signs were proliferating as fast as Pizza Huts. "It's just about impossible not to find a job here," said Ed Trupp, a retired New York City narc-squad cop who was living on a sailboat in Red Hook Bay, helping out at the Island Resources Foundation, and running an active little blade-sharpening business. For sailors, peace and good snorkeling lay only minutes away from St. Thomas, at a beautiful anchorage off St. James Island called Christmas Cove. But for the land-bound, St. Thomas was more Las Vegas than Tahiti, and every day a little more of the former charm surrendered to the bulldozer.

The blight extends across the two-mile channel to Great Cruz Bay at the western end of St. John, where a prominent landmark is a lavender-roofed 150-unit hotel complex, built on the basis of a permit authorizing the construction on the site of seven condominium units. The raffish town of Cruz Bay, a short distance away, also flaunts its share of new condo units, as well as a multi-level shopping and eating complex called Mongoose Junction in honor of the "savage little beast," as Peter Matthiessen called it, that was introduced on several Caribbean islands to suppress snakes. But on St. John, disorderly development comes to an abrupt end as you travel eastward. Just beyond Cruz Bay is prim Caneel Bay, where long ago the Rockefeller family's Rockresorts company (now owned by a large corporation called CSX) installed a discreet hotel and beach retreat whose rules remain so respected that the regional cruising guide implores yachtsmen to honor them. Example: you can radio in for dinner reservations, but be sure to inquire about the dress code. Just beyond Caneel Bay is the formidable and well-managed National Park, now occupying two-thirds of the entire island, which had its beginning in 1954, when Laurance Rockefeller quietly bought up the properties forming its core. Though development threatens at the island's eastern end as well as at Cruz Bay, it is still the tranquil, trail-studded park that sets St. John's tone.

Sanderling spent several placid nights at anchor within its boundaries. For some days we had been exploring the British Virgins in the good company of Allen Putney, a resource manager from the mainland who has spent ten years promoting rational development in the Caribbean, his wife, Lilia, and three enthusiastic children: Allen's sons, Colin and Alexander, then twelve and nine, and Lilia's beguiling eight-year-old niece, Pascal. On our final afternoon we cruised westward along St. John's rugged south coast, little frequented by the yacht-charter crowd despite easy access, and put in at Salt Pond Harbor at the park's southwestern corner. Rocks and a wide reef protect this little anchorage from the sea. Ashore, a clean white crescent of finely ground coral beach. Beyond the shoreline, a band of cactus scrub vegetation gives way, on the hillsides, to dry woodlands composed largely of deciduous species that lose their leaves for a month or two each year.

Though it was a sunny Saturday and you can drive to within a short distance of this idyllic place, no one there had come by land. Off the beach only a few boats lay at anchor: four other sailboats, two power cruisers tethered together and sporting Puerto Rican flags, floodlights, loud music, and boisterous laughing families. We anchored surrounded by small hawksbill turtles. Ashore we walked along short trails, flushing little rock doves and eating the conical magenta fruits of the Turk's-cap cactus that flourished along the way. At sunset the breeze dropped to a whisper.

The crew—now Peter, Leslie, and me as well as the Putney brigade—sat in the cockpit enjoying the evening. Without warning a spotted eagle ray, neither as powerful nor as big as a manta but still an impressive creature, broke through the surface, close aboard, and leaped a good five feet into the air. The next morning, the harbor even calmer for want of the Puerto Rican flotilla, which had vanished in the night, we snorkeled above the reef. Pascal, just learning to swim, donned a large

Allen Putney aboard *Sanderling*.

orange life preserver, and a mask and snorkel, and pushed her face into the water. She emerged spluttering and excited. "*Les poissons, les poissons*," she kept saying, as if in disbelief that they would actually be there. We also saved from the reef's hull-grinding peaks a small sailboat whose unset anchor was dragging as the trade wind came up while its mom-and-pop charter crew was happily exploring the shore. "What are you doing on my boat?" bellowed Pop as he reappeared on the beach at the height of our rescue mission. No good deed goes unpunished, we were reminded. On New Year's Day 1988, *Sanderling* returned to Salt Pond Harbor with a revised crew, usually consisting, from now until our departure for Brazil, of Peter and me, Flo and/or Leslie, and various others (now the refreshingly upbeat Emily Wilson, eighteen, of Baltimore). Hemmed in by strong "Christmas winds" that reminded us of how capricious and difficult Caribbean weather can be, we spent three glorious quiet days there.

We did not visit St. Croix, but we heard a thing or two about its uncontrolled development from Putney, and he is hardly an environmentalist radical. A Peace Corps alumnus first posted to southern Chile in the early 1960s, he spent eight years there and in Costa Rica and Ecuador, working mostly for the United Nations' Food and Agricultural Organization (FAO), before shifting his flag to the Caribbean in the late

1970s. At that time his good friend Kenton Miller, then head of the University of Michigan's School of Natural Resources, persuaded him to undertake a six-month consultancy to look into how to go about conservation among the small islands of the Lesser Antilles. Working with steady patience and a keen eye for the need to achieve local participation in conservation efforts, Putney and others founded a loose confederation that carries the awkward name of ECNAMP (Eastern Caribbean Natural Areas Management Program).

With international backing long led by the Rockefeller Brothers Fund, ECNAMP has discreetly gone about the tasks of establishing conservation priorities on the various islands, drawing up management plans for critical areas, lobbying to get them declared as parks or reserves and to improve the legal framework for conservation action on islands that only yesterday had no pertinent laws at all and were being overrun by feral goats, cats, mongooses, and resort developers. The organization has been especially successful at getting local community people to participate in its activities, at finding alternatives to nonsustainable use of resources, and at persuading universities and other educational institutions to include coverage of these subjects in their curricula.

Though Putney lives in St. Croix, holds a position at the University of Puerto Rico, and dreams of including the U.S. Virgin Islands in an international biosphere reserve, he spends little time working on U.S. issues. Yet he cannot but observe what is happening around him, and he gives relatively undeveloped St. Croix low marks, looking with marked disfavor on a new beachfront hotel that has done a "remarkably sloppy job" of obeying such regulations as there are. Overall, Putney's assessment of the situation in the U.S. Virgins is negative.

"You have two-thirds of one island well protected," he said, "and nothing on the rest."

British Virgin Islands

The publicly owned Seal Dogs are two among a number of small islands named Dog (West Dog, George Dog, Little Dog) at the northern end of the British Virgin chain extending from the Tobago cays at the west to little-visited Anegada at the east. From a distance, the Seal Dogs are not much to look at: mostly barren craggy rock, no sign of a reef, a few birds about. Soon after *Sanderling* had crept closer on a quiet afternoon, we began to see frenzied bird activity. Brown pelicans wheeled and dove with awkward splashes. Laughing gulls crowded close to them, often standing on their backs, and snatched fish remnants as they dribbled away from the pelicans' quart-sized bill loads. Least terns cried from on high, frequently joining the larger birds in the fray. Sleek-shaped brown boobies too formed part of this dense, hungry pack.

Several bird species nest on the Seal Dogs, we read in the literature. What we did not know, until we went over the side with mask and snorkel and fins, was just how much food for them there was. The Seal Dogs were completely encircled by clouds of brightly colored one- to two-inch fish that moved close to the surface in dense shoals so thick that it was hard to see through them to the bottom. In tightly coordinated reflexes, thousands of them would veer off as a swimmer approached, sending ripples of iridescence across the clear, sun-dappled water. You could paddle softly through the rainbow, then flick your fingers and send hundreds or thousands of them briefly sheering off. Power! Larger reef fishes nibbled and circled below, and the spines of black sea urchins swayed gently in the lazy current. When we could see it, the bottom was cluttered with coral of every description: delicate undulating blue and purple and mustard fans, tubes and gently waving boughs, the large orange elkhorns with their proudly spreading antlers, red fire sponges. Where air met water we would, from time to time, see towering explosions, then gradually subsiding patches of white bubbles and the emerging webbed feet of a newly landed pelican, or the aerodynamic shape of a booby slicing tidily into the water from a yard above its surface.

The profusion of life around these rocks reflects the degree of interest that authorities in this self-governing British territory, where a governor appointed from London has little but ceremonial responsibility, are taking in conservation matters. A vigorous and professionally run National Parks Trust, in existence since 1961 and supported in large part by public funds, manages a comprehensive system of marine and terrestrial parks. In partnership with ECNAMP and the Ministry of Natural Resources, the Parks Trust has identified a number of additional sites to be incorporated into the parks system and has established priorities for these. The current challenge is to get them officially declared as parks, then find the funds for their acquisition. Development project proposals were undergoing careful scrutiny by conservation-minded government officials. Recently the BVI government, which had already won an international award for "significant advances in the field of natural resource management," announced the addition of several additional sites to the growing parks system.

Good intentions do not always guarantee hoped-for results in a small place whose economy, shattered after slavery came to a thankful end in 1834, underwent more than a century of deep depression until tourism came to the rescue starting in the mid-1960s. During that period Laurance Rockefeller built Little Dix Bay on Virgin Gorda. The first five-vessel fleet of bareboat-charter yachts, now numbering several hundred, was launched in 1967. Explosive growth ensued. While the spirit of conservation is now abroad in the BVI, its economic welfare is also so dependent on tourism that, paradoxically, no power exceeds that of the hoteliers, boat operators, and other development-minded citizens.

Sanderling's wanderings included a stop at the BVI's sole existing marine park: the wreck of the *Rhône*, a British steamer that in 1867 was driven onto the rocks near Salt Island, having almost succeeded in fleeing from a hurricane out into open water. The *Rhône* lies in shallow water and close to the shore. Though divers have long since stripped her of anything that had value, the wreck remains interesting to snorkelers and scuba divers. In order to avoid further destruction of the bottom, already badly battered by yacht anchors, the government has placed a number of yacht moorings in a cove near the site; dive-boat operators have cooperated by installing their own moorings directly over the wreck. "These are important steps," Putney said. "Yacht charterers make up two-thirds of all BVI tourism, so it's a sector that they simply have to pay attention to."

Alan Baskin, president of the BVI Dive Operators Association, was enthusiastic as well: "Those moorings have been in there two and a half years now, and it's unbelievable how much regeneration we've gotten. There's new growth all over the place." Baskin lacked the resources to install his own moorings at many of the fifty other dive sites within half an hour's powerboat ride from Road Harbour in Tortola. But he had a clear view of what he was after: at all of them, strong slim cables tidily epoxied into three-inch holes bored by scuba divers into the bedrock. If the plan succeeds, tourism will win, because the principal threat to the integrity of the dive sites will have been removed, and the environment will, of course, win as well.

It is not always so easy. Sixty-five feet of one reef was destroyed not long ago when the captain of a small cruise ship allowed six tons of anchor and rode to scrape the coral clean when a wind shift caused the vessel to swing. At the Baths (recently acquired by the government), a remarkable area on Virgin Gorda where pink sand beach alternates with massive square boulders that look like giant rounded dice tumbling down to the shore, as many as thirty yachts at a time anchor even at the height of the off-season. When *Sanderling* pulled in, inflatable outboards were noisily shuttling between them and the shore. But the real problem is not so much the yachting crowd as the land-bound horde arriving daily at the seven-acre site from hotels and ferryboats. Managing this park will be a tricky exercise.

The North Sound, at the bitter end of Virgin Gorda, is a snug and reef-studded anchorage that was frequented by Francis Drake during the years when he preyed on galleons along the Spanish Main, as the north coast of South America became known after Columbus discovered it. Several resorts are already scattered along the North Sound; half a dozen proposals for new ones vie for space with fish nursery and watershed management areas. To prevent the St. Thomasization of the sound, whose ecologically sensitive development is a top priority for BVI conservation, Putney, working with BVI's National Parks Trust, was hoping to append the land areas to the existing park at Virgin Gorda Peak and turn the sound itself into a well-controlled conservation district. The Parks Trust's former director, Nicholas Clarke, did not underestimate the complexity of the task. "There are all sorts of rules," he said. "But the developers are so confident that their proposals will get approved that often they just start. And the government's never penalized anyone for doing anything wrong—once they've done it, that's it."

Already, while development has cracked the still calm of many virgin BVI beaches, at least a good part of the North Sound is likely to be spared. The going is tougher on the capital island of Tortola's south coast, where soon only Trunk Bay will remain untouched. At remote Anegada, a low island completely encircled by healthy coral, protection is a complex matter because of the difficulty there of establishing who owns what. The safest bet is that permanent protection will be found for smaller islands such as the Dogs and the Tobago cays at the territory's western end. Even here, private landholders may hold out in hopes of rising prices.

If you sail northwest from North Sound, passing the Dogs and leaving Beef Island to port, you enter a narrow channel between Tortola and the Camanoe Islands, and breast swift currents. Soon to starboard you will find tiny Guana Island, high and craggy and, almost uniquely in the Virgins, virtually unchanged from pre-Hispanic times. Quakers settled there early in the eighteenth century and raised sheep. Ever since they left, the island has been owned as a single unit; its land has never been cleared for sugar or pasture. Today its natural beauty remains unbroken except for two tennis courts, a hilltop cluster of buildings constituting a small hotel (maximum: thirty guests), and a few roads. *Sanderling* rounded Little Camanoe and turned northward into Guana's principal anchorage at White Bay, where the purest sand gives way, almost at the water's edge, to little tendrils of healthy reef. Putney and I rowed across to the beach used by the hotel guests (but not by the public, which to the chagrin of many BVIslanders is not welcome there) and found a man to drive us, in an ancient Land-Rover, up the steep road to the hotel. Its panoramic view was breathtaking but, we soon discovered, no more of a surprise than the unique scientific program run by the hotel itself.

"I'm big on conservation," said Paula Selby, its cheerful young manager. "I was a zoology major in college." She went on to explain that in 1980 a scientist named James D. ("Skip") Lazell, Jr., visiting the island, had begun to suspect that, for a place its size, it has more than its share of biological diversity. Lazell established contact with the island's owner, Dr. Henry Jarecki of New York. The result was Science Month, Selby explained. "We used to close at the end of June and not open again until November. But each year since 1984 we have been remaining open, exclusively for the scientists Skip invites, during the month of July. We've had botanists, ornithologists, experts on reptiles and insects, marine biologists. It's wonderful for them and it's wonderful for us, because we get to learn so much about our island."

In part, the scientific program consists of basic research that tends to confirm Lazell's impression of Guana's unusual diversity. "I expected to find only two species of termite here," said Dr. Margaret Collins, a Smithsonian Institution research associate and a Science Month regular since the program was inaugurated. "But I've already found nine species, and I may find more. I'll certainly keep on trying, for this is as close to paradise as a research place can get." The reason for the unusual diversity, Dr. Collins went on to explain, is that at the height of the Pleistocene ice age, when sea levels dropped dramatically, Guana, like all the Virgins, was part of a continuous land mass extending westward all the way to Puerto Rico. According to the theory of island biogeography, as promulgated in 1967 by the scientists E. O. Wilson and Richard MacArthur, species attrition is the invariable consequence of isolation upon newly formed islands. So it was on Guana, which has lost a number of species—the white-crowned pigeon, an iguana, the rock tortoise, the Caribbean flamingo—that probably once lived there. In the absence of disturbance since the Quakers left the island, the loss rate has been far slower than expected. Science Month participants have found more than twice as many reptile species as classic island biogeography theory would forecast, and 325 plants vs. a predictable 200. Lazell himself has recorded three bats that he had hardly expected to find on Guana.

The second part of Lazell's program, which consists of efforts to reintroduce some of Guana's vanished species, is not universally popular. On Anegada, people remember that Lazell made off with some of their large herbivorous iguanas without letting anyone know of his plans to collect them. To some, the zoo-bred flamingos now adorning Guana's salt pond, air-freighted down from Bermuda, seem more a decorative than a substantive addition even if what happens to the new colony is of interest to the scientists. Yet it is hard not to applaud the general thrust of Lazell's efforts, given Guana's biological history, and difficult to look with disfavor upon the support that Dr. Jarecki and his Mocatta Metals Corporation are giving to research there. This is not merely an effort to create a quirky zoo, but a basically honest inquiry into a fascinating 600-acre corner of the globe.

After our visit we took *Sanderling* around to the north end of the island, anchored within spitting distance of the bold shore, and snorkeled there in utter privacy. The BVIs still contain places like Guana Island and the Seal Dogs, I mused, and people like Putney and Alan Baskin and a shrewd and beautiful lady named Lorna Smith, who serves as permanent secretary of the Ministry of Natural Resources and Labour and manages to win most of the decisions. Could things be hopeless?

St. Maarten/St. Martin

Sanderling slalomed, between the cruise ships, into the shallow end of the principal harbor on the Dutch, or southern, side of this schizoid little island. In Philipsburg on the Dutch side, you can go to the bakery and get fresh croissants for your morning breakfast; five miles away in Marigot there is no lack of Dutch chocolate. But for touring sailors or even hotel-bound vacationers, proximity in a tight space provides no relief from bureaucracy. "Remember, we are two different countries," a St. Maarten customs man solemnly told us, explaining why, if we sailed around the corner to St. Martin, we would have to clear in all over again.

A great step forward for the Lesser Antilles would be a blanket yacht visa that could be issued by all participating countries: enter one, enter all, and the same on departure; a kind of Eurailpass for cruising sailors, most of whom are on tight schedules, seek parties or tranquillity, are neither drug nor arms smugglers, and would never squander the time to come near a place like Philipsburg if they did not have to. It will not happen soon. Even easygoing West Indians cling to notions about sovereignty, and want to know as precisely as possible who is around

The scene at St. Maarten.

their land at any given time. Throughout the Caribbean, the United States also applies heavy pressure to pursue drug traffickers. If impractical, mine is every bit as splendid a scheme as political union for Western Europe.

Though we had a good dinner at an odd place called the West Indian Cafe, which was festooned with brightly colored draperies, we found St. Maarten to be little more than a stage set for cruise-ship passengers who were being ferried to the beach, like General MacArthur returning to Bataan, on World War II landing craft. Strings of tourist-trade shops lined the single main street, which led to marinas at one end and beachfront hotels at the other. A casino dominated the scene. The skyline was an eclectic profusion of architectural styles, from pseudo-Dutch colonial to U.S. beltway glitz. Beyond town the hills were pocked by scars caused by making more of the same. Even Orient Bay on the French side, a haven for nude swimmers and sunbathers, was marred by ugly shacks and a nearby garbage dump. Greater charm and good food were to be found at Marigot, the principal town on the French side. Overall, though, the island seemed indifferent in comparison to most of its neighbors. Allen Putney called it "the classic example of what happens as a result of a completely laissez-faire policy."

St. Kitts and Nevis

Here for the first time, having not been able to pause at the interesting but remote Dutch islands of Saba ("Looks just like a breast," said Frederick Walsh) and St. Eustatius, we were beyond the utter domination of tourism. *Sanderling* arrived at Charlestown, principal city on Nevis, on a Saturday evening. We lay protected from the trade wind by the mass of the high extinct volcano that dominates this small island; the lowering sun shone warmly on the softly rounded hills at the southern end of St. Kitts, only five miles away across the narrows.

Peter and I went ashore the following morning to enter. We found Nevis closed. After a vexing morning-long search for the only customs official who could clear us in, we cornered her on the phone just after she had returned from church. She requested time to "breathe a while and get something to eat," but with little further delay received us cordially at her house and completed our paperwork. Since it was still only midday, we had sufficient time to motor past splendid beaches to the reef at the northern end of the island, where the snorkeling, said to be spectacular, was no better than good. On the way, we saw the few small resorts to be found on the island, whose tourism consists largely of the same people who return, year after year, in search of peace and solitude. The operators of these hotels, we heard, are the island's most avid conservationists. "The developers *started* the preservation movement here," a resident urban planner named Blanche Hobson said. "The government is what we have to worry about."

Later *Sanderling* spent a night rolling around in the open roadstead constituting the harbor for Basseterre, capital of St. Kitts. In the morning we bought supplies in the listless town. Men lazed around the docks and the movie theater. En route from St. Barthélemy, we had passed the imposing Brimstone Hill fortifications, said to be "the Gibraltar of the Caribbean," upon whose heights the British in 1782 held out while the French captured the island. At the other end of the island, now served by planes as big as DC-10s and boasting a growing hotel/tourist industry to replace the traditional sugar economy, we passed a mellow night at anchor in Majors Harbor, a cove on the island's southern end that is surrounded by vivid hills of scrub and cane. Plans exist for the further development of this scenic corner of the island; it is to be hoped that this will not come to pass too quickly.

View of English Harbour Antigua Bay

Early view of Antigua

Antigua

Sanderling lay stern-to at Nelson's Dockyard (restored) in English Harbour, an important port in the Caribbean's turbulent naval history and today the best-equipped yachting center anywhere "down-island" from St. Thomas, with a boatyard, well-stocked markets and stores, an inn and several restaurants, even a good bakery. Flo and I were lounging about, tired from having accomplished many humdrum errands. She had arrived the evening before. Having her aboard reminded me of a classic Alfred F. Loomis passage in which he says of his wife, P.L., on the occasion of her arrival aboard his *Hotspur*: "When I cruise either singlehandedly or with friends, each day's sail is a separate entity— pleasant, strenuous, exciting, or lazily satisfying, but distinct from the days preceding and succeeding it. Each evening when we're anchored and snugged down I am in a state of suspended animation, far from home. But when I cruise with P.L., *Hotspur* is my home and a day is a closely integrated part of life."

Now, as Flo and I sought to make *Sanderling* a home, a tall man dressed in a blue polo shirt and tan slacks loped up to the edge of the stone pier. "I'm Desmond Nicholson," he said with a slightly fiendish smile. "I heard you were looking for me." Indeed we were, for Nicholson, a member of the yachting family that arrived from England in 1949 and has been a principal force on Antigua ever since, is known to be a passionate conservationist. Though keener on archaeology and historic places than on the natural world, he had been highly recommended for his general knowledge of the island and its evolution. Briefcase in hand, he swung aboard and arranged his lengthy frame in the cockpit.

He talked first of how the institution he was directing, called the Museum of Antigua and Barbuda, was progressing. It is the only museum of any sort here, and the plan for its development incorporates all aspects of these affiliated islands' natural and cultural history. The government supplied a partially restored air-conditioned building in the island's capital of St. Johns, and was paying routine bills as well as the salaries of a three-person staff, including a curator. Nicholson was canvassing the private sector for material to add to the collection and for support for exhibitions and special programs. He also sometimes puts on a robe and a black wig, plays a primitive Arawak flute, and tells local schoolchildren stories of the island's Stone Age past. We saw him do this sitting on a little stool at the entrance to a wigwamlike structure. "Now, children," he commanded, waggling a finger at us as he began his show. Despite his status as a colonial, Nicholson enjoys an easy relationship with the authorities. "They are fine," he said. "They help the museum, and they don't interfere."

Though Antigua makes only Putney's "B" list for conservation progress, Nicholson had encouraging news with regard to archaeology and historic preservation. Thanks to the support of an enthusiastic doctor from Washington, D.C., an old sugar plantation called Betty's Hope—occupied by the same family from 1668 to 1944—is being restored with the energetic assistance of Lydia Pulsifer, an archaeologist from the University of Tennessee. A young Brown University scholar had just received a Fulbright award to study forty pre-ceramic (i.e., pre-Arawak) sites that have been discovered on the island. "This is very good news for our archaeology," Nicholson said. Several hoteliers have shown interest in incorporating historically important elements into their designs: an Italian group was "very excited" by the presence of Arawak remains on their Nonesuch Bay building site. Tulane University students were digging among the battlements of Fort Shirley, the large installation that looms on the hills above English Harbour, where lately Nicholson played a part in shooing away a busload of American tourists carrying metal detectors. "You'll let us come back, won't you?" the nervous leader of this Lost Horizons Discovery Tour asked Nicholson. The point, Nicholson said, is that what such groups find is "almost all worthless unless you know exactly where it came from." Antigua, a principal British fortress in the eighteenth century, remains rich in unsurveyed archaeological sites and shipwrecks. Nicholson is determined that they remain intact until people and funds materialize to explore them properly.

With regard to the island's natural attributes, there is less reason for encouragement. During the sugar era Antigua was almost completely deforested. Many extinctions occurred. Introduced acacia trees and goats, now feral, and mongooses have done further damage to native communities. The lobster fishery is almost gone, and conch is scarce. Though two reef areas are protected as marine parks, Nicholson suspects that little control is exercised over the coastal areas beyond their boundaries. Severe pollution problems afflict Dickenson Bay, along which many of the island's hotels are arrayed. "There ought to be a master plan for that place," said Ivor Jackson, a former ECNAMP associate who now works as an independent consultant. "They have all the problems: sewerage, erosion, garbage disposal, flooding, access. Once we took a politician out to one of the hotels there to show him what was wrong. All you had to do was step outside, where you could see and smell the problem, and figure out that the hotels themselves were the big losers because of it. The politician said that of course something should be done, and called on the technical people to do it. Nothing ever happened."

One day Flo and I and Mauricio Obregón, back aboard *Sanderling* to take a close look at some of the eastern Caribbean places that Columbus visited while on his second voyage, stopped at the abrupt end of a long dirt road on Antigua's wild, mangrove-lined northeast side. In a small rowboat we crossed the narrows to a dry island called Guiana and walked up a rocky dirt road. Sheep and fallow deer peered at us from the roadside, then scampered away. As we approached a run-down house, surrounded by animals and rusting machines, a rooster crowed and a dog barked. We clapped our hands and yelled hello. No response for a long time. Then an amply proportioned, very white man hove into view from around a corner. He wore a pair of makeshift shorts and carried a pistol on his hip, and he gazed at us with suspicion as he approached the fence where we waited. I said something about my affiliation with the World Wildlife Fund. The man's face broke into a beefy smile and he greeted us warmly.

Thus we met one of the Caribbean's more unusual conservationists, Taffy Bufton. When independence came, Bufton was suddenly eager to leave the farming nations of central Africa where he had long worked. He welcomed an offer from Guiana Island Farms to move to Antigua and manage the company property. For most of the past quarter-century, he and his wife, Bonnie, have been the sole human inhabitants of the 478-acre island. It started well, Bufton explained. He and Bonnie lived in the Great House that stands as a sturdy monument to Antigua's eighteenth-century plantation grandeur. The Buftons tamed Guiana's wild sheep, saved its introduced population of fallow deer (the only such in the Caribbean) from excessive hunting, raised chickens and guinea hens, planted and tended 70 acres of Sea Island cotton. Taffy fiddled with engines and water systems. Bonnie bustled in her rustic kitchen and made tea and baked bread.

In the mid-1970s, there began a ceaseless round of disputes with the company's owners and, after their death, with their representatives. Money stopped coming, and the Buftons were ordered off the island by someone with unclear authority who claimed ownership. Afraid that the island would be developed and its sheep and deer all killed if they were to depart, they decided to stand fast. They reduced expenses any way they could, abandoning the Great House for a small outbuilding, letting go all the previous help, living almost entirely off the dry but fertile land. Taffy gave up smoking because "I couldn't afford it anymore," and spent all the family's savings on a prolonged legal battle to establish their de facto ownership of the island; he then arranged for its sale to the government at a knockdown price and subsequent establishment as a national park. This, the Buftons thought, was the only way to keep the island out of developers' hands. But neither the Antiguan authorities nor the international conservation community were enthusiastic about pre-serving the islet, which has little of biological importance upon it except Antigua's only colony of tropical mockingbirds (they are common else-where).

After a decade of fighting their lonely battle, the Buftons became paranoid. Fearful that the enemy was lurking in the bushes awaiting a chance to take over the island, Taffy took to leaving it as seldom as possible, and only to get essential supplies. Bonnie had been "across" only four times since 1984. Legend has it that Taffy uses his pistol against intruders, and he described to us several occasions when he "disarmed" people wandering on the island. Recently, he said, he had been forced to drive away a group of Puerto Ricans attempting to shoot deer with marine spear guns.

In the end, the Buftons' story is more one of pathos than of violence. In our two hours with them, Taffy showed us the Great House, now boarded up and used only as a hurricane refuge. He led us carefully across breaking floorboards while alarmed fruit bats rose from their roosts and fluttered about. Then he introduced us to Bonnie, a shy and pleasant sixtyish woman. She dusted off her armchairs, gave us tea (from a pot covered by a cozy) and cakes and fresh bread, and complained about not having had time to fix us a "proper lunch." Taffy showed us many documents suggesting the falsity of others' claims upon the island, and told us of his own despair. "We've given up all hope," he said. "We are quite penniless now, we've spent everything we had to save this island. Unless some big surprise occurs, we will have to leave soon and go back to England, and throw ourselves upon the mercy of the dole." I said I would try to help, but doubted I could. We signed the Buftons' guest book (joining "Snowdon," who had come to Guiana to photograph not long before). Taffy drove us, in a shiny Suzuki jeep that a sympathetic government official had arranged for him, back to the narrows. Now garrulous, he was still shouting information to us as we landed on the mainland and drove away in the spattery start of a squall.

During the course of the giddy tour he gave us of Fort Shirley, Nicholson skidded his Japanese car to a halt only feet from a plunging vertical cliff, unfurled himself from behind the wheel, and bounded out to the edge of the precipice. From this vantage point he showed us an egregiously ugly resort complex recently built on Mamora Bay by the St. James's Club, an allegedly classy London gambling joint. (A later glimpse of this prompted Obregón to tell the story of a snobbish Spanish friend who, upon first sighting a gaudy Hilton Hotel, said, "*Es magnífico. Pero no es para nosotros.*") "We hope this won't happen again," said Desmond with a wicked little snarl.

The odds are long, for tourism development remains the essence of the government's economic program, pushed relentlessly by the various members of the reigning Bird family. Business schemes of other sorts tend not to succeed. Though much of the island is fertile and capable of supplying meat and citrus and produce for the hotels, the anti-farming stigma dating from the sugar infamy remains so strong that few Antiguans bother with it. Agricultural cooperatives usually fail, we were told, and only 8 percent of the island's workers list farming as their occupation. A Peace Corps forester told us of his almost total failure to generate interest in reforestation even on an island that was once fully wooded before being laid bare for sugarcane. "I guess I'm learning to be a generalist," he sighed.

I had confidence that the values of the Nicholson family, which had also earned them a pretty penny, would prevail, on part of Antigua, over those of businessmen with less tasteful ideas. English Harbour would almost surely stand fast. Other areas will surely succumb to bad planning, corruption, and a quick-buck mentality. The island's budding

Waikiki at Dickenson Bay, replete with strolling vendors and Jet-Ski rides and Jolly Roger day-tripping sailboats laden with rum-soaked passengers, is already well down the slide. Much of the east side of the island, in the hands of the exclusive Mill Reef Club, is safe from random development unless authorities decide upon a program of outright expropriation. To some Antiguans, the integrity of the Mill Reef Club represents a mixed blessing. In bitterness little can match the writer Jamaica Kincaid's description of this place in her recent memoir, *A Small Place*. The club, she wrote,

> was built by some people from North America who wanted to live in Antigua and spend their holidays in Antigua but who seemed not to like Antiguans (black people) at all, for the Mill Reef Club declared itself completely private, and the only Antiguans (black people) allowed to go there were servants . . . we Antiguans thought that the people at the Mill Reef Club had such bad manners, like pigs; they were behaving in a bad way, like pigs. There they were, strangers in someone else's home, and then they refused to talk to their hosts or have anything human, anything intimate, to do with them.

I left Antigua confused. The island is four or five different places— some wonderful, none yet so tawdry as St. Thomas or Philipsburg. Once, when coming ashore at English Harbour, Peter and I were asked if we would like some "black meat." The incident reminded us that this too was a poor, rapid-fire, tense place. Ironically, it was also still beautiful. On our last night *Sanderling* anchored in a deserted cove on the east end. We were alone. We snorkeled the reef and watched a spectacular sunset. An evening zephyr dappled the water. Then, attended by the crystal pinpoint of a nearby planet, a crescent moon appeared.

12

Among the Windwards

FROM THE LEEWARD ISLANDS <u>SANDERLING</u> PROCEEDED SOUTHWARD
to the Windwards, so named because they lie closer to Europe in more
easterly longitudes than the Antilles at the northern end of the chain—in
fact, with the prevailing easterly trades, to windward of the Leewards.
The Windwards, too, are rich in history and variety. They vary from the
four-lane urbanism of Martinique to the rain-forest wilderness of Dominica to the fading Britishness of Barbados. Each deserves its own
book. At the very least, it is important to disaggregate these islands
rather than present them, as is so often done, as a single lumpy
bouillabaisse called the Eastern Caribbean.

The French Islands

Martinique, to the south, and Guadeloupe with its attendant Columbus-
named Iles des Saintes, to the north of Dominica, somehow remained
French through the din of the eighteenth-century Caribbean. Today
they are *plus français que les Français*, the shopkeepers and officials
surlier, the bread crustier, the hunters deadlier. *"Qu'est-ce qu'il y a?"*
barked the *douanier* as we approached his house in the picture-book
little town of Ste. Anne on Martinique. We explained that we would like
to reenter France even though it was already four on a weekday
afternoon. Not before the next morning at seven, the man muttered,
then slammed his door in our faces. Nowhere did a French merchant
express anything but contempt when we tried to make purchases with
the Eastern Caribbean (EC) common currency that is valid from Antigua
to Grenada. *"Absolument pas,"* snorted the dour lady in the *boulangerie*,
with no further explanation, when we tried to use the stuff to buy a loaf
of bread. On the islands we ate wonderful *steak frites* and *poisson fumé*
and morning croissants, and in the busy town at the Iles des Saintes
celebrated Bastille Day, complete with fireworks and dancing between
cloudbursts on the streets to an orchestra right out of a Pagnol film.
Though two species of the parrot genus *Amazona* are holding out in the
forests of Dominica, such birds are long gone from the French islands.
"Over there they shoot anything that moves," said Paul Butler, a British
wildlife manager who was living on St. Vincent and working on a project
to save its endemic parrot.

The dramatic high peaks and green slopes of these islands still give
strong hints of the verdant beauty they radiated before they too were cut
over to make farms and sugar plantations and before the massive
eruption of Mount Pelée on Martinique in 1902 sent lava flows careening

down steep slopes. A little fishing town called St. Pierre was abruptly obliterated. Forty thousand people died. In recent times values transmitted from France accelerated the rate of change. Tall modern apartment buildings crowd the shore along the coast near Fort-de-France, capital of Martinique. New Renaults and Citroëns fan out from town, along broad highways and boulevards masterminded in Paris. Few still practice fishing here, preferring to buy from the market the seafood caught and delivered by fishermen from poorer neighbor islands who have no recourse to the elaborate French welfare system. Pleasure yachts outnumber fishing craft in many harbors; a fleet of several dozen cruising boats from Guadeloupe joined us for Bastille Day at the Iles des Saintes. At Anse Mitan, the hotel-and-restaurant strip across the bay from Fort-de-France, several hundred yachts bob at anchor. One quiet evening there, we watched in horror as a handsome chartered sailboat motored at high speed directly toward a small, well-marked shoal in the middle of the anchorage. The boat hit hard, with a loud crunching noise, and the stern rose high out of the water. With hardly a backward glance, the helmsman charged on.

In such places conservation is defined as having more to do with parks and scenic overlooks and history than with the preservation of species or wildlands. Still, said Allen Putney, "they have an interesting approach, very different from ours on the English-speaking islands. We can learn some things from them." On Martinique the government closes some beaches from time to time, so that vegetation can recover and self-cleansing take place. Martinique has also become the first Caribbean island to break free from the sun-and-sand stereotype and promote tourism to rural inns away from the shore. Caribbean conservationists are also heartened by the growing French (for these islands are fully so) interest in participating in regional movements such as the Caribbean Conservation Association, whose 1988 annual meeting was held on Martinique.

Dominica

Stephen, a motor vehicle driver who works for the government's small but competent Forestry Division, led me down a narrow path in the forest. It was late on a sunny, windy afternoon. We reached a lookout point from where, Stephen had assured me, we would have a good chance of seeing both of Dominica's endemic and very rare parrots: the large sisserou (*Amazona imperialis*), of which at most only one hundred still exist, and the smaller red-necked (*A. arausica*), with a population of three or four hundred.

In the course of half an hour of intent watching, we saw little but swifts, hawks, and fast-flying little brown birds that disappeared so rapidly into the dense forest that even experts would have had trouble identifying them. Then three red-necked parrots, looking mostly green with little ornamentation, flew fast down the valley at treetop level, quickly vanishing from sight. Another long wait. "Sometimes you see the sisserou right away. Sometimes it takes a little longer," said Stephen encouragingly. Then in the distance we saw a brownish fleck of movement and heard a throaty squawk before two large birds plunged back into the canopy. "That's the sisserou," Stephen whispered. "You can't miss the call." If only for an instant, surely not long enough for me to have made the identification on my own, I had just sighted, Stephen assured me, one of the world's rarest animals.

Edouard Benito-Espinal, an ornithologist from Guadeloupe who was mist-netting in the forest while I wandered off in search of parrots, said he was convinced that the sisserou population would continue its decline toward extinction unless a captive-breeding program is established. Others disagree. Arlington James, one of Dominica's growing number of well-educated young forest managers, bases his hopes on better protection of the sisserou's high-mountain habitat. The government owns much of this, and has declared it a reserve; Rare Animal Relief Effort (RARE), an American organization, is acquiring an adjacent 200-acre parcel that remains in private hands. Though much land in Dominica is being cleared to plant bananas, James and his associates are making a determined effort—backed by strengthened wildlife-protection laws—to prevent squatters and loggers from violating the reserve's boundaries. James also thinks that the installation of nesting boxes within the habitat would help by reducing competition among females, which have long vied for cavities in a dwindling number of the old trees that the species prefers. A spirited public-education campaign is designed to persuade people not to shoot or capture the parrots for food or sale to the international pet trade, but rather to respect them as national treasures. Despite these measures, and although efforts to save some species have doggedly continued right down to almost the very last surviving individual, the bird may not survive in the wild because its population is already so small.

Saving the sisserou, which adorns the national flag, forms part of a broad strategy in Dominica. Thirty miles long and ten wide, this fertile volcanic island contains more natural wonders than any other in the Lesser Antilles: a mountain 4,747 feet high, dense rain forests, a bubbling hot sulphurous lake that is the second largest of its kind in the world, a rich plant biota in which ferns are particularly prominent. Ten percent of the island is already within the national park system and another 18 percent protected as forest reserve. Abundant in natural beauties but deficient in white sandy beaches, Dominica is the Caribbean's second-poorest country next to Haiti. Jobs are so scarce that many citizens emigrate in search of work, reducing the annual population growth rate to a scant 0.57 percent a year. Tourism in Dominica is still in its infancy, with only 24,000 annual visitors in 1986, few hotels, and taxis harder to find in Roseau, the capital, than even in New York City.

In view of this configuration, government and private-sector leaders hope to position Dominica as "the nature island," forming one stop on packaged tours or cruises to several places. You come to Dominica and hike in the mountains and see the Boiling Lake, then move on to Antigua for the beaches and the shopping. One champion of this idea is soft-spoken Gerry Aird, a prominent businessman with interests in shipping, insurance, retailing, and tourism. The red-mustached Aird, as chairman of both the Dominican Conservation Association and the Tourism Development Board, is in an excellent position to promote it. Nor does it hurt that Maria José Edwards, who in 1988 was head of the government's Tourism Department, had previously worked with Arlington James and his current boss, Felix Gregoire, in the Forestry Division.

A principal asset for Aird and Edwards is the large Morne Trois Pitons National Park, protected since the 1970s and with a solid infrastructure of roads, trails, and other conveniences already in place. Aird also hopes for the further development of the 1,300-acre Cabrits region near the town of Portsmouth at the northern end of the island. Located on a peninsula forming one arm of Portsmouth's Prince Rupert Bay, Cabrits contains an ample supply of dense forest ranging across two steep hillsides yielding fine views. On the shoulder of one of these is another Fort Shirley, a compactly handsome eighteenth-century complex of stone buildings and battlements. Columbus visited the bay twice, once in 1493 on his second voyage, then again in 1504 on his fourth and last expedition. From 1535 until 1763 Spain controlled the harbor, using it as a supply station for treasure-laden ships en route back to Europe. The entire island was then ceded to Britain, which in 1774 began to build the fort. After the French captured Roseau in 1778, Fort Shirley also surrendered. But in 1782, after Britain's Admiral Rodney defeated a far superior French force near the Iles des Saintes, the entire island reverted to British hands. Without ever firing a shot in anger, redcoats manned Cabrits until 1854, when, for want of further reason to maintain a garrison there, they left it to the goats and weeds. The fearsome

Hurricane David that in 1979 battered the island with 175 mph winds caused further deterioration. In 1982, under the inventive leadership of an artist and writer named Lennox Honeychurch, and with financial support from the Armand G. Erpf Fund and other international sources, Cabrits (named for its goats) was declared a national park and restoration work was inaugurated on the grounds of the fortress.

Sanderling anchored in Prince Rupert Bay, at the foot of the site, and we arranged for a visit. With Stephen at the helm of a four-door Toyota pickup and Arlington James along as well, we drove to Fort Shirley and spent a morning there. We walked from the parking lot up a short path to the gateway, a well-preserved assembly of smooth rectangular rocks fitted together almost as tightly as at the Inca sites around Cuzco. Continuing our climb, we passed experimental groves of young teak and mahogany trees (they were not doing well), then a well-tended lawn area (Aird, perhaps uniquely for a business leader, drives out from Roseau on weekends to push a little red power mower around the premises), and entered what used to be the barracks kitchen. Its large oven remained intact. Another level up, three adjoining rooms once used to store gunpowder were being turned into museum spaces. Two of these rooms were well restored with red brick and whitewash; a third awaited funds to pay for a similar renovation. Another few steps up: hurricane-battered barracks for enlisted men and cannons scattered about, some having recently been hauled up from the beach below by strong-backed volunteers from the crews of passing British naval ships.

At the compound's uppermost level, which commands a superb view of the bay, Portsmouth, and high mountains in the distance, the unrenovated ruins of the officers' quarters had the solid square look of a large Georgian house. Honeychurch intended, we heard, to transform this building into a small inn. According to his plan, cruise-ship passengers would soon begin visiting the site from a pier to be constructed right at its foot—the world's first such facility to be located within a national park. Nearby, a German investor, having bought part of a swamp containing one of Dominica's few patches of white mangrove, was regrettably draining and dredging the wetland to make way for a marina. After visiting Fort Shirley's principal buildings we also walked along a path through the "dry" forest (only 50-70 inches of rain a year vs. as much as 300 only a few miles away) to the ruins of the house where the commandant lived and kept his horses. For want of funds, no restoration work is in progress here. Still, a fine start has clearly been made at Cabrits, with expenditures of no more than $200,000 to date on a project that would benefit Dominicans and tourists alike.

Back down at the Purple Turtle, an unpretentious open-air restaurant and two-bedroom hotel on Portsmouth's unspoiled crescent beach, we dodged intermittent rain showers while awaiting Tom Sage, then a resident American fieldworker. He would show me his part of the island's conservation program: a fascinating, if complex effort to motivate a group of small-scale sawyers to spare the forest by using its resources sustainably. Eventually Sage appeared, tall and bearing the girth of a pro football tackle, another former Peace Corps volunteer, who has more recently lived around the Eastern Caribbean as an AID official and freewheeling consultant. He welcomed me aboard his pint-sized pickup. Crouching behind its wheel, he drove off into forests near where, the day before, Stephen had shown me the rare parrots. We were on private land for which, Sage explained, he had drawn up a management plan for a timber company a decade before. While providing for an adequate timber yield, his scenario would also shelter resident parrots and an important watershed area. This land would thus act as a buffer between full-throttle development below and the core of the parrot habitat on protected public land higher up on adjacent mountain slopes.

Now the area was threatened by a wave of deforestation for banana planting, thanks to a high price and the introduction of efficient new harvesting methods, and by indiscriminate logging as well. Sage's herculean task, underwritten by a U.S. foundation, was to get to know the loggers; help them form an association and define and enforce criteria for prudent use of forest resources; create the legal structure and leadership for the association; seek cooperation from sawmill owners (mostly for the use of their lumber kilns—the independent sawyers somehow fashion boards with chain saws); try to computerize the entire activity; and raise funds for all of these projects—all on a tight budget and with little help. This was Sage's first full day on the job. I watched with admiration while he stopped and chatted in semi-patois with two woodcutters we ran across. His was a challenging mission for a well-trained Dominican, I thought, let alone for even a sensitive gringo import. Not long after I met him, I was not fully surprised to hear, Sage abruptly bolted and left the island.

In his office overlooking the grounds of Roseau's botanical garden, Felix Gregoire discussed the political need for this sort of project. "In former times our approach was too conservationist," said Gregoire, a strapping career forestry official with a direct gaze and a strong clear voice. "Today we are still trying to do the same things, but we call it something different. We don't talk of saving the parrot anymore. We talk of protecting water catchment areas." It's not that conservation had become unpopular over the decade since the introduction of its principles in the mid-1970s, Gregoire continued, but simply that the combination of high unemployment, the ravages of Hurricane David, and propitious conditions for banana cultivation had resulted in sharply conflicting national aspirations. Accordingly the conservation-minded must grapple delicately for the souls of the country's most senior officials, principally Prime Minister Eugenia Charles, a formidable woman often compared with Margaret Thatcher. Aird was encouraged, he said, when the Minister of Agriculture called on Dominicans to press for higher crop yields rather than clear more land. Opposition to "indiscriminate clearing of forest land" remains a principal plank in the platform of Charles's political party, and the Prime Minister has personally pushed the issue over the radio. On the other hand, she has been known to suggest that protection for 28 percent of the entire island is quite enough. She did not oppose an AID project to run power lines smack across the middle of the Morne Trois Pitons National Park. Despite adverse environmental consequences, Charles has also expressed her determination to increase the island's already substantial ability to generate hydroelectric power. "She has said that she is going ahead with a project that will raise the high-water level of one of our finest lakes by thirty feet so that the runoff will make more power," said Arlington James. "This means major changes in the vegetation and will cause a strange appearance during the dry season. But when the Prime Minister says she is going ahead, she is going ahead."

It is hard not to be impressed by the general commitment, expressed by many people on this appealing island, to keep environmental as well as development goals in mind. Dominica today is not greatly changed from the Sunday when Columbus first saw and named it. With luck its beauty will far outlast that of St. Thomas or St. Maarten, even if more people stay home and the population spurts.

St. Lucia

"Hello, darling," Paul Butler said loudly into a phone. "What was that you wanted, darling?" Then an expatriate employee of St. Lucia's Forestry Division, a pale Briton with little round eyeglasses and shoulder-length dark hair, Butler was having a routine conversation with an official in another government department. He solved the problem, rang off, then began barking instructions to workmen passing by outside his street-level kiosk of an office on the grounds of the old botanical gardens in Castries, St. Lucia's capital. Two pretty girls, in search of

Along the St. Lucian coast two hundred years ago.

information, pressed their noses against the louvers. "What's your name, darling?" Butler asked one of them. "Angela, is it? That's a pretty name." They told him their problem and he said he could not help—he was about to leave the island to attend an international conference on endangered species. Such was Butler's frenzied office life that all too rarely did he have time to get out to where he really wanted to be: in the field. No Terry-Thomas caricature of a British colonial, but a dedicated wildlife manager and parrot specialist, Butler came to the island in 1977 on a six-month consultancy and stayed ten years. More than any other individual, he is the savior of *Amazona versicolor*, St. Lucia's endemic parrot.

As a graduate student, off for a stretch of fieldwork, Butler first arrived on the island at a time when this striking bird, locally called the jacquot, was in a period of sharp decline. Its poorly protected mountain habitat was shrinking as banana planters chewed away at the forest. Local people were in the habit of shooting the jacquot when they could. "If the bird died, they'd eat it. If it survived, they'd make it a pet," Butler said. "In older times here, people killed anything that moved—to eat or for money," said Gabriel Charles, the island's forest supervisor. "All our wildlife was close to extinction." Punishments for violating wildlife-protection laws were light, and enforcement was lax. Using a careful scientific approach, Butler surveyed the jacquot population and estimated that about one hundred individuals remained on the island. Unlike many scientists, who would conduct such a study and then simply walk away, Butler went on to prepare a report to the government that contained proposals for ways to save the bird. He recommended further research, the initiation of a captive breeding program, improvements in legislation, community-education initiatives, and habitat protection.

Despite the shambles that the August 4, 1980, Hurricane Allen made of the jacquot's habitat, Butler said that the government's response had been effective: "A parrot sanctuary was declared. The shooting is almost completely gone, with the fine moved up from $48 to $5,000 EC. There hasn't been any parrot hunting for a long time. We've had people deported for catching boas, let alone a parrot. Protected areas have well-marked boundaries, and squatters get caught and removed. Our breeding program, on the isle of Jersey, is doing well and we're planning to reintroduce captive-bred birds into the wild in the near future."

The education program is a model of its kind. At an international parrot conference held on the island in 1979, the jacquot was declared the national bird. Schoolchildren were taken on hikes through its forest habitat and told how it protects watershed as well as wildlife. "When we started the walks all we got was tourists," said Gabriel Charles. "Nobody here knew what a forest was. People thought it was just for birdwatchers and naturalists. We've put a lot of material on the radio. Our little newspaper, *Bush Talk*, has been running for more than ten years without a cent of help from outside this island. Now the local people are asking the visitors if they've been on the forest walk. Ten percent of our children have been on the walk. Today any child here knows the scientific name of that parrot." Flo and I took the forest walk with a young woman appropriately named Christina Plante, at twenty-three a veteran of six years' work in the Forestry Division, as our capable guide. Christina saw the jacquot. We missed it. But we learned a lot.

As a consequence of the well-coordinated effort on its behalf, the jacquot is back from the brink. In 1986 Butler conducted his fourth and most recent survey of the parrot habitat. He then estimated the population at two hundred to two hundred fifty. More recently Gabriel Charles hazarded three hundred, with no boost yet from the reintroduction of captive-bred birds. St. Lucia's parrot has made an impressive comeback. By 1988 it had become so secure that Butler departed to launch a new effort to shore up the beautiful Amazon parrot that is endemic to St. Vincent.

A prominent sign guards the entrance to the Forestry Division's modest headquarters. It reads: "Let's Change Our Attitude to Forestry from Hate and Apathy to Love and Concern." The sign is an indication that the struggle to save the parrot is but the most visible tip of a larger effort to establish on the island the principles of sustainable, conservation-minded development. Not settled by Europeans until the seventeenth century, studded with steep hillsides and high mountains, the island suffered more from bitter bouts of warfare between the British and the French (who named many of its bays and mountains and contributed much to the local patois) than from environmental degradation until well into the current century. The country has been British seven times and French seven times.

As late as 1942, St. Lucia remained sufficiently wild for a German U-boat to have been able to hole up in tiny, landlocked Marigot Bay on the west coast (where *Sanderling* spent several happy nights) and from there mount a torpedo attack on two ships berthed in the principal harbor at Castries. In the 1970s departing British colonial administrators, who thought little about the welfare of any sort of wildlife, left behind a forest management plan calling for a concentration of timber operations in the very heart of the jacquot's habitat. Resort development was beginning to leave ugly marks. To create Rodney Bay, today a successful haven for yachtsmen and vacation-home owners, engineers drained a productive mangrove swamp, turned historic Pigeon Island into a peninsula, and blasted away a reef containing at least twenty-six coral species and three hundred kinds of shells.

"It wasn't long before we realized we couldn't just be talking about the parrot and the forest," Gabriel Charles said. "We had to consider the whole environment." Concurrently, the parrot-based education program began to produce political dividends. "The politicians were talking about forestry now because the people were talking about it," said Paul Butler. He cited a survey showing that, while people on the neighboring island of St. Vincent professed little concern, St. Lucians considered deforestation as grave a threat to their environment as a big hurricane. "In the interest of the nation, the government today is willing to risk a few votes," Butler added. A Naturalists' Society, founded in 1977, had about one hundred and twenty members and was becoming quite a powerful force. In 1975, partially in response to outcries about the Rodney Bay affair, the government founded the St. Lucia National Trust "to preserve and promote the natural and cultural heritage of St. Lucia for the enjoyment of all." To this new entity the Rodney Bay Company was persuaded to donate Pigeon Island and its historic fortress, today visited by 12,000 paying customers a year as well as by thousands of students. Since this beginning the Trust's budget and responsibilities have been vastly expanded. Legislators have voted full protection for almost 11 percent of the island.

The Forestry Division, once solely concerned with timber operations, has changed greatly. "We now have a management plan for all our forests," said the graying but vigorous Gabriel Charles, a veteran forester who is himself a convert to environmental concern. "CIDA, the Canadian foreign-aid agency, has put in $10 million over five years for training. We have complete control of all the wildlife on the island. We have the best laws in the Caribbean, and our magistrates are getting better and better at enforcing them."

Charles and Butler both expressed admiration for the World Wildlife Fund's role in helping to bring about these changes. In 1976, Thomas Lovejoy, who was then the Fund's senior scientist and remained so until 1987, when he shifted his flag to the Smithsonian Institution, paid a visit to the island that resulted in the parrot conservation program. After the 1980 hurricane, Butler phoned Lovejoy for emergency help in assessing the damage; twenty-four hours later an ornithologist from Jersey, his plane ticket supplied by WWF, was in the forest helping Butler count parrots. "People here still remember that," Butler told me. WWF long ago donated two motor vehicles and a single-sideband radio to Charles's division; all three machines were still functioning in 1988.

By phone and by mail from Washington, WWF has also been helpful in encouraging St. Lucia's shift from protecting a single species toward a broader conservation approach. Of this there is no better example than the effort to bring about the balanced and sustainable development of the entire southeastern end of the island around the town of Vieux Fort. The originator and manager of the program is a tall, stoop-shouldered, widely respected Guadeloupe-born Frenchman named Yves Renard, a leading figure in ECNAMP and in the Caribbean Conservation Association, and a St. Lucia resident since 1981. To dramatize his explanation of the program, Renard drove Leslie and me up to Moule a Chique, a high mountaintop with a commanding view of the area. A shock of black hair tumbling across his brow in the afternoon trade wind, he began to talk.

Vieux Fort, he said, was a quiet place until World War II, when the United States paved a sugarcane field to create an airstrip. When the war ended, the military abruptly departed. The region, now more populous, sank into torpor until 1971, when the opening of a new civil airport on the old base was meant to precipitate a new wave of tourist development. Only one hotel was ever built, however. After several bankruptcies and changes of ownership, it fell into the hands of Club Med. The change did little good for the local economy, since the Club does not encourage guests to stray off the compound and go to town, and employs St. Lucians

Yves Renard of the Caribbean Conservation
Association and ECNAMP.

only at menial levels. For the 27,000 people who live in and around
Vieux Fort, prospects therefore remained uncertain.

From the hilltop where we stood, we could see the town and the
airport. In the distance were the dramatic heights of the Soufrière region
with its needle peaks. Closer by was an area of rolling hills and planted
sugar; directly below us a small bay with two islands at its mouth and a
reef extending from one of them. Board sailors whizzed to and fro in the
gusty breeze. Beyond, along a coast of great beauty, lay a succession of
bays heavily used by inshore fishermen, the hotel, a mangrove area, the
dark blue deep water. For Renard the challenge was how to preserve the
region's natural values while, at the same time, addressing the severe
and sometimes conflicting economic difficulties of its human population.

"We came here to see if we could put sustainable development
theory into practice at the local level," he said. "We began with these
two little islands here, the Maria Islands. They have two endemic species
on them, a small grass snake and the Maria Islands ground lizard, and
they are a prime habitat for nesting seabirds, terns and noddies. The
parks people came to us and asked us for a plan to protect the islands. We
have done that. The islands have now been under active management for
more than two years. Already the nesting-bird population has more than
tripled! We know the name of every lizard out there. We have built a
little nature center on the shore facing the islands, and already it is being

thought of as a museum. Once we started, we began to see the islands as part of a broader, integrated, community-based coastal zone management program linking conservation and development, and incorporating most of what you can see from up here, which are most of the resources you would find along any Caribbean coastline. Here we have two bays, beaches, reefs, mangroves, fisheries, high mountain ridges, a town, some industry around the airport, sand mining from the beaches for construction projects. With all this we felt that we might serve as an interesting model."

One principal sector of Renard's broader effort involves the region's mangroves, which have long been under heavy attack because charcoal remains the principal fuel for most St. Lucians. To preserve them, Renard has established a fuelwood plantation up in the hills, and has helped form an association of charcoal producers to set and enforce criteria for sustainable use of the natural resource. While this project has yet to show positive results, other aspects of the program have made great strides. Thirty fishermen working from eight canoes based in Savannes Bay work cooperatively thanks to Renard; he said that they had become more conservation-minded and that their technology was improving (though technology is hardly the whole answer: an Island Resources Foundation study convincingly shows that elaborate equipment and big boats perform poorly in this region of spotty and fast-changing fishing). The fishermen had worked together to construct a building at their landing site. It is used for marketing and to store equipment, and has been a major reason for new prosperity among the group's members.

Renard and his local partners are also trying to manage the white sea urchin, or "sea egg," greatly prized as a delicacy but beset by the sort of overharvesting that has already wiped out the island's conch; and are successfully cultivating sea moss, an aquatic plant that is used to make a popular local tonic said to have aphrodisiac qualities. These activities are accompanied by workshops and other training programs, and invariably involve the participation of community groups. Students, enrolled in the diploma course in environmental science that is newly offered at the Barbados campus of the University of the West Indies, have found south-eastern St. Lucia attractive as a place to do their required fieldwork.

I asked Renard to look ahead. "Agriculture is the most difficult thing," he replied. "Other than fuelwood gathering, the principal cause of deforestation here is land clearing for banana cultivation. Bananas get a good price now, and the country badly needs the export earnings, so there is great pressure." Paul Butler worried along similar lines: "Sixteen percent of this island consists of private land that is still in forest, and we have no jurisdiction over private land. It's going very fast and there's not much that we can do about it—even though the island is running out of water. What I see for the future here are small patches of protected forest amid barren seas of bananas."

The banana sector is particularly difficult to control, said Robert Devaux, head of the St. Lucia National Trust, because it is the small farmers, controlling about 90 percent of the banana crop, who are moving onto marginal lands and bringing about instability. Driving from Vieux Fort back to Castries, I passed billowing hillsides of banana trees, their branches of ripening fruit encased in the ubiquitous blue plastic. Close to the capital a small noisy yellow plane buzzed to and fro spraying upon them an anti-nematode chemical that, Devaux snorted, is a marked-up waste product from a factory in Trinidad, of which, given the limitations of aerial-spraying technology in very hilly country, little reaches its intended target.

His main obstacle, Renard also said, is often the purist fanaticism of some conservation people. "They are so uncompromising. They say, 'Let's stop it, let's close it.' They never want to bring the local people, the users of the resource, into the discussion. We're often in the middle, the mediators, and if we were not here I don't know who could play this role." Renard was there, though, and so was Gabriel Charles, and to back them up were solid laws and a growing tradition of conservation-mindedness. Unlike many of its neighbor islands, St. Lucia seemed far from a lost cause. In 1988 even the world economy was cooperating: slow British demand for bananas was forcing St. Lucians to dump some of their crop. "Of course, it means hardship for some of our people," said Gabriel Charles. "But there's a good side to it as well. It's a warning about the dangers of depending on a monoculture, and it comes at a time when the bananas are badly damaging our forests and our streams and watersheds."

Heading south toward St. Vincent, *Sanderling* spent a night tied to the rocks below the dramatic twin peaks called Les Pitons on St. Lucia's west coast, near the pretty old town of Soufrière. The Pitons and the verdant valley between them, an old plantation, constitute one of the crown jewels of the Caribbean—a site that is a natural for a national park. Tourist facilities alongside would pep up the lagging economy of Soufrière and surrounding villages. St. Lucians generally support the idea of a park. But the key 500-acre parcel of land between the Pitons is in private hands; the owners have placed before the government a proposal to build a hotel and residential complex. Though construction jobs would be created, the long-term relationship between this "club" and the rest of the island would be about as satisfactory as that between

The Pitons, St. Lucia.

the Mill Reef Club and Antigua. A government thumbs-up for the developers would also kill the park. As 1988 ended, Renard was following this issue closely, in partnership with the Soufrière Development Commission and others in the remote, staggeringly beautiful region. How it is resolved will say much about St. Lucia's future course.

St. Vincent and the Grenadines

On a calm morning, after a night of hushed admiration beneath the Pitons, *Sanderling* motored along the lush, intricately folded hills of St. Vincent's leeward shore. We passed this island's Mount Soufrière, an active volcano that last erupted in 1979 and spread fine dust over a large portion of the island, and the capital city of Kingstown. Then across nine miles of lumpy open water and into the large clean harbor of Admiralty Bay on the island of Bequia. Northernmost of the chain called the Grenadines that lies between St. Vincent and Grenada, Bequia proudly boasts a long tradition of honesty and hard work on the part of its population of 6,000 fishermen and boatbuilders. Still without an airport, the island had by the late 1980s become a popular haven for yachtsmen and for land-bound tourists arriving via the *Friendship Rose*, a well-worn island-built schooner that was making a daily round trip across the channel to Kingstown. Ashore: a friendly welcome from the efficient lady at the tourist information center near the Port Elizabeth ferry dock, and a string of pleasant hotels and bars along the beach.

"It's a nice place to live," said Athneal Ollivierre, a handsome, deeply tanned Bequian who one calm afternoon welcomed me into his sparsely furnished living room. "We all own our own homes here. No renting." Ollivierre's special distinction was his role as doyen of the island's old, if lagging, whaling tradition; on his wall hung a painting showing him as a young man aboard a small boat attacking a whale. "The Last Harpoonist" reads the caption. In a lilting English (I would have found subtitles helpful), Ollivierre talked of his passion for this activity, practiced here for three hundred years and by him since 1957, when he registered his first score. Using two open 27-foot boats, Ollivierre and his crew of older Bequians (six men per boat) hunt for a limit of four humpback whales during each three-month season. They ply local waters, using only sails and oars, to harpoon whales in the traditional hand-held way: "We lose a lot of them because we have to sneak up." The quota is stern; transient whales in the region face far greater dangers, including, said Ollivierre with a mournful shake of the head, yachtsmen who try to shoot them with rifles.

Ollivierre had no intention of stopping his own whale-hunting altogether, despite mounting pressure to do so. "I get letters from all over the world asking us to stop," he said. "But I write back explaining how much whales are part of our lives here. They supply food for many people. We use the oil as fuel for our stoves, and the bones make furniture. And our whaling brings many tourists here. They line up on the beach when we bring one in. Asking us to stop is like putting a knife to our throats. I'm trying hard to keep it going." A catch of three whales during the season is ample for Bequia's whalers, since they also fish conventionally, Ollivierre explained; they could even get by with two, and some years they only manage to catch one. Later, when I walked down the beach to inspect his trim gray-and-yellow whaleboats, though I have little use for whaling in general, I found myself sharing Ollivierre's distaste for a reduction of the Bequia quota to zero.

At Port Elizabeth, I boarded the *Friendship Rose* for the early-morning run across to Kingstown. After a quick breakfast at the Hi-Tide Snackette & Bar, which advertises that it is "Licensed to Sell Intoxicated Beverages," I walked up to the Forestry Division. There I found Paul Butler, newly arrived on St. Vincent and busily setting up shop to replicate his St. Lucia parrot conservation model. With limited support from RARE, Butler had a year, or two hundred working days, to get the job done. *Amazona guldingii*, the St. Vincent parrot, remains more plentiful than either its Dominican or its St. Lucian equivalents, with a population of some four hundred fifty individuals. But banana-growing was placing stress on part of the bird's habitat, and its high value in the international pet market ($7,000 U.S. per bird, according to a British source that Butler quoted to me) made it a grave temptation for many job-hungry islanders. And enforcement of the protection laws has been sporadic.

With characteristic energy, Butler was setting up his program. Already a tough bill, drafted but pigeonholed since 1982, had been dusted off and made into law; all over town I saw posters warning violators of the high cost of noncompliance. With the help of a newly arrived Peace Corps volunteer, Butler was planning, on behalf of "Vincie"—the nickname he coined for the bird—a broad environmental education program for teachers and schoolchildren. Meetings with district forest rangers were being scheduled, and with their help a knowledge-and-opinion questionnaire was being distributed to a thousand islanders. The upcoming media blitz that was to make 1988 St. Vincent's Year of the Parrot included a locally composed calypso tune entitled "Leave de National Bird in de Wild."

Butler took half a day away from his manifold chores to drive me, in a shiny pickup donated by the World Wildlife Fund to the Forestry Division three years before, to a nearby parrot habitat. We reached the end of the road, then walked up a steep, slippery path into thick forest. "This parrot quacks like a bloody duck," Butler said. We failed to see the bird that morning, but we clearly heard its distinctive quack. On a second visit we saw both it and, as a result of a mist-netting program being conducted by summering British students, St. Vincent's only other endemic bird—the whistling warbler.

Under a hot midday sun I walked toward the botanical garden, oldest in the Caribbean and beautifully kept. At an open manhole men were working. I asked them directions. "You're on de track, mon," one replied. Moments later I was in the presence of Earl ("Doc") Kirby, head of the St. Vincent National Trust and director of the small museum on the grounds. Kirby, Ivor Jackson had told me in Antigua, is the best-informed man on St. Vincent's ecology, and in a short time I found out why. Kirby talked about the folly of introducing Holstein cattle, which adapt badly to heat and humidity, onto this hot and humid island; about the difficulty of harvesting arrowroot; and about the general unpopularity of farming even though the St. Vincent soil is rich with volcanic nutrients. In turn this means that above 1,000 to 1,500 feet, where most of the biological diversity is to be found, there is as yet little cultivation or disturbance of any sort. "Our real problems are micro-environmental," said Kirby. "One is that of garbage disposal with new foods and packaging like that introduced by Kentucky Fried Chicken."

Barbados

Sanderling's last port in the Caribbean, before we jumped off for Brazil, was Bridgetown, capital of Barbados. The most windward of the Windwards, this island long enjoyed special attention from the British, who at one time prized it more than their North American holdings. To attack Barbados the French would have to fight their way upwind for at least twenty-four hours and would be fatigued before the battle even began. Britain consequently invested heavily in sugar development on Barbados, fortified the island well, and stationed a substantial garrison there; it was never conquered, not even during the Revolutionary War when London's attention was diverted northward. The care that the British lavished on Barbados, and the fortunes made from sugar growing there during the boom times, in turn gave it a dominant place among the islands: it is known as the most sophisticated of them, even in terms of thinking about conservation. "If it's happening on Barbados," Allen Putney had told me, "you can be sure that the other islands will be wanting it too."

What I found, after completing the exacting and expensive customs and immigration formalities for entering yachts, was an island upon and around which little is left to conserve. Almost all of it had long since been stripped of its original vegetation to make way for sugarcane, the most suitable crop for an island made of coral with only a few inches of rich topsoil; today erosion has become a serious problem in major agricultural areas. As sugar production has declined and farming diversifies, agricultural chemicals are increasingly being used, and these in turn pollute land and water. In the cane fields the dominant species today is the green monkey that was introduced from Africa and has become as much of a pest as Antigua's mongoose.

Reef fishing of all sorts has declined because of overharvesting. The white sea urchin population is severely depleted. The reefs themselves have suffered considerable attrition, though some say that storms and wave action are as much to blame as the usual sources of pollution. Sea grass beds have dwindled because of sand deposited upon them as a result of construction projects accompanying the tourism boom of recent years. Not even the abundant flying fish, a staple of the Bajan diet, has remained unaffected. "You used to be able to just scoop them out of the water," fisheries officer Patrick McConney said. "You couldn't get any easier fishing than that. But now they are scarcer, and you have to use a gill net."

At least 80 percent of the Barbados fishery is pelagic, McConney continued, and little is known about what is happening to the high-seas populations of wahoo, dolphinfish, and other species taken by Barbadian fishermen. Closer to shore, new efforts are being made to manage reef fishing and to safeguard nesting beaches used by hawksbill and logger-head turtles. These species have never been heavily exploited by the Bajans and the department is pressing for a total moratorium. It has also made a major, and by several accounts effective, effort to educate schoolchildren about sea turtle behavior. A couple of marine protected areas have been established, and limited reef recovery has been noted around them. The hotel industry is said to have discovered the importance of environmental health; though it has since been dismantled, one recent government even established a Ministry of Environment and Tourism.

Such programs struck me as no more impressive than many others I had seen on islands thought to be less advanced. Where I found Barbados more of a leader was in the level of education that its principal conservation people had achieved. Both McConney and Yvonne St. Hill, a determined young woman who was then holding an environmental position at the Ministry of Labour and was also the founder of a private group called the Barbados Environmental Association, had earned graduate degrees from Dalhousie University in Nova Scotia. Also in Barbados is the headquarters of the Caribbean Conservation Association, which, though more concerned with regional than with local affairs, is able upon occasion to bring its expertise to bear close to home. Michael King, CCA's executive director, said that from time to time he could impress Bajan government officials with the importance of taking conservation actions, although "you cannot realistically look at them from an aesthetic point of view." Jill Sheppard, a determined Englishwoman who ran CCA for many years, continues to live on Barbados and remains active with regard to several cultural-heritage projects.

An exciting innovation at the University of the West Indies, one of whose principal campuses is at Cave Hill on Barbados, is a new multi-disciplinary program in environmental science. The idea first surfaced late in the 1970s, said Dr. Euna Moore, a biologist who was serving as its director. "Environmental problems were cropping up throughout the islands, and the time for new actions was clearly at hand.

It took a long time to get the new program worked into the system—you know how things work in academia. But we are now entering our third year, and everybody is happy. The students—we try to have all the Eastern Caribbean islands represented—take courses in several different departments here, and they also do solution-oriented fieldwork that addresses real problems." The results of this part of the program are already being felt. Though the work was still entirely for undergraduates, Dr. Moore said that plans were in progress to advance the program to the M.S. level and make it equal to that at Dalhousie. Canadian funds had just become available to support this expansion.

According to several people I talked to in Barbados, the principal challenge here is to move from thought to action. The island boasts a fast-growing bank of knowledge about conservation issues and increasing numbers of people with skill and sophistication. Public awareness is on the upswing. "A lot of people are concerned, and a lot of people have ideas about what can be done," said Yvonne St. Hill. "The biggest task on Barbados now is to get the mechanisms in place." (Soon after our talk, St. Hill left the island and went to work for a regional organization in Guyana.)

As THE 1980s were reaching their end, the notion of sustainable development remained on the tips of many tongues in the Eastern Caribbean. Leaving the drug question aside, it was widely recognized that no commodity—not sugar, or bauxite, or winter vegetables for the U.S. market, or spices—is likely ever to replace tourism as these islands' principal source of income and employment. The trick would be to attract tourists while at the same time neither killing the golden egg that brought them to the islands nor abandoning all sense of local culture and pride in the face of the tourists' materialistic, hedonistic values. The bitter pill was there to be swallowed, and the hope was that somehow it would make West Indians feel better.

Outsiders—the Canadian and U.S. development assistance programs, the Organization of American States, several United Nations entities, a variety of U.S. conservation organizations—were uniformly eager to help. Too often, though, the assistance proffered consisted of flying visits by expensive consultants to pick local brains, then write reports calling for actions never implemented. Local conservation and historic preservation groups struggled on, with far too little money available to them to carry out their plans. Though one could point to a success here or there, and to an impressive array of individuals on the barricades and making heroic efforts to stem the tide, the general tendency along the chain seemed clear enough: yet another depressing chapter in the tormented history of these already battered, if still remarkably beautiful islands.

With such grim thoughts in mind, we aboard *Sanderling* now addressed an Everest of our own: negotiating the tedious 1,640-mile passage, against the current and upwind, from Barbados across to Fortaleza on Brazil's north coast.

Part III

THE BRAZILIAN
MIRACLE

13

Climbing Everest

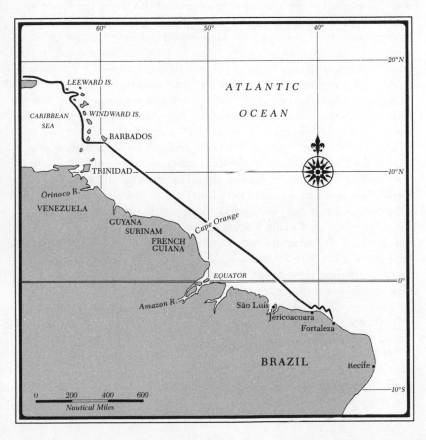

THE SEAS CONTAIN AN ELABORATE NETWORK OF FREEWAYS AND HIGH-
ways, roads and paths and trails. Large tankers and freighters thrum
along well-established routes between major ports, entering them along
"sea lanes" so burdened with traffic that they represent grave peril for
small vessels of *Sanderling*'s dimensions. Coastal and pelagic fishermen
follow age-old tracks from harbors to shoals, banks, or places where the
sea-floor contour changes sharply and fish gather to feed. Pleasure craft
too have their habits, moving in herds from anchorages and marinas out
into the harbors and bays. So cluttered are coastal and even offshore
waters, a naval officer had told me in Norfolk, that a modern aircraft
carrier often has trouble finding an available area large enough to
conduct operations.

Ocean sailors have their routes as well, following prevailing winds and
favorable currents to classic rendezvous points in the Canaries, the Bahamas, Barbados, Antigua, the Galápagos, the Marquesas, Tahiti, Tonga,
Fiji. Specialized support systems work around this trade; the Peace and
Plenty Hotel in the Exumas, and the Boatyard in Barbados are two such
facilities that *Sanderling* visited. Hamburgers, people looking for crew
positions, and forwarded mail are to be found there. By staying on the
familiar paths, a skipper of average capabilities, equipped with modern
devices like satellite navigation and Weatherfax machines, can undertake
a long ocean passage at no great risk. In Barbados I asked a young British
teenager how she had liked the twenty-day passage from the Canaries that
she had just made aboard a catamaran with her parents and two younger
siblings. "It was quite boring, actually," the girl unhesitatingly replied.

At the time I planned *Sanderling*'s itinerary, I was not fully aware of
how seldom ocean sailors hazard the direct passage from Barbados to
Brazil. Our destination, the port of Fortaleza on Brazil's north coast, lay
1,640 nautical miles to the southeast—against the prevailing winds and
against the strong Guiana Current. This invisible stream flows along
South America's northern coast, from Cabo São Roque at the northeastern corner of Brazil to Trinidad, at speeds of up to a fearsome four knots.
Since *Sanderling*'s best speed is about five and a half knots when sailing
close-reached against ocean swells, we risked being jostled and battered
by adverse winds and seas while making virtually no forward progress.

At best, the crossing would involve two weeks or more at sea. At
worst, we faced the possibility of having to give up the bone-jarring beat
to windward and revert to the easier but far longer and more time-
consuming conventional route, which consists of long off-wind passages
north toward Bermuda, then east to the Canaries, then a southwesterly
run down the prevailing trade winds to Brazil. Hoping to avoid such a
time-consuming, if less arduous cruise, I decided to take a shot at the

direct crossing. Ever practical, Flo suggested that instead I hire a delivery crew, fly to Fortaleza, and meet *Sanderling* there. Hardly sporting and not affordable, I sniffed, though I preferred the comforts of the coast and was barely qualified to lead an ocean passage of any sort. I was eager, moreover, to discover how far from shore one can still find evidence of coastal pollution, and perhaps also learn something of the effects of deep-sea contamination through ocean dumping.

Careful preparations would give our perhaps quixotic venture the greatest likelihood of success. The process began long before our departure. An early stop was at New York Nautical in lower Manhattan, a first-rate purveyor of marine charts, instruments, and other paraphernalia essential to the ocean navigator. Here I purchased a set of the Pilot Charts that, for all major oceans, indicate average wind and current directions and velocities for each month of the year. From these I established that our best chance of encountering the most northerly (that is to say, favorable) slant in the trade winds was during January and February; we timed our arrival in Barbados accordingly. At New York Nautical I also bought copies of the Sailing Directions published by the British Admiralty (which tell you to attempt practically nothing without local knowledge) and by the U.S. Defense Mapping Agency. These provided somewhat contradictory information about the strength and whereabouts of the Guiana Current. They also, to my great interest, suggested the likelihood of westerly countercurrents close inshore, from the mouth of the Amazon to Brazil's northeast corner, during periods of the northeasterly trades for which I was hoping. The best strategy, then, would be to aim for a February departure, hoping to pick up favorable slants to carry us past the Amazon more or less on the rhumb line (direct course) for Fortaleza. Once past the city of São Luís, at the western extremity of the Amazon system, we would edge in close to the beach in hopes of avoiding the full sweep of the Guiana Current, which achieves its greatest strength well offshore, and perhaps picking up the reported countercurrent.

I also bought a sextant and copies of the various publications required to work out sun, moon, and star sights. Our Satnav had been a gem, but we could not discount the possibility of engine or electrical power failure, or of lightning striking the antenna and knocking out the system. Though my ability to succeed at celestial navigation had never been put to the practical test, I had, admittedly more than thirty years ago, taken a detailed course in the subject at the U.S. Navy's Officer Candidate School. A distinct memory is of the leathery chief warrant officer who taught the course, filling several blackboards with numbers and hieroglyphics, then turning to the class with a smile and saying,

"Now you know where you're at." Fuzzy recollections of how to work the tables and do the calculations would get clearer with practice, I reckoned, and short of a disaster we would have the Satnav to give us a check on where we really were while sharpening our arithmetic skills and also getting used to shooting the sun from a pitching deck.

Health was another concern. Some long-distance sailors, I had read, voluntarily have their appendices removed prior to departure in order to reduce the risk of medical emergency at sea. Since we would never be more than a couple of days' sail from land, I opted to keep my organs in place. I did, however, think a good bit about how we might cope with various medical problems. My nephew Matthew, who has done several long passages, sent along an awesome checklist compiled by the committee that organizes the biennial Newport-to-Bermuda yacht race. It recommended sutures, scalpels, endless types of bandages and medicines—almost enough equipment for an operating room. I groaned and took the list to Dr. Tabb Moore, our family physician in Washington. He mercifully trimmed it, wrote me prescriptions for standard painkillers and antibiotics—and failed to cross out the sutures and scalpels. Off I went in search of these. The clerk at a hospital-supply store snorted. "Whaddaya mean, sew up people at sea with no experience?" he asked. He solved the problem by handing me some heavy-duty butterfly tapes, and some even stronger materials, which many doctors now often use in preference to the old catgut and needle. With Dr. Moore I also set up a system wherein I could radiotelephone him either at his office or at the Georgetown University Hospital emergency room, in case of a serious illness or injury.

As for calamities that might require us to abandon ship in the open ocean, we already had aboard a standard emergency kit, including a radio signal broadcasting device called an EPIRB; a six-man inflatable life raft containing its own comprehensive inventory of survival equipment; and our regular Achilles eight-and-a-half-foot rubber dinghy. I added supplements: one-liter plastic bottles of fresh water, stored handily in the lazarets (the storage bins under the cockpit seats); a dozen tightly sealed packets of the kinds of Army rations that require no cooking; fishing lures. If we were forced to take to the lifeboats so far off the beaten track, I figured, our chances of getting picked up by a passing ship would be poor. More likely, with the wind and current at our backs, we would eventually wash up somewhere in the Caribbean; my hope was to be well enough supplied to enable us to survive en route.

Our diet aboard *Sanderling*, I decided, would not consist of the spartan fare that some racing skippers inflict upon their crews: tube number one, tube number two, etc. Nor, while I am normally willing to slave long hours at the stove to eat well, could I raise my sights too high. Though we would probably be able to keep our refrigerator functioning well enough to keep the beer and sodas cold and the butter from melting, we could not expect things to remain frozen for more than the first few days. Even with a well-designed gimbaled gas stove boasting three burners and an oven, I had learned, cooking when the seas are running is a game of hazards and frustrations, spillages and expletives, bruises and burns. The level I would aim for was what we came to call Baute Cuisine. Our basics were frozen meat and chicken for the outset, and a large ham. This we supplemented with an inventory of durable fresh fruits and vegetables, plus a wide variety of pastas, packaged rice dishes, couscous and other grains, and canned goods. Into seven large boxes of food that I had mailed from Washington to St. Thomas (in order to avoid sky-high local prices) I had also slipped a few special treats, such as good olive oil and vinegar, various herbs and sauces and spices. Aboard was also a substantial supply of fallback foods—canned chili, baked beans, and the like—to which we would turn if we failed to catch the expected volume of fresh fish. (As things turned out, I suspect that some of the crew members actually preferred Heinz's beans, with great lashings of catsup and taco sauce and *salsa picante*, to my own carefully constructed Under Way Poulet.)

Peter, my loyal first mate, had been spending endless hours in St. Thomas getting the boat up to scratch for the long voyage. With some professional help he renovated or replaced large sections of the engine (which had suffered greatly from an unscheduled saltwater bath one night in Tortola), fiddled with the electrical system, moved the electronics to a new place where they would stay drier, bought extra tools and other supplies. In Antigua, on the way to Barbados, we paused to have *Sanderling* hauled and her bottom scraped and repainted. We also checked the rudder mountings, the stuffing box (where the drive shaft emerges from the hull and meets the propeller), and the other through-hull fittings. Peter ascended the mast and activated our long-laggard wind-speed indicator. We added a scoop to the hull that, according to the Antigua Slipways manager, would probably force enough seawater into our balky refrigeration compressor's cooling pipes to keep the system going even while we were under way.

As ever, Pete would constitute the mainstay of the crew and would alternate with me as watch captain. By the time we reached Barbados he had been aboard almost full-time and for almost a year. With the help of the Perkins manual, a slim and priceless volume called *The 12-Volt Doctor*, and many friends he had made along the way, Peter had learned the boat almost by heart. He had become far more confident of his nautical abilities and, in many ways, more of a man. Steve Riehemann would be aboard for the crossing. We would find most useful his fishing skills, the detailed knowledge of the rules of the road that he had acquired during a recent successful quest for a captain's license, and his bull strength. In Barbados we would, finally, welcome Matt, a recent Harvard graduate, son of my childhood neighbor Lawrence Huntington. Over the course of three Bermuda races and many shorter sails around northeastern U.S. waters, Matt had become an accomplished yachtsman, sail handler, and jury-rigger; we would also come to appreciate his unflagging good nature, keen sense of humor, and inability to balk at even the least agreeable assignment. The four of us would split into two pairs (Pete and Steve, Matt and me) to stand deck watches on the Swedish system: 0600 to 1200, 1200 to 1800, 1800 to 2200, 2200 to 0200, 0200 to 0600. One man would tend the helm; the other would remain on standby on deck or below. With five watches a day instead of the conventional four on/four off system, the more hazardous and more tiring nighttime duties would be shared equally among us. I would act as meal planner and cook and also, though all hands were invited to take their own sights and run their own plots, as official navigator.

In Barbados we spent a week anchored in Carlisle Bay off the Boatyard while an amorous, temporarily beached professional captain named Eric made us a Bimini awning to shade the cockpit from the tropical sun, and an auto mechanic named Darcy wrestled (ineffectively, as it turned out) with a burnt alternator. We stocked up on food, ate a last excellent Boatyard hamburger, began listening to weather broadcasts, eventually screwed up our courage and began. Here is a selection from the journal I kept during our venture out into the open seas:

Sunday, February 7. Day One

In the morning we hunted Eric down after an evening during which, he informed us several times, "two women" had cooked him dinner. He showed up at 1030 to finish our Bimini. By soon after noon he had the Naugahyde, or whatever it was, stretched tight and secure over the cockpit seats. We had finished our other last-minute chores; jerry cans of extra fuel and water lashed to the stanchions on deck made us look salty and very high-seas. We upped anchor and headed for the gas dock near the deep-water port. While *Sanderling* awaited a space at this busy place, Steve ferried me in the dinghy across to the port terminal building, where I attempted to complete three necessary pre-departure stops: port clearance, customs, and immigration. On this lazy Sunday

Sanderling preparing to leave Barbados.

afternoon *none* of the three men I needed to see was on hand when I arrived. Within an hour, though, I lacked only immigration's clearance and posted myself at the foot of the locked office door. Eventually the duty officer sauntered in, a *Penthouse* magazine under his arm. He placed it on his desk and whistled me through.

Back aboard *Sanderling*, I was greeted by a strong rainsquall. We decided to return to nearby Carlisle Bay, drop anchor again, have an early dinner, then make our belated launch. We accomplished this sequence on schedule, motoring definitively out of the anchorage under a slight drizzle to the accompaniment of cheery radio goodbyes from neighbor yachts and the Knowles brothers, the Boatyard's fun-loving owners. As darkness fell we watched the lights of the island's southwest corner twinkle on, then fade as we moved out into what became a messy night with frequent squalls alternating with periods of near-calm. Many sail adjustments required. Matt and I stood the first watch, up to 2200, since we all agreed that, if anyone, it should be the captain to put a premature end to the expedition by running the boat up on the reef off the Hilton Hotel.

Luckily I avoided this fate. After clearing the island we could for a while almost fetch our rhumb line of 140 degrees magnetic—southeast by south on the old compass rose. We sailed close-hauled on port tack, the wind blowing across our port bow. But soon we were sagging off in the general direction of Trinidad. We'll need better than this to avoid a truly miserable passage.

Monday, February 8. Day Two

Squalls, some heavy, marked our full night along with choppy, confused seas. It blew at 20–25 knots as well. The combination soon reduced all three of my crew members to a semi-comatose state, and in a communications foul-up I failed to register with them that a potent seasick remedy was to be found in Dr. Moore's medicine kit. We made good time, soon leaving Barbados well astern as we dodged heavy ship traffic. Morning brought our first misfortune when the refrigerator cooling system's pump failed to perform despite our Antigua scoop, and the compressor switch dutifully turned it off when the overheating point was reached. For all our efforts we *still* lacked a refrigeration system that works reliably at sea.

The squalls dwindled as the day advanced. By afternoon we were sailing smoothly, laying the rhumb line, in 20 knots of breeze. At nightfall I temporarily resurrected the refrigeration system, at least enough to get the beer cooled down. The crew, still feeling lumpish, managed to choke down hamburgers for dinner. With our balky fridge we'll have to eat our way through the fresh stuff fast, and hope to catch some fish later on.

Almost exactly 100 miles for the first twenty-four hours. Not bad.

Tuesday, February 9. Day Three

Overnight we had smooth water and fast sailing, and were able to head a little above the rhumb line. The breeze freshened and in the morning we shifted from our large genoa to the working jib. 180 miles made good by midday. Had our last fresh avocado for lunch. Radio, engine, and Satnav all working fine. In the afternoon I had another heroic go at the refrigeration system and this time had better luck. The procedure is no fun. Turn on the engine, activate the switches, open the starboard lazaret, uncouple the seawater cooling exhaust hose, SUCK until you taste salt water. Get water running steadily through to supplement the feeble pump, drain into a bucket. When bucket full, hand-pump into self-bailing cockpit. When dribble stops, SUCK again to revive the stream. This action required about fifteen times in the forty-five minutes or so that it takes to chill things down.

We decided to switch off the freezer (already, not much left to keep frozen), but try to keep the refrigerator section going for cold drinks, eggs, butter, cheese, etc.

Wednesday, February 10. Day Four

Matt got the morning off to a rousing start when, going off watch at 0600, he spotted a tear in the mainsail. After breakfast all hands turned to and we wrestled it down for resewing. During the process Peter found a major sag in the cable around which the sail rolls as it furls into the mast. We hauled him up to the top of the mast, fifty-four feet above the sea. Hanging on tightly as the seas swung him around in long arcs, he discovered that a three-quarter-inch stainless-steel rod at the upper end of the rig had sheared right off. We had no replacement aboard and, as we sewed away at the main, we wondered if we would be able to get the mainsail back up and the essential roller-furling system working again.

I scanned charts and sailing directions for clues as to where we might go to get what was left of the pin rethreaded or a replacement made. The entries to coastal towns of the Guianas looked forbidding. Each has a river with a shallow bar at its mouth and all sorts of other hazards to navigation, and we had no large-scale (detailed) charts for this portion of the coast. Turn back under jury rig? To where? Barbados? Trinidad? I juggled the options as we continued sewing under a bright sun. Then I found what I had previously missed in the Sailing Directions: the easy-access deep-water port that serves Cayenne, French Guiana—only 300 miles away, on a heading that we might well achieve under jib and engine if we could not rehoist and refurl the main.

By 1700, the crew had made the heartening discovery that the pin was not integral and that the mainsail would function adequately without it. With the emergency ended, we got back under way in a fair breeze. The Satnav was telling us that the Guiana Current was behaving like a kitten and having no major effect on our progress. We were, however, already well south of the rhumb line and I faced the choice of whether to continue closing with the coast or to tack away to the north and away from our destination. Recalling the possibility of a countercurrent, I chose the coast.

Thursday, February 11. Day Five

Am having trouble being systematic about writing this. There is much to do with six hours a day on the helm (the autopilot's not much good going to windward), navigating, cooking, sleeping, and coping with crises such as yesterday's. So these entries will become anecdotal rather than formal daily records. It's now 0830, Matt sailing, I due to relieve him in half an hour, Pete and Steve sleeping as usual (at least for Steve) when off watch. Overnight we continued to make good speed—four to four and a half knots over the bottom despite the adverse current which must be unusually weak at the moment. We've even picked up a more northerly slant on the wind, and edged back a little closer to the rhumb line. No further troubles with the sails, or anything else, for that matter. Pete's worries about mildewed clothing may resurface as a high priority. "That's my entire wardrobe down there," he bellowed when I joked about his concern.

The main cabin is full of wet and dirty clothes and beginning to smell like a locker room after a basketball game in an overheated gym. Matt, mindful of previous blue-water experiences, has suggested that we belay the personal remarks, no matter how bad things get, until we're safely ashore.

The Satnav says 1,242 miles to Fortaleza. We're almost a quarter of the way.

Friday, February 12. Day Six.

At dinnertime yesterday I reviewed our progress and the charts and what they say about the currents, and discussed our options with the crew. We decided that we would abandon sailing as close to the wind as possible, trying to claw our way back to the rhumb line (we were about forty miles south of it). Instead we would loosen our sheets a little, gaining some speed, and head inshore toward less current against us. So we steered 135 degrees all night, about ten degrees lower than we could have. It should have made the going easier. But we had a splashy, confused sea that made the first two watches wet and uncomfortable—even with the Bimini and the dodger up, the man at the wheel still often gets a good soaking. But then as the half-moon rose the weather mellowed and we had a pretty dawn this a.m. with the Southern Cross still high in the sky.

A ship passed in the night—only the second we had seen—and then a freighter this morning. The latter radioed us a position which coincided almost exactly with what our own Satnav was telling us. Further excitement when Steve hauled in a five-pound tuna (our first fish). He cleaned it and we ate it for lunch. Just before lunch he also caught a ten-pound wahoo, which we'll have for dinner—three of us, that is, since Matt is, of all things, allergic to almost all kinds of seafood. Timely, since we ate our last fresh meat last night, and from now on it's either fresh fish or into the cans and paper boxes.

In the morning we bore well off (to 160 degrees) to get into shallower water and out of the current. By this evening we should be there and able to make better progress over the ground, on our rhumb-line heading. We're now due north of the western end of French Guiana, headed toward Cayenne and Cape Orange at the northwesterly corner of Brazil. We've covered better than 500 miles and will soon reach the one-third mark. Steve points out that this leaves two-thirds of the way to go. But if my strategy works the last two-thirds will be quicker. It's beautiful today, with the breeze down to 12–15 knots. A good time for drying out and cleaning up.

Saturday, February 13. Day Seven

0645. The wahoo (with Muscadet alongside) was great, and the overnight sail balmy with hardly any sea and a 15-knot breeze on the beam. But I'll have to eat those words about the current. No sooner did we get into the shallower water than the current accelerated and we *lost* headway. Forward progress reduced from about 4.5 nautical miles an hour during previous days to only an average of 2.75 from 1600 yesterday to 0600 this morning. Now we're bearing off a bit to get even closer inshore. The Sailing Directions disagree about just how close we need to be to get out of the current's full blast. DMA (the U.S. Defense Mapping Agency) says that the band lies 60–120 miles offshore; the British Admiralty says that it's 150–300 miles out, with the current diminishing within the 200-meter depth line. We're already within that, only about 70 miles offshore and headed closer, so soon we'll be in good position according to both sets of directions. At the moment we're moving through the water at six knots, or almost. There is hope.

All hands are in better spirits after yesterday's lull, and the final traces of the crew's *mal de mer* (to which I am apparently immune) gone. It was good to be able to report high morale to Flo last night on the SSB radio—by prearrangement we're checking in with her every three days—and it does *my* morale good to hear her voice from time to time. It's interesting to be doing this, but in any number of ways I won't be sorry when it's over.

1500. Soon after dawn we began to make better progress—30 miles in the five hours ending at 1100. So we must have just hit the corner of the bad stuff. Cayenne is now due south, 75 miles away, and Cape Orange will be abeam when we've gone another 120 miles. 1,024 miles to Fortaleza. We've had a nice breeze all day—changed back to the big jib at lunchtime—and are rolling along in hot hazy weather.

Sunday, February 14. Day Eight

1015. Valentine's Day. Ham and baked beans for dinner last night since Steve failed to catch a usable fish—only a bonito that he unhesitatingly rejected because of its bloody flesh and oily taste. Then a night consisting in large part of quite a bit of wind (over 20 knots) and confused seas. At 0200 we reduced the jib and the wind and sea eased a little too. Then a beautiful dawn watch with a crescent moon and Scorpio high in the sky. We are still averaging four to five knots over the bottom. Not bad, though I'd still like to be picking up some of that alleged countercurrent. I guess we'll have to wait at least a day for that. This morning we're chugging along under gray but not threatening skies.

Cape Orange is now past due south and we're therefore in Brazilian waters with 944 miles to go. This morning we shifted to a new, larger-scale chart: Cayenne to São Luís. Had Real Coffee for breakfast. Not easy to make with things jumping around on the stove. Almost a week without a cup and can't say I missed it a lot, though it tasted good.

How am I doing physically? O.K., I think, though sleep is sporadic. But I feel alert and focused and am constantly busy with navigating or cleaning up or writing or something. Even Pete feels optimistic, so we must be doing something right. Today we're conducting a pool on our arrival date/time. Secret ballots, not to be opened until we get there, due tomorrow a.m.

Monday, February 15. Day Nine

How could it be that I haven't gotten back to this journal since yesterday morning? Well, that's the way it is on this kind of a trip. On watch all yesterday afternoon, at the helm or navigating for much of it. That meant going to sleep right after dinner, so as to get ready for Steve's by now famous wake-up call ("Fahve minutes, y'all") and be on deck for the 2200 to 0200 watch. Then back to sleep. Then on watch again from 0600 to 1200. Then a radiotelephone call to New York to propose to an arriving crew member, Tim Hogen, that we rendezvous in Natal on the 29th and to ask him to bring: (a) a new voltage regulator, (b) a new and more powerful pump for our famous compressor cooling system, and (c) a new jib roller outhaul line to replace the one we are now using, which parted and is tied together. Then refrigerator sucking, lunch, a short nap, and here we are.

Good progress. 140 miles achieved (808 to go) since my entry of yesterday morning. The northeast wind blew a steady 20 all day yesterday and all last night, putting five to six knots on our speedo at all times. Mostly cloudy weather but no rain. Our only problem is short, confused seas because we are not in deep water but up on the bank. Every now and then comes a warning THUMP as our bow crashes down, once with enough power to tear loose a well-installed shelf above the starboard berth in the forward cabin. Then a breathless little delay. Then a sheet of water slants across the cockpit. We're seldom dry. I've taken to wearing only a bathing suit under my foul-weather jacket and assuming the worst. In order to air out the main cabin, where things have gotten a little fetid, we often leave open the little overhead hatch, which is covered by a dodger. Still, sometimes a rogue wave sneaks around the dodger and drenches things below—often including either me or Steve on the starboard bunk, as well as the stack of charts that I keep just above. Steve had a rare tantrum when he recently took this kind of a washdown.

Other than these sorts of waterfalls, we have few weather-related complaints at the moment. The big question is what lies ahead when we reach the so-called Intertropical Convergence Zone with its alternating squalls and flat calms. The zone supposedly moves up and down near the equator, reaching its southernmost point at São Luís in December and then edging gradually back northward. But here we are at below 4 degrees north latitude, and no sign of it yet. The optimist would have us ride the northeast trades right on into Fortaleza. But we shall see.

Now we are well east (90 miles) and even a little south of Cape Orange, and therefore in what one might in a broad sense call the mouth of the Amazon, though the water remains clear and with no sign of the river's muddy outflow that allegedly extends several hundred miles out into the sea. It is a striking fact, though, that it will take us several days to cross this mouth (past Marajó Island, itself larger than Switzerland)

and reach São Luís, still almost 400 miles away. How mighty and vast the ocean seems from this perspective: the Amazon spewing out a volume of water equivalent to two World Trade Centers *per second*, and yet not a trace of sediment in the water here. Could it be that we have exaggerated the ocean's frailty, unnecessarily lost our long-standing belief in its might as a cleansing agent? Perhaps not, but out here, from this vantage point, a speck in this great emptiness, it's tempting to think that you could dump many bargeloads of garbage and never find a trace of it again. Heresy: don't print that, Stone. But it's the way being out here makes you feel. We, anyway, continue to separate our garbage, filling and sinking our bottles and cans and setting adrift only what is biodegradable.

As I write, a squall is hitting—our first, really, since leaving Barbados.

Today was the deadline for our arrival-pool submissions. I guessed at 0800 this coming Sunday, which means that we will have to maintain an average speed over the bottom of 5.9 knots. This means, in turn, that I have bet on our finding the favorable inshore countercurrent that has formed the basis of our navigation strategy. As we search for this we are holding about 60 miles south of the rhumb line. No sign yet of anything in our favor. At least we may have been shielded from the worst of the adverse current.

Few birds, no fish striking at Steve's wonderful pink lure, few ships (though one did pass last night), no airplanes overhead. We are occupying our own lonely stretch of planet. No wonder we spend so much time stargazing. Venus and Mercury are up early in the evening. Then comes a parade. With Orion directly above, we get Pleiades and Aries to the north, then southward along the Milky Way to Sirius the Dog Star and his constellation Canis Major, Leo, Libra, Virgo, and finally the splendid Southern Cross in the southern sky with the Scorpion in the southeast. The Starfinder, a floppy rubber yarmulke, has been in heavy use and Matt and Pete have begun to identify even the obscure stars and groups with some ease.

More than halfway to Fortaleza now. Impatience to "get there" settling in.

Tuesday, February 16. Day Ten

0830. The near-squall of yesterday produced nothing more than a few spatters of rain. Then it began to clear slightly and remained so overnight, with little dark clouds scuttling fast under brightening stars.

With the wind continuing northeast at 20 knots or more, we crashed along fast, doing six knots or better through the water. Under other circumstances one might have called this wet sleigh ride "exhilarating." This far out and this waterlogged, I yearn for a calmer, if slower trip and less of a wrestling match at the helm. Nevertheless, we are eating up the miles—119 in the last twenty-four hours—and one senses the beginning of a fast homestretch. The question is still whether we will carry these strong northeast trades all the way in, or whether we will in fact have to endure the calms and squalls of the doldrums.

Late yesterday afternoon, just as I was about to break out hash for dinner, we reeled in a fifteen-pound wahoo and gladly ate lots of it instead, with pasta and a good bottled red sauce. As I was dishing up, Matt, a hearty eater, looked into the pasta pot and, crestfallen, asked if the amount I had cooked was supposed to be for all of us. I said yes and he accepted a moderate portion. Quietly, a little while later, after we had eaten and the dishes were done, he whipped himself up another large bowlful. Even with his large appetite, and Peter's, which is no slouch, the stores are generally holding up well. We could go for weeks beyond Fortaleza and still not starve. We also still have plenty of fresh water in our big tanks, and have used only ten of our eighty-five gallons of fuel to run the engine for battery charging and to keep up the refrigeration.

To make my predicted arrival time, we now must average a good six knots for the rest of the way. That countercurrent better start shaping up!

1700. Blew quite strong all morning, mellowed at noon, and we've had a pleasant afternoon with 15–18 knots of breeze and a dry cockpit. Peter called his parents, our close friends, on the radiotelephone and it was good to hear their voices. Peter's father, also a keen sailor, has been monitoring our progress on a chart that he keeps in his office in Santa Monica. He is worried about our being too far south.

Must break now to cook dinner. *Wahoo à la escabeche ce soir.* 680 miles to go, says Satnav. 120 miles a day of regular progress, plus 200 extra because of a lift from the current, if we are to make our arrival prediction. I fear I was a touch optimistic.

Wednesday, February 17. Day Eleven

A sunny morning with the breeze at just the right strength and direction. We bowl along, in relatively calm seas, at six knots through the water. Moreover, since 0200 we have made good 46 miles over the bottom, meaning that we are getting a one-knot lift from the current! About 580 miles to go, or one-third of the total distance. It should go faster than the first third.

We are now more or less due north of the Rio Pará, the easterly entrance to the Amazon. Along the Pará lies Belém, the principal city at the river's mouth. Though we are now only about 75 miles from shore, we still see no indication whatever of Amazonia or any land of any sort being close by except for large swells that signal a shelving bottom.

Last night's wahoo was damn good. The classic combo of butter, olive oil, onions, garlic, canned crushed tomatoes, a little hot sauce. Just cook this a while, then poach the fish in it for a few minutes and it comes out "real tender," as Steve put it. Matt got by with a large can of corned-beef hash, rice, and the balance of the tomatoes. This morning we had pancakes. Everybody approved.

If we are to arrive at Fortaleza at my forecast time we shall have to average seven knots. Even with a favorable current, that's improbable.

Thursday, February 18. Day Twelve

Under a gray squally sky we are approaching a point about 90 miles due north of São Luís and we are flying! From 1600 yesterday to 0400 today we did in fact average seven knots. Only 425 miles to go now. At about 0400 we crossed the equator—the first time for Pete and Steve. I didn't have the heart to wake them up and play Neptune. We also crossed from winter to summer, and were now picking up commercial Brazilian stations—as well as the portentous BBC World Service and U.S. Armed Forces Radio—on our little battery-powered Sony radio. Carnival had just ended, the announcers were lamenting, and listeners would simply have to face the reality of struggling through another year before the beginning of the next one.

All of us have sore butts (red, welts) from spending too much time sitting at the helm in salty wet pants.

1815. Enter the doldrums! All went well until late this morning, when the breeze started to slacken. By noon our speed was down to three knots and rain clouds were building. A squall was imminent and the wind shifted against us, pushing us closer to shore. We've spent the afternoon mostly in rain, heading well to the south of where we want to go, and navigating to avoid the unmarked (except by a wreck) reef called Manoel Luís that lies well off the coast. Funny currents around here, and strong ones. Despite corrective actions under power, we have still been swept to within ten miles of this hazard.

Everything and everybody wet. With the humidity near 100 percent, nothing dries. Spirits still generally high, but what next uncertain.

Friday, February 19. Day Thirteen

1200. Last night, by means of some attentive coastal navigation, we managed to avoid Manoel Luís. But we could accomplish little more than that. The doldrums gave us their share of flat or almost calm, which meant many sail adjustments and much slatting around. I considered motor-sailing, but for the sake of the sleeping off-duty watch abandoned the idea. Eight stinking miles made good between 0200 and 0600. Dawn broke under a threatening bank of low dark clouds, and soon we were in a long one-hour squall. It carried hard rain and plenty of wind right out of the east. Now we're motor-sailing and doing all right but not brilliantly.

Fortaleza seems very far away. 317 long miles to go. At this rate it looks like a Monday a.m. arrival. But perhaps we'll still get some good wind or current to speed things up. I'm sleepy now and about to retire for a siesta even with the engine blasting.

Saturday, February 20. Day Fourteen

0615. What a difference a few good hours can make. Yesterday afternoon everything happened at once—the squalls stopped, the seas calmed, the breeze settled at the ideal 18 knots, and we sailed through a splendid red cloud-spattered sunset into a starry night. The new moon rose, with Venus and Mercury lined up above it. Though we could not make our way back toward the rhumb line, we were able to stay even with it and make good speed.

Dawn came at 0400. We still don't know what time it is locally; as we have worked our way eastward, we have remained on Barbados time and daylight has come progressively earlier. Overnight we saw the flashing light on the Barra das Preguiças (Sloth Beach)—our first direct indication of land, though we have not yet seen this low coast. Many terns are flying now, after many days with practically no birds, and the sea has turned from deep blue to a milky green.

Soon we shall finally have to tack for the first time in two weeks. Even though the straight-line distance to Fortaleza is down to 233 miles,

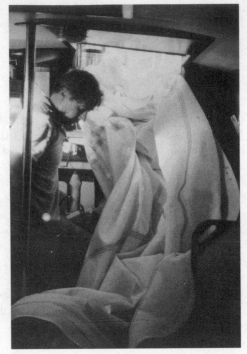

A crewman at work en route to Brazil.

I fear that we will have to sail some 300 to get there and that—with still no sign of the favorable current—we will not get there until late Monday. At least, apparently, we are clear of the Intertropical Convergence Zone.

0915. Terra. Soon after they came on watch at 0600, Pete and Steve sighted low dunes. Two fishing boats inspected us. At 0700 we finally tacked. It was too hot for good sleeping; I played Steve's game and lay along the lee rail, letting the beautiful green water wash over.

In shifting winds and still against the current, we managed to gain only six miles toward Fortaleza all morning. At noon I decided to motor straight into the dead-easterly wind, a tactic which infuriated Peter, who wanted a quiet, relatively cool cabin to sleep in. By 1500 the wind shifted back toward the north; tonight we will continue tacking along the shore, doing our best to stay out of the current. At least the weather is good and the breeze moderate. Thus we creep toward Fortaleza. It's still 212 miles away, meaning that since early this morning we've made good only 21.

Sunday, February 21. Day Fifteen

0830. For a while last night we perked along pretty well, making good headway in shallow water, close inshore and out of the current. During the night we sailed close under the point at the head of the broad golden beach at Jericoacoara, said to be one of Brazil's most beautiful, populated by few but fisherfolk. It was tempting to stop and anchor under the lee of the point, even though it would not have been cricket. Tired, I slept soundly after going off watch and dreamed about golf. Then awoke to hear Peter fuming about no wind and squalls and not fucking getting anywhere. I suggested the engine and Pete complied. But forty-five minutes later he shut it down, alleging that it had again fallen victim to its old Bahamian and Caribbean ailment, surging. "I can't work on it now," said Pete. "It's too hot." "No," I replied. "You're too hot. Go to sleep." Pete did so and now we're tacking along the coast in a light easterly that's full of holes. We do not know exactly where we are, for the Satnav has not yielded a fix in almost five hours. It seems not to like this time of day.

1600. Late in the morning, revived, Peter cleaned a very dirty air filter and thought that this simple fix would cure the surging of the engine. We ran it to charge up the fridge and batteries, also to give us extra speed in the light air. Soon came another agonizing surge. Peter has yet to crawl back into the pit and probably will not until tomorrow morning. It always takes him a while to work up to the grimy business, and he's the only one of us who knows how to try to fix the surging.

By current standards we have been making reasonable progress today. Still, this is dreary stuff with the end so near and yet so far. The pattern now is that the easterly wind has a southerly slant to it in the morning as a result of the overnight land-breeze effect. Then, as the sun warms the land and the sea breeze fills in, the wind comes on stronger from the northeast for the afternoon and evening. If the pattern holds, we should by tomorrow morning be off the Banco Aracau, where the coast turns southeast, with perhaps 120 miles to go. This would indicate an arrival around midday Tuesday and a sixteen-day sail in all—still not bad, but not the fourteen-day sail that at one point we thought we might accomplish.

Two small fishing canoes passed us, close aboard. Occupants seemed curious but said nothing, hardly even waved as they passed. No birds around now.

Monday, February 22. Day Sixteen

0645. Where, I keep asking myself, are the trade winds "at right angles to the shore" that we're supposed to get along here? Right now the wind is coming dead out of the *south*, the ocean swells are slapping against our lee rail, and we are poking along at three knots or so. The norther should be coming along later this morning, and when it does we'll be well positioned to give it a good ride. We can expect to hit Fortaleza sometime tomorrow. Now we are having an extra-close look at the low sandy coast and the milk-green water lying off it. Peaceful, if slow.

Talked with Flo on the radio last night. Only three weeks till she gets to Salvador for our March 14 rendezvous, then Leslie a week later. Going to sleep now.

Tuesday, February 23. Day Seventeen

0630. Don't know why I never got around to writing anything further yesterday, as it was lazy, calm, easy going all day. We tacked quietly along the shore in light to moderate air, enjoying the scenery of high dunes, green water, blue sky. Little fishing villages dotted the shore, clusters of small white red-roofed houses. At one point Peter counted seventeen fishing canoes at work a mile or two off the beach, each with a crew of several dark brown men dressed in tatters, all standing upright as spray flew over the low topsides and their vessel bucked and pitched. When clouds came later in the day, and a few thunderstorms built up over the land, the light turned a striking silver. Dry desolate coast; no condos here.

The same conditions prevailed overnight, though as usual the wind veered back toward the south as morning approached. Yesterday morning we had broken the 100-miles-to-go barrier. By afternoon the magic number had dropped to 75, and now we were truly closing in. Conversation was turning to reminiscences of the voyage and the boat's performance, and of showers and steaks. At this writing, a bit more than 40 miles to go and the scent of victory, even though there has been no sign whatever of the alleged favorable inshore countercurrent. We shall use the engine if necessary, even though Peter has wanted to baby it for fear of renewed surging and a flameout at some critical moment.

Yesterday morning, while Pete was still asleep, I started the engine in full knowledge that he would jump up at the sound and appear on deck to urge caution. He did exactly that. "What are you smiling about?" he asked. "Oh, nothing," I replied. "Well, I'm the one who'll be down there working all day if it quits," he snarled, and returned to his bunk.

We have no harbor chart for Fortaleza, but the Sailing Directions make the entry look quite easy—one reef to get around, and that one well marked. Anyhow, we'll have to hurry on to get there by nightfall.

1330. Just before noon, shimmery spikes appeared close aboard the port bow. Gradually they turned into buildings, grew larger, and became—Fortaleza! From a distance it resembled Atlantic City or even Miami Beach, a line of white high-rises massed against the shore. For the last couple of hours we have been skirting the beach west of town, watching the abrupt transformation from the pristine emptiness of the Brazilian coast we have seen so far to coastal resort development and now to the outskirts of a large city. Now we are passing ugly large hotels or apartment buildings and housing subdivisions hard on the dunes: high rolling mounds of sand behind, golden beach in front, dune buggies scurrying about.

11.2 miles to go as the crow flies, probably 15 including one last tack out to sea, so we will not be in until late afternoon. But we WILL BE IN!

Wednesday, February 24, 0630

And we were. Slowly, as we tacked along the shore, the city rose before us, whiter and larger than we expected. Several tankers lay anchored in the roadstead behind the point that forms the harbor, and as we rounded the reef we could clearly see the large modern quay for the large ships. Lacking a detailed chart, we radioed for directions, in Portuguese and in English, to a large seagoing tug that flew the Union Jack, but received no intelligible reply. As we continued our gingerly approach, now in fading daylight, a small motor vessel materialized and a smiling man pointed to the end of a large finger pier. "Go around there," he yelled. "You'll find the yacht club on the other side." We followed his directions. At 1730 we were at anchor—15 days, 23 hours, and 51 minutes after our final departure from Carlisle Bay.

Adjacent to us was a sturdy motor-sailer called the *Clymene*. After we got squared away and our dinghy was reinflated, I rowed over and hailed the occupants, a pleasant South African named Martin Henning, various members of his family, and one unrelated crew member.

Henning asked me aboard, offered fruit (not exactly what I had in mind), and told me his sad story. Several days before, *Clymene* had arrived off Fortaleza after a trouble-free 4,000-mile sail from Cape Town to St. Helena, Ascension, and Fernando de Noronha islands. Playing it by the book, the Hennings requested and received aboard a pilot to guide them into the harbor. The pilot brought them in very close to the yacht club at high tide, told them it was safe to anchor there, and departed. The tide went out and *Clymene* grounded on jagged rocks, badly damaging her rudder. Now Henning was in search of a place to get his boat hauled and repaired. The only offer he had received so far was from a man who handled large ships and would do the job for a mere $6,000.

Understandably suspicious of Brazilians after this reception, the Hennings passed on somber warnings about the behavior of the fishermen aboard the many small vessels anchored nearby. Many yachts had been robbed of gear left on deck; in the dead of night, unless one exercised extreme care, thieves might sneak up on a foreign yacht, haul up its anchor, unshackle it, and replace it with a stone. To prevent such eventualities, the Hennings always left one person aboard at night; even during daylight hours, at the very least, one of them would keep an eye out from the terrace of the yacht club. Since they were planning to remain aboard for the evening, they added, they volunteered to keep an eye on *Sanderling* so that we could go in and have dinner at the yacht club.

I accepted this invitation with enthusiasm, rowed back to *Sanderling*, and reported the Hennings' grim news. All hands turned to, stowing all loose deck gear we could lay our hands on: jib sheets, emergency raft, man-overboard pole, life preservers. Then we rowed to the yacht club float and stepped ashore, lurching and careening at this first experience of steady dry land in more than a fortnight. With the instinct of a dazed bloodhound, Matt made for the shower tucked in beside the ultramodern, brand-new club. We weaved after him into a froth of fresh water, shampoo, soap. Then we sat down to a fine dinner. During the course of it we opened our ship's pool ballots. We had all been far too optimistic, except for Steve, whose prediction was only eight hours ahead of our actual arrival time.

Reviewing the voyage, we agreed that we had been extraordinarily lucky with the weather—only a few hours of calm in the doldrums, no severe squalls or storms. Conditions had in fact closely resembled what was forecast in the Sailing Directions. "What went wrong with your boat?" Mrs. Henning had cheerfully asked. I was almost ashamed to admit to practically no trouble except for the three-inch tear in the mainsail, the engine gasps that now seemed a distant memory, the balky refrigeration system (which limped through to the end, sucking required at each start-up), and the problem with the mainsail roller-furling rod that may have long predated our departure. In all, not a long gripe list. On the positive side, we could point to a number of heroes: the Satnav, so precise that we knew we were more right than one passing freighter that gave us a slightly sloppy position; the head, the stove, indeed the *boat*, which sailed well indeed in heavy seas and made good overall progress for a cruising vessel not designed for speed.

One might not want to try our route a second time. But we have done it and I am pleased. Not the elation one feels at the end of a physically draining sailboat race, nor the sense of relief that comes from tying up after a bad storm or a cold wet ride. More, in this case, a mood of quieter satisfaction, and the unexpected confidence of thinking that if Fortaleza had been twice as far away, we would still have gotten there in good shape.

14

Around Calcanhar

"P'RA INGLÊS VER"—FOR ENGLISH EYES. BRAZILIANS OFTEN USE THIS sardonic phrase to describe sand castles they build to create, for foreign visitors, favorable impressions of their land and cities, their morals, their levels of efficiency and modernity.

Much in today's Brazil is worthy of a demanding Colonel Blimp's admiration. Even midsize Brazilian cities now boast elaborate multi-level shopping centers, some including the chic storefront names of the Faubourg St.-Honoré, Rodeo Drive, Madison Avenue, Via Veneto. The tidy Bom Preço supermarket has largely replaced the hurly-burly of the street *feira*, at least in upper-class sections of town. Airline offices have computer reservation hookups that actually work; many small towns have airports and scheduled service that usually shows up. The phone system, still sporadic in the mid-1960s when Flo and I lived in Rio, is greatly improved. Four-lane highways link the big cities, and along them whir cheap, comfortable, clean express buses. Tall new buildings and expensive first-class restaurants abound in Fortaleza and Salvador and Rio de Janeiro. The towering new skylines convey a sense of tropical modernity, of the sleeping giant finally stirring.

Beneath the veneer spreads the vast province of scores of millions of landless and homeless who have reaped no benefit from the past two decades' burst of development. In mid-1988 Greater Rio de Janeiro had 4 million slum dwellers; only a million lived in the fashionable Zona Sul. The pressure of hyper-inflation, reaching levels of up to 20 percent a month, and of prices rising faster than salaries, was causing most gasping citizens to run hard to stay in place. More crime was one consequence. Bank robberies were daily occurrences. Well-organized gangs of armed gunmen held up buses and streetcars, seized entire apartment or office buildings and kept the occupants captive while they did their work. The law, never widely respected in Brazil, was being disregarded in even its most routine aspects. For fear of being held up, motorists habitually ran red lights. Tax payments remained sporadic after two decades of "reform." Newspapers printed gleeful daily reports of gross corruption in high places. Without cheating a little, not even the most scrupulous Brazilian could make his way through the labyrinth of rules and bureaucratic impediments that insanely complicated daily life. The verb *agüentar*, roughly meaning "to cope," remained a staple of Brazil's slushy Portuguese.

P'ra Inglês ver. With the smooth flow of a trombone, the Brazilian slides between the formality of the "English" and the sleaze of the "real." Brazil is the world's largest and most promiscuous Catholic country, a land of emptying churches and busy brothels. This morning's banker, a chauffeured Mercedes at the door, is tonight's Casanova, at sport with

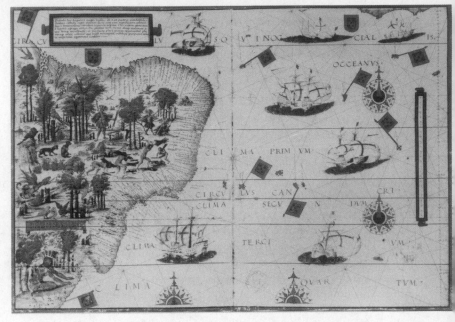

1519 depiction of the east coast of South America.

mulatto girls in a heart-rated motel out along the highway. Hardly a man is faithful to his wife. Some women respond with resignation. Others react by finally leaving their husbands or by living freely themselves. "I never was a virgin," a lady from Natal told us. Brazil's girls, who wear the world's most revealing bathing suits, seem to enjoy having men look at them. They look straight back.

Rouba mas faz, he steals but he gets things done, was what they said on the street about one well-liked and prodigiously corrupt politician who kept a wife in São Paulo and, flagrantly, a mistress in Rio de Janeiro. *Qualquer coisa*—anything you need, just call me, a Brazilian will say—knowing or hoping that you won't bother him again. Oblivion for a project often begins with a Brazilian saying, *Deixa comigo*—just leave it to me. A Brazilian once flew a friend to a remote wilderness ranch, far from any road. The pilot said he would be back in a couple of days. Twenty-two days later he showed up to fetch my anxious pal. "I had to go to a wedding in Miami," the aviator explained. "It exists," the Brazilian shopkeeper will tell you (the British façade), "but we don't have any" (the Brazilian reality). "It would be difficult" means "no way." Hypocrisy and good humor lie side by side in this land of slippery values

242

and very funny jokes, where a wry sense of the ironic is all that keeps many citizens merely despondent. For all their misfortunes, no people are warmer or more sentimental, cleverer or better company.

If God's revenge was to give Brazil the Brazilians, as they often say about themselves, the natural beauty of the land places the country in a class of its own. Mostly out of carelessness, the Brazilians have managed to do considerable damage to this heritage. During *Sanderling*'s cruise along 1,500 miles of the Brazilian coast, from Fortaleza to Rio de Janeiro, we saw sights of great and rare quality, untouched miles of golden dunes descending through mauve evening light to trackless beaches. We also experienced gross forms of coastal degradation. In Rio de Janeiro, as our voyage was ending, I looked skyward from our marina berth. In the foreground was the charming colonial church of Nossa Senhora da Glória. The green hills of the old Santa Teresa district loomed behind. Cristo Redentor, the very symbol of Rio, flew high overhead. Closer at hand, rafts of plastic sacks and bottles bobbed about in the highly polluted water of almost dead Guanabara Bay. The harsh light of day softened to a lulling dusk. A used condom, jumbo size, floated by.

Our eclectic Brazilian experience began in Fortaleza, which along with Recife is one of the twin anchor cities of Brazil's long-downtrodden Northeast. This drought-prone nine-state region had a population of 42 million, most of whom were still living and trying to work in the rural villages of the interior. But the rains are intermittent, the soils poor, the life hard. Largely because of grievous imbalances in the land-tenure situation, things were little better for most people in a greener belt along much of the Northeast's coast, where 300,000 square miles of tropical forest have been almost completely felled to make way for plantations, roads, towns, and some factories. Peasants fleeing the region's poverty have swollen all Brazil's cities, including those in the Northeast, which still has 30 percent of the nation's people but only 15 percent of its gross national product. The beleaguered coast offers more hope with the ongoing productivity of its fisheries and new income from a national and international tourism boom.

Soon after getting *Sanderling* securely anchored near Fortaleza's ultramodern, empty Yacht Club, I phoned Priscila Holanda, a young biology teacher who was developing a marine environmental education program for local educators. From the club, through midafternoon haze and showers, she drove me on a two-hour tour of the spread-out city's eastern flank. We hurried past a district of open prostitution called Farol (lighthouse), whose muddy half-paved streets were lined with bars named, for instance, Pink Panther and Hamburger. Why? I wondered: few visitors to the region speak English. The bars and their occupants served sailors from the nearby commercial port. We continued toward Praia do Futuro, a beach to which middle-class Fortaleza flocks on weekends. Along the garbage-strewn strip were small thatch-roofed snack bars and soft-drink stands, forlorn on this gray weekday.

The dunes behind the beach, Priscila explained as we drove uphill into them, had long been the scene of conflict between rich people who built "mansions" there and poor squatters and homesteaders in search of a better life than that available out in the arid interior of Ceará state. One landowner on these rolling hills, now lightly covered with new grass that sprouted during the rainy season, was obliged to tear down a wall he had built because it obscured the full range of the nearby lighthouse. Overall, few rules applied. Indigent immigrants would build small shacks on empty land. Then someone would acquire a tract and bulldoze down the shacks. Their occupants would disappear. Then a new mansion would materialize. Cows wandered the sandy-green terrain, on which roads were built more often in ad hoc response to political pressure than according to a plan. Trash was piled high in various sections; a sign reading "No Litter" marked an especially dirty place. We drove to a polluted river at the end of the road, then turned back toward town. On one bridge new refugees from the interior were assembling cardboard houses. A few hundred yards away, the pavement had barely hardened on a new road leading to an elaborate shopping mall.

While the textile industry maintains a strong presence here, the sea still supports many people. Swarms of small fishing boats in the harbor, and an abundance of seafood at fresh-air markets around town, attest to the continuing vigor of the trade. Lobster, though scarce because of overharvesting, is a local delicacy; the region consumes and exports a wide variety of finfish and shellfish. What is remarkable, said Priscila, is how little is known in the region about the marine environment and its biology.

It is this gap that, with help from the World Wildlife Fund and an educator from New Hampshire who makes occasional visits, Priscila was trying to bridge. She was planning a series of teacher seminars, exhibits, and public relations activities to draw attention to the sensitivity and danger of overstressing the coastal ecosystems that surround the town. In her new office at the marine research lab in the federal university, Priscila was gathering materials for a display. A large piece of whalebone was ranged along one wall, and paper cartons of newspaper and magazine clippings were piled on the floor. Though she did not have much to show yet, Priscila expressed optimism about her project. "No one's ever tried anything like this around here," she said. "For a long time I've wanted to do something about it. Now at last I have a little money and a chance. It's a dream come true."

A native Fortalezan with a hundred cousins living in the region, Priscila left me to fetch her daughter from the convent school that she and her mother had also attended. I returned to *Sanderling* to find the crew enthusiastic about Fortaleza's food, shopping, and agreeable people. I saw instead a city suffering the distortions of rapid and uncontrolled expansion and heading toward mediocrity. The next day Priscila took me on a second drive, out past the western end of town. We passed a cluttered section once entirely owned by Priscila's great-grandfather before it was all expropriated without any form of compensation. We traveled briefly along the broad main road toward São Luís, 400 miles to the west, then turned off through verdant country to the beach town of Icaraí. Now, though the harsh dry interior was only minutes' drive from the coast, we were in a well-off tourist belt of vacation homes, condominiums, hotels. Near the village of Cumbuco a developer had simply helped himself to land previously occupied by resident fishermen, thrown them off, and built vacation homes that he was selling for prices in the $300,000 range. We sat under a *barraca* (straw hut) here and ate a grilled red snapper while tourists rode dune buggies and burros on the beach and boarded for-hire *jangadas* (fishing canoes) for wave-tossed passages out through the surf.

On our next and final day in Fortaleza, we mounted yet another expedition, this time to the newly completed Pôrto das Dunas, an elaborate development built among high dunes between a lagoon and the ocean. It was windy and the surf a dirty yellow. At the entrance to the complex a sign warned investors: (a) to have their land carefully surveyed, lest they build on someone else's property, and (b) not to throw garbage onto their neighbor's land. That night at dinner Priscila, continuing our conversation about changing conditions in Fortaleza, chose to overlook the region's shortcomings. She could live nowhere else, she said. "I cannot imagine life without the sea and the music."

Our crew briefly sampled the Fortaleza *boate* (nightclub) scene. I acted as translator. "Steve doesn't realize how much I love him," a striking tall brunette confessed. "Help me make him understand." At this task I failed. Between sightseeing excursions, we had been successful in getting some of the kinks out of *Sanderling*. We found a machine shop that in a jiffy made us a replacement for our broken roller-reefing rod, and once again hauled Peter up the mast to install it. We cleaned and polished, and got our laundry done, and for $40 U.S. (you could live very well in Brazil in 1988 if you had greenbacks) restocked our depleted

Sanderling rounding Cape Calcanhar.

galley at the Sugarloaf Supermarket. We saved from a premature end a newly arrived French yacht whose anchor was poorly set. The solo skipper was soundly sleeping while his boat dragged through the fleet toward the reef. Then we were ready to push on and did so after I obtained clearances from the three separate agencies that I was obliged to visit twice in each port: the Navy's office of the captain of the port, the maritime section of the Federal Police, and the Receita Federal, or customs section of Brazil's Internal Revenue Service.

February turned into March as *Sanderling* pounded another 200 miles eastward from Fortaleza to Cabo Calcanhar, Brazil's northeastern corner. It was almost as if our crossing had not ended, for the frustrations of head winds and foul currents and rainsqualls and slow progress continued for more than three days of dreary sailing. At lunchtime on March 1 we finally had the impressive Calcanhar lighthouse abeam. The air was light and we ghosted through opaque yellow-green water past the 203-foot freshly painted tower with its bold horizontal black and white stripes. Peter and Matt inflated the dinghy and boarded it to take photographs of *Sanderling* at this turning point, beyond which we expected fair winds and fast passages. Steve dove over the rail and swam, casually raising himself back aboard with one arm. We celebrated with beer, Doritos, and guacamole made from a football-sized avocado we had found in Fortaleza. Under threatening skies we motored the 20 miles of the Canal do São Roque, a smooth narrow passage with reefs to seaward and endless empty sandy beach to starboard. At 2230 we at last dropped our anchor in the Rio Potengi, the swiftly flowing brown stream that flanks the city of Natal.

We were fully a day late for the rendezvous we had scheduled with our arriving crew member, Tim Hogen. The following morning, relieved that we were not even later, he swung aboard bearing many welcome gifts, including a new pump allegedly able to cure our long-standing refrigerator problems. From our anchorage off the small and pleasant yacht club, we later set forth to explore this quiet, arid, sandy city at Brazil's far eastern end—less than two thousand miles from Senegal. Fish was a prominent factor in people's lives here, and there seemed to be a greater degree of prosperity about the seafaring than we had found to the north. Instead of the primitive *jangadas* to which we were now well accustomed, the Natal fishermen had larger and stronger boats, many equipped with diesel engines. The markets were flooded with fresh fish, which seemed still the source of a far greater share of protein in the local diet than beef from the scraggly steers of the parched northeastern interior.

Not supply but politics was their biggest threat, they said when I visited the crowded little section of riverbank that, as one of the fishermen put it, "has been ours as long as there has been a Natal." Now, it was believed, the state oil company, Petrobrás, had its eye on a portion of the fishermen's port, and the city on another portion as a site for tourism development. The fishermen had been promised a replacement area across the river, far from the market, among people considered to be dangerous. "I'll never go over there," said one fisherman. "Those people will steal everything I own." As they sat around on this hot afternoon, talking and mending nets, Natal's fishermen said they felt helpless to affect the final outcome. "The politicians can do what they want," said one man, shrugging.

Since we had come to Natal only to fetch Tim and drop off Steve, who was headed back to the States for a summer of fishing and travel aboard a motor vessel in Alaska, we moved on after a brief look. Our course was due south now that we were around the bend; for once we had an easy beam reach and good speed. The towers of Natal dropped quickly out of sight; soon we were back in an older world of undeveloped dunes, uncluttered beaches, small fishing villages with tile-roofed houses. Even the flies, of which there had been a heavy invasion while we were at anchor in Natal's river, vanished as abruptly as they had arrived. We spent a short night in the unattractive port of Cabedelo, at the mouth of a shallow river. Its oil refinery, whale-oil plant, and railhead offered few charms, and early the following morning we continued our southward run toward Recife. Hogen had been living there when I first met him, and we now counted on him for local knowledge. Instead of proceeding directly to the city, he suggested that we pause at a break in the reefs twenty miles north, at the Canal do Santa Cruz, where a seventeenth-century fort guards the pretty river mouth and the water was clear and clean. The fort, called Oranje, had been built by the Dutch, who had occupied the region briefly while trying to crack the sugar monopoly that Portuguese Brazilians had already established there.

As we had learned in the Bahamas, finding passages through unmarked reefs can be tricky in bad light. Now, again, we found ourselves in unexpectedly shallow water while still far out at sea, and had to motor slowly, parallel to the coast, until the fort reached a precise bearing. Then we turned in, drifting gingerly shoreward past a narrowing succession of reefs and sandbars concealed now by the high tide. These hairy harbor entrances tend to make me feel a little queasy in the stomach (my own version of seasickness), and now was no exception as we ghosted in, eyes glued to the depth indicator. We passed through the needle's eye without incident, however, and were soon anchored in a swift current between the mainland and a sandbar, fashioned by the fast-flowing waters only a few years ago, called the Ilha do Amor (Love Island).

The area, we discovered the next day, is a magnet for tourists and weekend homeowners from nearby Recife. Though a fishing fleet sails forth each morning from upriver, many of the area's *jangadas* get no farther than the beach in front of the fort. There they line up, each mainsail bearing an advertising slogan, in wait for passengers to ferry across to the long line of *barraca* restaurants that have sprouted on the Ilha do Amor. While a falling tide emptied the basin around us and turned much of it into sand flats, we went ashore and sampled the excellent grilled shrimp and fish, and rice and beans, and cold beer at one of these. The family that ran the place, we learned, lived on the sandbar even though it has neither housing nor sanitary facilities of any sort. Their capital consisted of a few chairs and tables; a couple of Styrofoam coolers; pots, pans, plates, forks, knives, and cooking utensils; and whatever food and drink they had on hand at the beginning of the day. We had arrived early. Before long, tourists began swarming off the *jangadas* to swim in the warm clean water, then set tables at the very edge of the beach to eat and drink while the tide rose around them. To our surprise, several motorized hang gliders buzzed above, frequently landing in the water nearby and taxiing up to the beach to pick up paying passengers for fifteen-minute rides.

Typical of Brazilian ingenuity, I thought, that this entire cottage industry should have burst forth, literally from nothing, over the course of just the couple of years since the island was born. On the mainland not far away, we discovered the next day, was a more orderly resort called Maria Farinha that was already popular during Hogen's time in Recife. An anchorage here harbored a collection of small Brazilian-made powerboats, loaded with chrome and fins, aquatic versions of U.S. autos of the 1950s, bearing names such as Bullet and Cobra Monte Carlo 32. Past the fleet we found a setting of great charm: brightly painted houses with tile roofs lined the waterfront of a narrowing little estuary. Palms and mango and cashew trees, bright green and lush in spite of the dry air, alternated with the pretty houses. Locals and weekenders were out doing quiet morning chores when Matt and I drifted by in our rubber dinghy.

Sunday, March 6, was hot and clear and picture-book. Tempted as we were by the attractions of the Ilha do Amor and Maria Farinha, we hauled anchor near the time of the afternoon high tide, motored carefully out the narrow channel, then set sail for a glorious romp down the sandy coast to the big port of Recife. Toward sunset we reached along the face of the harbor in smooth reef-guarded water, past several tankers and an odd little Japanese vessel. At the end of the dredged big-ship facility a shallow bay opened up, a drying mud flat at its center and barely navigable channels at each side. The more easily accessible yacht club was at hand to port. But adjacent to it was a dangerous slum; Tim, who had been told of a viable channel leading to its narrow entrance, recommended that we try to make our way farther in to the more central Cabanga Yacht Club. We took down the sails and edged forward under power, my stomach again jumping as the depth indicator began to give us truly alarming readings. While I veered from side to side in a futile search for deeper water, Matt and Pete quietly munched cold steak with hot sauce. "How the hell can you be eating at a time like this?" I hissed. One hundred feet from the club, ironically close to a dredge, we firmly grounded in fading light. I had visions of spending the night in place, heeling over in the falling tide, our hull taking a beating from rising seas. But we managed to power off, and Hogen, who had rowed into the club for help, eventually returned with a guide who led us down the unmarked, razor-thin channel to a place where we could tie up bow-to to a concrete wall. Water bugs, crabs, and rats scuttled. At least we were secure.

Recife's downtown was little changed from what I remembered from 1960s visits. The dramatic difference was in the section called Boa Viagem, then an empty beach strip, almost a cow pasture, with an occasional modest house. Since then, with a big boost from national and international development agencies bent on solving the Northeast's poverty problem, Boa Viagem had become Waikiki: mile upon mile of high-rise buildings facing a beach protected by an offshore reef. Here lived povertycrats and businessmen who had taken advantage of government subsidies and tax holidays for regional investment, as well as the few surviving barons of Pernambuco state's feudal sugar industry, which flourished until slavery was abolished in 1889 and still limps on. Hotels for German and French tourists had sprouted as well. Along with them had come restaurants and nightclubs. A few years ago the only available food was mediocre regional, its emphasis on dishes like salt cod. Now the many cuisines of Brazil and the world were readily at hand. We had a good Italian dinner and wandered the aisles of Boa Viagem's traditional Sunday market for local handicrafts.

A couple of days was ample time in Recife, though Hogen's friends, who entertained us with great spontaneity and style, could not understand why we would want to leave so soon. Jockeying for position at a busy dock, we managed to fill *Sanderling*'s tank with diesel fuel for the first time since leaving Barbados, and also top off our supply of fresh water. Then we set forth in hot dry weather, with a beautiful quartering breeze from the east, to continue our run down the coast. Soon we were past the incongruous oil port of Soape, set among coconut palms at the mouth of a little-used river and near nothing but small fishing villages. Only one ship was tied up in this ghost harbor. We spent a night at anchor off the privately owned Ilha do Santo Aleixo, one of the very few islands anywhere along the northeast coast, and the next morning snorkeled the reefs in only slightly cloudy water. From there it was another three days to Brazil's colonial capital of Salvador, first with a perfect reaching breeze under clear skies, then with thundersqualls and adverse southerly winds alternating with periods of dead calm.

Against long odds we had run into the kind of frontal system that is typical of winter weather along here but unusual in the early Southern Hemisphere fall. The freak weather made the run something other than the picnic we had envisioned; at times we had solid downpours and were thoroughly wet and uncomfortable. Peter was fretting about our electrical system, which was manifesting irregularities despite the new voltage regulator that Tim had bestowed upon us, and our freshwater pump suddenly went onto the sick list. At the very moment when theoretically we would accelerate as we hit the homestretch of the entire voyage, things seemed to be turning against us once more. Moods began to sour. At least, thanks to Tim's persistent efforts, *Sanderling*'s head and galley were becoming cleaner; he also became my generation's principal vigilante in keeping the younger crew members' possessions from piling up in the main cabin. Any loose stuff he sees around, explained the *chefe* (chief), as he had become known aboard, "I just throw it up forward" into the cabin now referred to as the boys' locker room.

As we proceeded southward, the coast to starboard was fast changing its character. We left behind the golden dunes of Pernambuco state and entered a region of low green woodlands bordered by red cliffs. Lights ashore were scarce and human settlement limited to the village often found at the mouth of the occasional shallow river. Even fishermen became infrequent sights, though we were remaining inshore, close to the continental shelf. The most visible sign of human activity was the ubiquitous oil-drilling rig, evidence of Brazil's relentless pursuit of self-sufficiency in petroleum, which cost her dearly in foreign exchange as consumption shot upward during the last two decades. Wildlife we did not lack along here. With each offshore breeze came butterflies, moths, many unfamiliar insects; bravely Peter dispatched with a flyswatter a fat sluggish red wasp that had taken up residence in the main cabin. Terns, long absent, reappeared. The most common seabird was now the attractive black-and-white Audubon's shearwater. Peter caught a large wahoo-type fish. Having carefully observed Steve's technique, he cleaned it expertly and (except for Matt) we gladly ate it in preference to the corned-beef hash that I had excavated from a back corner of the food bin.

Closing in on Salvador we passed many miles of untouched, reef-lined beach. Then came the beginnings of a major urban industrial complex, signaled first by the twin smokestacks of the Tibras plant, a titanium-refining installation that had been sited at seaside because of the heavy seawater demand which the highly polluting process involves and because the toxic effluent could simply be piped into the sea. From Tibras, which we had abeam soon after dawn, it took us an entire day to reach our Salvador anchorage. We passed thickening concentrations of tourism development and fishing settlements of ever greater size. Some fifteen miles out, on sandy beachfront land that a quarter-century ago was as empty as Recife's Boa Viagem, we now found hotels, large buildings, and residential subdivisions. One after the other, big jets settled onto the airport runway that had been cut into the golden dunes. Near Point Santo Antônio at the eastern entrance to Salvador's magnificent All Saints Bay, a Hotel Méridien and many modern high-rise residential buildings rose from the rock-strewn beach. There surfers

An early view of Salvador.

were gathered on this weekend afternoon, and uniformed barefoot soccer teams vied with each other, dodging dramatic crashing waves when the ball bounced out toward the sea. We passed the beach called the Barra, nestled between two sixteenth-century forts, near which Flo and I had stayed in 1965, and rounded up into the bay to seek our anchorage. At last light (why the hell is it always getting dark when we're in unfamiliar territory and looking for a place to drop the hook?), we nestled in near the famous Mercado Modelo, large indoor-outdoor market for food and crafts, squeezed among a large grotty-yachtie fleet and many locally built wooden *escunas* for the tourist trade.

Over the course of the next two days, I succeeded in completing boat-entry formalities—more languidly conducted here than elsewhere in the Northeast. "*O chefe*," said one barely covered young secretary at one of my stops, "I'm so tired and I think I'll have to take the rest of the day off." She leaned against her boss as he sat in his chair, her elbow pressing down on his shoulder. "All right," he said weakly, not *p'ra Inglês ver*. At least one British visitor had not been fooled. In his account of a 1920 steamship ride to South America, William J. McKenzie called Bahia "the most corrupt and effete state in the Republic of Brazil," a fetid place that is "usually a hotbed of disease" and where "little attention is paid to sanitation." McKenzie had that secretary's number as well. He wrote: "Warm climates tend to lethargy and lassitude, which we northerners cannot understand. We must be active to keep us warm; they must be passive to keep cool."

A day late because of airline delays, Flo arrived, and we settled in to the Pousada do Carmo, a former convent converted into an attractive hotel in the city's mostly run-down but wonderful colonial district. It lies in the heart of the Cidade Alta, high above the bay, and yields spectacular views across to scattered islands. Close beside is Pelourinho, a zone of narrow streets leading into a steeply sloped triangular cobblestone plaza. At its upper end stands a house (now a museum) once occupied by the novelist Jorge Amado. He has written much about this lowlife district, which, like New York's East Village, has been partially recycled for tourism. From this base we explored the old city, far more agreeable than the seaside hotel and pizza-hut strips in the Barra district and a new area called Pituba. We also began to investigate the region's ecology.

At eleven o'clock, half an hour late, the chemist Tania M. Tavares bustled into her lab at the Federal University. Short, frizzy-haired, vivacious, Tavares had much to say about the Recôncavo, as the All Saints Bay region is called, and its environmental degradation. "You must remember that we have quite a history. This was a busy place during colonial times. Then came a century and a half of decay. Absolutely nothing happened. Then, in the 1950s, oil was discovered in the bay and a big refinery, Brazil's first, was built. A big wave of development activity based on the oil began about twenty-five years ago. No thought was given to nature or the environment. First there came the Aratu Industrial Park at the upper end of the bay. Then they built the Camaçari petrochemical complex, which is already the country's biggest and is now doubling in size. Overall, in what was virtually an untouched area, full of fish and shellfish, we now have over two hundred factories."

During the 1970s Tavares and other young scientists, concerned about the environmental consequences of this industrial concentration, began pioneer efforts to study the situation. They first selected the Enseada dos Tainheiros, an inlet just north of Salvador around which 110,000 people live—most of them in wooden shacks built on stilts over the mud. Over twelve years, they found, ten tons of inorganic mercury from a nearby caustic soda plant had been dumped into the Enseada. Most of the sediments in the area were polluted by the mercury, and concentrations exceeding World Health Organization limits were discovered in a common edible bivalve. Although they could not document high mercury levels in the people who ate the mollusks, in part because of the manner in which they are usually cooked, they were able to persuade the state government to move the plant to a less populated area that was already polluted. The scientists then turned their attention to the town of Santo Amaro at the head of the bay, where it was known that a foreign-owned lead plant—accounting for 80 percent of Brazil's total exports of the metal—had been "throwing out mountains of lead" for many years. Dross from the plant was being used as a pavement ingredient at one of the town schools. Using analysis of hair samples as well as other techniques, the group established that 10 percent of local children were suffering from lead poisoning, a condition that provokes anemia and inhibits mental development. This finding again moved the government to action. It ordered the company to close 50 percent of its production for a year while a filter system was installed.

If such reactions suggest governmental responsibility, Tavares produced other information indicating a general lack of adequate rules or control around the 390-square-mile bay (Brazil's biggest). A copper smelter was continuing to generate ten times the normal concentrations of arsenic. A detergent spill had put ten tons of hydrocarbons into the water in ten minutes; six months later, local shellfish were still loaded with the stuff. Airborne pollution is becoming a problem. The city's water supply is so affected by pollution in the watershed that it is overdosed with chlorine. Uncontrolled runoff after heavy rains renders most of Salvador's beaches unsafe for swimming for long stretches of time.

Because of organic as well as toxic contamination, Marlene C. Peso, a biologist whose lab we also visited, would not allow her children to swim from any beach within ten miles of the city. Peso, who had worked with Tavares on many studies, also reported "complete ecological disorganization" around the Enseada dos Tainheiros as a result of a relatively new phenomenon: the use by fishermen of a poisonous acetylene residue called *carbureto* to coax crabs out of their holes—the local equivalent of Bahamians with their Clorox. More toxic to some species than to others, the *carbureto* had brought about an explosion in the population of an immune worm, while totally eliminating at least one bivalve species. Up in the bigger freshwater rivers, Peso continued, a popular fish called the *surubim* (*Pseudoplatystoma coruscans*) was edging ever closer to extinction because of overfishing. Crabs around Santo Amaro were "full of lead and cadmium," with consequences that were not yet clear.

In the Santo Amaro region, the North American anthropologist Charlotte Cerf was examining pollution's effects on artisanal fishermen. She had selected for comparative study two villages, one relatively free from pollution and the other, São Braz, whose anoxic water was laden with wastes from two paper mills, sugarcane refineries, and the relocated lead smelter. The decline in the São Braz fishery had brought about dramatic change. Fishermen, forced to compete with growing intensity for ever scarcer resources, had reduced the size of their net meshes so that they could catch smaller, often juvenile, fish. The prestige of crabbers, low when fish were plentiful, had greatly increased. Among São Braz children, malnutrition was four times more prevalent than among children in the village with less polluted water (almost two-thirds of all northeastern children under the age of five are at least somewhat undernourished). Cerf achieved these findings with the help of research assistants provided by Earthwatch, a Boston-area nonprofit group with an ingenious idea: to have teams of volunteers participate in scientific fieldwork activities all over the world, collectively paying enough to cover their own costs—and the cost of the project as well. Flo, wearing her hat as director of the Earthwatch office in Washington, spent several days with Cerf at São Braz. She returned depressed by the conditions she found but warmed by the humor and kindness of the environmentally beleaguered villagers she met.

Lack of sewers, lack of control over industry, lack of scientific knowledge were all contributing to the continuing decline of the Recôncavo's environmental quality. Sloppy personal and institutional habits had also filled it with garbage. Yet Peso has found that many marine species have held their own in the face of the human assault upon their habitats. The western side of the bay, protected from the industries by fast-flowing currents, was "still almost completely unpolluted," Tavares said. "The shrimp farms there are still doing very well." With public concern on the increase and the local government becoming more responsive, there was some chance that the decline of these waters could be arrested if adequate people and resources were applied. This, at least as long as Brazil's debt burden and economic crisis persist, would be the principal obstacle. Dr. Clea Bastos, an official at the Salvador office of the Brazilian Forestry Institute (IBDF), put the matter succinctly: "Just as we are getting more and more public demand for action, our ability to do anything is shrinking."

The easiest way to put together a sound environmental program on Brazil's northeast coast, I discovered during our stay in Salvador, is to control an entire region in the manner of a colonial-era feudal baron and apply enlightened policies to it. This Flo and I discovered at Praia do Forte, a small beach resort town some fifty miles from Salvador. To get there we drove past the airport, past fast-growing subdivisions of vacation homes, past the Tibras plant, past quiet fishing villages due shortly to succumb to the pressures of fast-buck coastal development. Then the freshly paved highway abruptly turned to dirt. A quarter mile farther on we came to a T. With no sign to guide us, we instinctively turned toward the coast. We halted at a barrier and explained our business to the gatekeeper. He let us through. Soon we found ourselves in a small clean village with low buildings, many with roofs thatched in a traditional weave from local fiber, a couple of handsome restaurants, a protected strip of beach lined with tidy *barracas*, a scenic lighthouse out on the point, and not a billboard in sight.

Our purpose in coming here was to meet Guy Marcobaldi, the director of Projeto Tamar, a national effort organized by IBDF to protect marine turtles and educate the public about their ecology. Since the beaches around Praia do Forte are used for egg laying by four of the five marine turtle species that frequent Brazilian waters, this village is the project's headquarters. For six years of living here, the handsome Marcobaldi explained after we had found him at his home near the lighthouse, he had been trying to make turtle protectors of fishermen accustomed to eating them and their eggs, and to explain to public visitors something of how these animals get along. Several tanks containing young turtles were on public view. Fishermen employed by Projeto Tamar were marking and protecting some nests on the beach; collecting and incubating eggs from other sites; and releasing for their dramatic return to the sea some 50,000 hatchlings a year. Though only a small percentage of these manage to avoid their many predators and reach adulthood, the program provided a new model for Brazil, a valuable educational tool. It was doubtless helpful to the turtles as well.

One of the project's benefactors, Marcobaldi told us, was Klaus Peters, the *patrão* who not long ago bought the 17,000-acre property, called the Fazenda García d'Avila, of which Praia do Forte is the keystone. When Marcobaldi asked if we would like to meet Peters, a São Paulo native who now spends half his time at Praia do Forte, we accepted with enthusiasm. We drove a short distance to his house. Marcobaldi ushered us through a doorway and out onto a terrace where Peters, a large blond man, was holding court. Pet macaws squawked in the trees. Peters welcomed Flo and me, quizzed us closely about our intentions, then relaxed and told us his story.

He and a brother, sons of German immigrants, had founded a company that manufactured street-lighting equipment. A runaway success during the rapid Brazilian expansion of the 1950s and 1960s, the company became a ripe takeover target. Early in the 1970s Peters succumbed to an "irresistible" offer from a multinational, and ever since had been applying the proceeds to rural and farming investments. As a very young man Peters had visited the Northeast and been struck by it. Much later, through a chance encounter with an acquaintance from those early days, he learned that what was left of the huge García d'Avila ranch—the world's largest recorded private landholding in the sixteenth century, when it was owned by the court finance minister in Salvador and covered more than 300,000 square miles—was for sale. With five miles of virgin beachfront, dunes, residual forest of a rare type called *restinga*, the remaining landholding was of considerable biological interest. The working farm, renamed Fazenda Sapitinga, was as irresistible to Peters as his company had been to the multinational buyer.

With the help of an international consulting firm, Peters embarked on an unusual development scheme. Instead of carving up the property into small lots and trying to sell them quickly in a blaze of promotion, he adopted a low-profile, word-of-mouth approach. The place would operate as an informal "club" along the lines of Mustique in the Grenadines; no one would be allowed to buy in without making a personal visit and obtaining letters of recommendation from two members. All architectural plans would have to be approved by Peters' people; a rigid thirty-three-foot height limit on all construction would be observed. For every coconut tree removed to make way for new construction (the trees on the property are direct descendants of those that Portuguese settlers imported from Goa), a new one would have to be planted. Peters built a model *pousada*, or small inn (where later he gave us a sumptuous seafood lunch), and expected that twenty of these would eventually dot the property. Refusing to accede to demands from Club Med, which could not tolerate his restrictions, Peters built his own prototype low-rise hotel. It attracts a European charter-flight clientele; strolling the airy grounds, we encountered hefty Scandinavian women doing aerobic exercises to rock music. A single golf course, tennis club, and boating center would serve all five of the hotels for which the plan allowed. Village development is also strictly controlled. "These streets will never be paved," Peters proudly told us. Land is freely available to farmers and fishermen who lived on the property before Peters bought it, but ownership is denied them. "If they owned it, they'd turn around and sell it to the first tourist that came along," Peters said.

The most striking aspect of Peters' plan is not so much its predictable economic success as its concern for environmental quality, which in Brazil has no precedent. An elaborate system of parks and nature reserves is included. Special protection for important resident species—caimans, a profusion of orchids—is a high priority. Deforestation is carefully limited. Peters used political pull to make sure that the asphalted coastal highway, which ended at Praia do Forte when we visited, would run behind his property, not along his beach. After our luncheon Peters took us on a lordly tour of the spectacular domain, on which Brazil's oldest castle, dating from 1552, also stands.

For all its charms, I concluded as we said goodbye to Peters with evening shadows falling across the softly waving palms, the scheme still gave me a slight case of the shivers. It had something of the precious snobby air to it of a Hilton Head Island; I could visualize the least drugged young people arriving there, being taken for hippies, and turned away at the gate. On the other hand, this was no Mill Reef Club, oblivious to its context. The success of Peters' environmental concern, which stood out in altogether pleasant contrast to the disorderly beachfront developments down the road toward Salvador, was apparent. "Tourism is the only economic activity in which the investor benefits directly from environmental protection," he told us. One could only hope that more shorefront developers would follow the example.

Back in Salvador, more comings and goings. We bid a reluctant goodbye to Tim the *chefe*, now obliged to return to business affairs in New York, and welcomed Ned Hoyt, a recent university graduate fresh from a year of working and studying Arabic in Cairo. Gifted in languages if not in sail handling, Ned soon twisted his Spanish into passable Portuguese and began leading the crew off on complex bus expeditions. Leslie Stone arrived for her third hitch aboard *Sanderling*, and we packed Flo off to the boondocks for her visit to Charlotte Cerf's Earthwatch project (she would rejoin us several days later at Ilhéus, 120 miles to the south). A mechanic named Manuel Santos, who had served for many years as a U.S. Navy enlisted man, came aboard with a sidekick named Nascimento to try to repair our faltering electrical system and cure the persistent problem of our refrigerator. Though hardly for lack of trying, they succeeded at neither task.

All week, while *Sanderling* lay at anchor in Salvador, the weather remained dry and picture-book clear except for brief showers. Now, as we prepared to depart on our odyssey's final 730-mile lap from Salvador to Rio, serious clouds gathered. The wind again came from the south and the rain poured down. For three days we stayed pinned within the Recôncavo, first at our cluttered Salvador anchorage, then off the pretty island resort of Itaparica on the bay's clean southern flank. As we made this crossing, I was briefly tempted to brave the pelting rain and head winds and slog on out to sea. We passed a fisherman in a log canoe. He pointed toward the sky, then to the large choppy swells entering the bay. Then with a big grin he gave us a thumbs-down signal. He was right, I reluctantly agreed, and we bore off across the bay.

15

Home to Rio

SOON AFTER COLUMBUS' 1492 DISCOVERY, TENSIONS AROSE IN SPAIN and Portugal over which empire would own what portions of the emerging New World. An initial period of jockeying ended with the 1494 Treaty of Tordesillas, in which Ferdinand and Isabella conceded to Portugal's Dom João all newly found territories east of a north-south line 370 leagues west of the Cape Verde Islands; Spain would own everything to the west of the line. The treaty, which would remain binding no matter what discoveries were made by whom, served to foster a spirit of cooperation between the two seafaring nations that prevailed past the end of the century in spite of suspicions lurking on both sides.

Dom João's interest in getting the line of demarcation moved westward, from a meridian that would have resulted in Spain's getting title to the entire South American continent, was based on his hunch that a substantial mainland would be found south of Hispaniola. Columbus was aware of this theory, which was supported by what he had heard from Indians during the course of his first and second voyages. Accordingly, he proposed to Ferdinand and Isabella that he undertake a third voyage, along a more southerly track than he had followed on the first two. Among his objectives would be to test Dom João's hypothesis and possibly discover new territories lying far enough to the west to be claimed for Spain. Columbus would also continue the search for gold and for the passage to the Orient. Spain's rulers agreed and Columbus sailed in May 1498.

At the end of July his fleet made its landfall at the southeast corner of Trinidad. Columbus then sailed westward, along the island's south coast. On August 1, he unknowingly became the first European to lay eyes on the South American continent when he spotted above the horizon a point extending seaward from the delta of the Orinoco. Less than a week later, having cruised the Gulf of Paria, which separates Trinidad from the Venezuelan mainland, Columbus and his crew achieved the further distinction of becoming the first Europeans to step ashore anywhere on the American mainland. Unable to communicate with the Indians the party encountered, Columbus thought that this coast was no more than another island. Nevertheless, he was so impressed by the extent and beauty of what he saw that he termed the region an *otro mundo*—another world—that would become ripe for Spanish and Christian conquest.

During his voyage along the Paria peninsula, Columbus encountered women wearing pearls. Though he did not tarry to harvest many of these, he wrote to inform Europe that a "pearl coast" existed in the area. The letter came to the attention of Vicente Yáñez Pinzón, captain of the *Niña* in 1492. On the basis of this information, Pinzón obtained a license and funding for a new expedition, and set forth late in 1499. From the Cape Verde Islands, which had already become a customary stopover point for the new breed of transatlantic sailors from Europe, Pinzón steered a more southerly course than any captain before him. Where he fetched up in January 1500 is a matter of dispute. Some say it was near Recife, others that his landfall was the Punta do Mucuripe at Fortaleza. Either way, he later admitted, he knew he was still too far east to be in Spanish territory. Nevertheless, he went ashore to conduct a formal laying-claim ceremony. Then he cruised north and west, entering the Amazon and sailing fifty miles upriver before continuing to the Gulf of Paria and from there northward to the Caribbean islands and eventually home.

Technically, Pinzón thus became Brazil's European discoverer. However, since his voyage led to no further explorations, the accolade is usually awarded to a captain whose did: the Portuguese navigator Pedro Alvares Cabral. A well-placed country squire, Cabral was a fixture in the Portuguese court in 1499, when Vasco da Gama returned from his pioneering and arduous sail from Portugal around the Cape of Good Hope to India. If the commercial ties with India that da Gama opened were to be made firm, a second trading voyage had to be quickly put together. Da Gama had no stomach for the job. He and Dom Manoel, who had succeeded to the throne after Dom João's death in 1495, shared confidence in Cabral, who accepted their invitation to lead the new voyage. By early 1500, an elaborate thirteen-ship fleet had been assembled and Cabral set forth. Following da Gama's careful sailing directions, he maintained a southwesterly course as he crossed the equator. Instead of turning back southeastward after he had passed clear of the equatorial doldrums, Cabral continued on his southwesterly heading; the prevailing current pushed him closer to Brazil.

On April 22, having already had indications that land was near, the crew sighted a prominent conical mountain 240 miles south of Salvador. Since it was the Wednesday of Easter week, Cabral named it Monte Páscoal (Easter Mountain), sailed closer, and anchored near shore. Without incident the crew made contact with a group of Indians assembled on the beach. But the exposed anchorage was uncomfortable and insecure; anchors dragged when the wind rose. In search of better protection the fleet sailed northward, keeping clear of many breaking reefs, until a gap in them was spotted. The ships then turned shoreward and made it into a large reef-ringed bay—now called Cabrália—where they could safely anchor in calm water. Cabral called this place Pôrto Seguro and remained there eight days. Though he wrote no journal, a sophisticated court writer and crew member named Pedro Vaz de

Caminha maintained a meticulous diary of what turned out to be a successful week of replenishment and contact with the local Tupinamba Indians. Caminha found the anchorage inside the reef "very good and secure, with a very wide entrance." The waters around were "quite endless," and ashore, "as far as the eye could reach, we could see only land and forests." Relations with the skittish but friendly Indians were good. Several parties were held ashore and afloat; the Indians "skipped and danced with us to the sound of one of our tambours," Caminha reported. A wooden cross was fashioned and a religious service was held. Although Cabral left two convicts ashore when he departed, there is little else to suggest that he had been attempting to make a new discovery and launch a colony. He diverged quickly from shore, eventually rounding the Cape of Good Hope and fulfilling his original mission.

Upon receiving the news of Cabral's discovery (from Pôrto Seguro he had sent one vessel home to spread the word), other Portuguese navigators were slow to follow. According to Morison, they perceived the Brazilian coast only as "a place to replenish food, water, and wood on a passage to India." Dom Manoel was, however, impressed by Caminha's report as well as by an enthusiastic account of a brief trip to the New World that the ship chandler Amerigo Vespucci, an employee of the Medici family, had published in 1500. Portugal's ruler commissioned an experienced captain named Gonçalo Coelho to undertake a more extensive exploration of Brazil, and invited Vespucci to join the expedition as its official scribe.

The three-caravel fleet left Lisbon in mid-1501, met the homecoming Cabral at a port on the African coast, then crossed the South Atlantic. On August 17, Coelho and Vespucci closed with the Brazilian shore, somewhere between Recife and Salvador. "This land is very populous and full of inhabitants . . . very pleasant and fruitful," Vespucci glowed. Though one love-seeking sailor was clubbed to death and roasted by a group of naked Indian women, the fleet experienced few other problems during the course of a leisurely exploration of the coast from Salvador at least as far south as Rio de Janeiro. On a second extensive voyage, the team of Vespucci and Coelho spent eight months along the Brazilian coast. Their base of operations was All Saints Bay, which they named.

"I fancied myself near the earthly Paradise," Vespucci enthused. Despite his euphoria the Portuguese hardly moved swiftly to consolidate their position in Brazil. For the first three decades of the sixteenth century, they did little more than send an occasional ship across to survey, trade, or leave behind unwanted persons. A town called Pôrto Seguro, at the mouth of a river ten miles south of Cabral's safe anchorage, was designated as the capital. But few Portuguese lived there

Amerigo Vespucci.

or anywhere else in Brazil until almost 1550, when Lisbon became more systematic in its approach. New surveys were conducted and a governor-general, Thomé de Souza, was sent out with instructions to found a new capital at Salvador. The French were, meanwhile, not sitting idly by. Not bound by Tordesillas and having long conducted trade activities along the coast, they set about at midcentury to establish colonies at São Luís and on the shores of Rio de Janeiro's Guanabara Bay.

The early French and Portuguese beachheads were small and tenuous, and the ragtag settlers occupying them not much for letter-writing. Little is known about how they got along on the Brazilian coast during the first half-century of their occupancy. By 1550, a few educated laymen had visited and the Jesuits had just established a series of missions along the portion of the coast that the Portuguese controlled.

From the books and letters of these later arrivals, a sketchy portrait of attitudes and reactions emerges. Clearly, the colonists had little use for the Indians they encountered. They were unwilling or unable to become slaves as land was cleared and farms established. Not fiercely cannibalistic, they did eat human flesh at occasional ceremonial events, and the Europeans made much in words and pictures of this habit. At a time when little was known about any other aspect of Brazil, the pot-boiling images of a German traveler named Hans Staden became famous in Europe. Many of the Jesuit letters foreshadowed later assertions by questioning why a land of staggering beauty would be so inadequately endowed when it came to human beings. Father Manoel de Nobrega noted that the "size, variety and beauty of the creatures" is an indication of the "greatness and beauty" of the Creator. In a wry footnote, Nobrega questioned why He should have placed upon this landscape "such uncultivated people." Father Leonardo Nunes found them very *revôlto* (ornery); Father João predicted that Brazil would turn out very well once the land had been populated by Christians.

Despite the sad fate of Coelho's sailor, Vespucci was but the first of many European visitors who expressed admiration for Brazil's native women; a later chronicler alleged that they "do seeke and practice all the meanes to move man to lust." The natural world also generated excitement. In a description first published in 1568, a French layman named André Thevet marveled at the "incredible multitude" of oysters, with shells that "shineth like fine pearles" along the riverbanks. Thevet found fish in "great abundance." Another Frenchman, Jean de Léry, devoted an entire chapter of his *Voyage to the Land of Brazil* to a description of parrots, toucans, and many other spectacular bird species. Father João, writing from Pôrto Seguro in 1555, told of good hunting for pigs, rabbits, monkeys, deer, mountain cats, jaguars, tigers, birds like partridges and pheasants. Unlike many groups of North American colonists, the early Portuguese in Brazil seem to have had no more of a problem with nutrition and health than they would have at home.

When *Sanderling* cruised between Salvador and Rio de Janeiro in 1988, we visited many places of great beauty still little changed from colonial times. After pinning us down near Salvador for several sodden days, the rains finally ended and we sallied forth from the pretty, brightly painted village of Itaparica on an island in All Saints Bay. We witnessed double rainbows that evening as we approached a point called Morro de São Paulo; a purple sunset lit dark fires across the sky. We anchored snugly under the point and out of the swells, with only a few fishing boats around us. The next evening, after a long day of beating into unexpected head winds, we found an untouched corner of a landlocked bay called Camamu, marred only by a small barium-loading facility. Our anchorage placed us in deep water but so close to a sandy beach that we could swim there in a few strokes (those who tried, under a bright waxing moon, got nipped by swarms of aggressive little crustaceans). Nowhere between Salvador and Ilhéus, 120 miles to the south, was there much to remind us of the modern world.

Ilhéus, an old seaside town that provided the setting for Jorge Amado's classic novel *Gabriela, Clove and Cinnamon*, provided an interesting contrast. Approaching in the morning after a balmy overnight

sail past empty, palm-lined beaches, we passed a new big-ship port—
Ilhéus is the center of Brazil's cacao trade—and a few tall buildings along
the shorefront drive. All too soon for my tender stomach, we reached
shallow water at the mouth of the Rio das Cachoeiras (River of the
Waterfalls); Amado's funny novel makes much of periodic political
struggles over what dredging this bar would mean to the local economy.
In calm air and intense heat, with a dark squall approaching, we crept up
the fast-flowing muddy river, managing somehow to remain afloat until
we reached a deep-water anchorage where it bends around the inside of
the town. Amusingly, we discovered as we wandered its byways, Ilhéus
seemed a place where each in a succession of mayors has worked to build
his own monument to civic progress: a square here, a statue there, a
redesigned waterfront street. Currently the beach facing the ocean was
being sculpted into new contours. An ugly nineteenth-century cathedral
has regrettably been renovated and recently reopened and gleams in
beige and white. Several rusted-out dredges, veterans of long-abandoned
harbor improvement schemes, littered the riverfront. We watched
young barefoot men play soccer on one section of the beach, and ate in
the Gabriela, Clove and Cinnamon Room at the Ilhéus Praia Hotel.

By admiring a fox terrier, Peter made friends with a striking
Japanese-Brazilian girl we kept calling Sashimi. As a result, he and Ned
temporarily jumped ship and stayed in Ilhéus an extra day while the rest
of us sailed on. Now we cruised a clean and unpeopled coast, protected
by reefs offshore and dotted with tall palms, far from the sludge and litter
of Salvador. A day out of Ilhéus, we began our approach to Cabrália Bay.
A miscalculation along unmarked reefs thrust us suddenly into bad
trouble. From a reading of eighty feet, our depth meter abruptly
dropped to twenty, then fifteen and twelve vs. our six-foot draft. I spun
the wheel hard and reversed our course with little time before an
untimely crunch. We eased our way seaward, along an invisible coral
band curving away from the shore. It was dusk as we passed through
Cabral's wide opening, approached the pretty little river-mouth town of
Santa Cruz Cabrália, then inside the reef turned hard to port. Under
moonlight we continued parallel to a broad expanse of unoccupied beach,
anchoring in a narrow calm pocket between reef and coast, a small village
close at hand. Morning revealed the clean water to be jade green.
Dolphins lazed nearby. We swam.

At midday we made our way back through the break in the reef, past
an ominous half-surfaced shipwreck, and toward the modern town of
Pôrto Seguro. Monte Páscoal's round summit, Cabral's beacon, duly
appeared above red cliffs. Then the picture-book town, well-preserved
colonial buildings in sharply contrasting colors ranging along the water-

The fashionable Ajuda Beach near Pôrto Seguro.

front, loomed ahead. As at Recife, the shoreline is protected by a long finger of old reef, now as strong and high as a breakwater. Inside is the narrow entrance to a small river with an even narrower channel; at low tide, half of it turns into sand flats. With the help of a passing fishing boat, we inched our way in behind the reef, past the shoals (now covered at high tide), and to an anchorage occupied by two other cruising sailboats—the first we had seen since leaving All Saints Bay. Peter and Ned rejoined us after a long bus ride from Ilhéus, and we set out to explore the region. Across the river we discovered a striking beach area known as the Ajuda, the name of a hillside church a short distance away. We walked the pristine sand past handsome houses concealed from the shore behind thick green shrubbery. Two French singers and the Brazilian film star Sonia Braga had houses here, we discovered: we had stumbled upon St.-Tropez. The sun set as we strolled along this breathtaking shore. We swam in the gleam of the rising moon.

On Good Friday, though even the food markets were shut down tight, we stocked *Sanderling* as best we could. Mineral water we purchased from the barman at the Arrastão restaurant, whose portly Levantine proprietor suggested that we return for lunch. We did so. As we ate, he told us much about Pôrto Seguro's recent history. Until 1972 it was purely a fishing village with no broader economy. Then electricity came, and summer folk from São Paulo with new money from the incipient "Brazilian miracle" of those years. *Pousadas* and restaurants sprouted, and tourism became the economy's mainstay. Two express bus companies were now serving the resort; a jet plane was arriving twice weekly. Though prices had risen sharply, the largest building downtown, with a spacious yard behind it, had recently been sold to a U.S. investor for a bargain $30,000. Development was quite strictly controlled, our informant said. A two-story height limit on all buildings remained highly popular. Such rules as well as the considerable effort still required to get to Pôrto Seguro, despite the new air connections, will probably prevent a runaway explosion of tourism development. Though stores in the principal square maintained large stocks of the gaudy T-shirts now prominent at almost every resort, and flocks of Easter-weekend visitors were snatching them up, Pôrto Seguro seemed unlikely to go the way of Provincetown or Ocean City.

Under a bright midafternoon sun we said farewell to Leslie, who would here embark on an eighteen-hour bus ride to Rio de Janeiro as the first leg of her return to the States. Giggling, three gay men hoisted a large barrel full of garbage—plastic bags and bottles, rinds of fruit and meat scraps, tin cans and beer and *cachaça* bottles—and dumped it into the river. The incoming tide swept the noxious mess toward the ferry dock. Wanting to make our way out past the shallows while the tide was still rising, we returned to *Sanderling* and hastily got moving. By midafternoon we were clear of all reefs, and sailing under a cloudless sky past the glorious beaches of the Ajuda. Our swift passage continued overnight in bright moonlight. By early morning we were among the Abrolhos, a collection of small islands thirty miles offshore. Declared a national park in 1983, the Abrolhos contain the southernmost coral reefs on South America's east coast, and are a principal destination for scuba divers and snorkelers from the little resort villages to the south of Pôrto Seguro.

"Oh, the Abrolhos," said a young Frenchman named Dominique in Pôrto Seguro. "The Brazilians talk about them a lot. But if you've seen the Caribbean they're nothing special." Wrong, Dom. Anchoring in calm clear water under the lee of the largest Abrolho, called Santa Bárbara, we found ourselves in a quiet paradise. Ashore, a little settlement is occupied by a small naval detachment, to man the communications station and the powerful candy-striped lighthouse, and a single park ranger. A Brazilian naval supply vessel was anchored among the islands, making a delivery. But by midday it had cleared off, and so had a couple of small tourist boats. Now we were virtually alone, amid an abundance of bird life, with nearby nesting colonies of boobies, frigate birds, and tropic birds with graceful long tails and screeching cries. We watched the soaring frigate birds, which cannot get airborne from the water and therefore refrain from landing on it, try to snatch food from the bills of other species. Under the water's surface we found vast stretches of healthy coral (including several endemic species), and particularly large parrotfish and other reef dwellers. The grandeur of the fish, and the isolation of the setting, separated this place from anywhere in the Caribbean that *Sanderling* had visited: the Abrolhos were as close as we would get to the Darwinian mood of the Galápagos or those islands' Atlantic equivalent, Fernando de Noronha.

Ashore, I chatted at length with Hélio, the pleasant young duty ranger for the National Park Service. Before the islands had been declared a park and fishing banned, he said, overfishing had been the principal threat to the region's stability. Now the dangers were beginning to come from too much tourism. Though the regular dive-boat captains were well known to the park staff and obey the rules, other "pirates" visited as well. They brought passengers intent on spearing fish, collecting coral, and doing other forbidden things. Though ours was the only yacht that Hélio had seen during his fortnight on duty (it was his first), the numbers of visitors had generally been rising: twelve to fifteen boats at anchor at the height of the season, two thousand total visitors during the most recent year. To protect the nesting bird colonies, Hélio explained, Santa Bárbara Island would remain permanently closed. As for policing the perimeter, the park service now had to rely on its single open boat, whose engine was currently not working. But by year end, Hélio reported, they would receive funding adequate for the task at hand. The next day, Hélio rowed out to *Sanderling* and we talked further as the tropic birds squawked and circled overhead. He was one of the few optimistic Brazilians we encountered anywhere.

We began Easter Sunday with a frenzy of Abrolhos snorkeling. Matt went ashore on one of the smaller islands and filmed fluffy white booby chicks and fearless parents remaining on their eggs no matter how close he came. All of the bird species seemed to be doing well, he reported, despite the constant threat of piracy by the frigate birds. It remained bright and calm into the afternoon. When a little breeze filled in, I reluctantly decided that we should begin our 170-mile run to the industrial port of Vitória, where we would again lose Flo. After a slow night, during which we were apprehensive about using the engine because we had little fuel left, we enjoyed good conditions for our final twenty-four hours and deployed our light MPS reaching sail for most of these. At dawn on the second morning we had Vitória in sight and soon were abeam of the giant iron-ore-loading facility operated by the Companhia Vale do Rio Doce (CVRD), a state-owned mining and

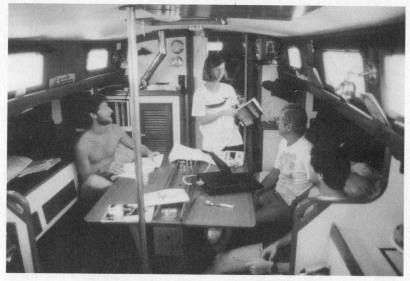

Crewmembers below and southward bound. *Left to right:*
M. Huntington, L. Stone, the author, E. Hoyt.

minerals company. To port was the large span, across the channel that makes the city an island, that is locally known as the "epileptic bridge" because of the many fits and starts during its long construction period. We asked a fisherman for directions to the yacht club and before long found it, tucked into a pretty little cove far up in the bay. The view gave out across to the giant CVRD facility.

Vitória was a bridge for us as well—from the rustic charms of the southern Bahia coast, to which we had grown accustomed since our departure from Salvador, to the mixed blessing of Rio that lay just ahead. Under the tutelage of Luís Carlos de Andrade Filho, a young man we met at the yacht club who ended up mothering all of us, we visited supermarkets offering far more variety than what was available in the North. At multi-story shopping malls, Luís Carlos helped us change dollars at a favorable rate. We ate at an excellent Chinese restaurant and at a streetside "trattoria," where we watched a guard assail a thief with a hot griddle, sparks flying. When time came to say goodbye, Luís Carlos came down to the float and filmed us all with his new video recorder. Then, representing once again the warm and generous side of this patchwork country, he drove off to the airport to put Flo on her plane while the rest of us put out to sea.

Two hundred and fifty-four miles now lay between us and our destination. I planned to cover them in a single lunge, in which, I hoped, we would be assisted by the favorable current and by winds almost bound to be favorable after we had rounded Cabo de São Tomé, about one hundred miles away, and fallen off toward the west. We reached this point about twenty-four hours out and indeed found a favorable breeze that would have pushed us in to Rio scarcely more than a day later. But Peter had lobbied for a stop in the area of Búzios and Cabo Frio, settlements and fishing villages from colonial times and now summer resorts. Though I did not concur, I agreed. At dawn we put in to the snug anchorage at Ilha Comprida, a craggy rock off the beach at the town of Cabo Frio. The one wooded section of the island provides a habitat for many parrots. As we anchored at sunrise, they left their roosts to cross over to the mainland and feed on fruit trees. We climbed to the island's crest and sampled spectacular views, across blue-green water, to the beaches and bays and bold headlands along the mainland shore. In the afternoon the breeze dropped. Gray hazy clouds began gathering as we prepared to depart at dusk. As we hauled up the anchor a blizzard of parrots returned, in pairs, and settled into the trees growing on a steep slope of the island.

Soon we learned the dimensions of the penalty we would pay for our Ilha Comprida layover. With the wind down to a whisper we motored toward the bold promontory also named Cabo Frio and famous for the storms that often swirl around the area. Faithful for weeks, the engine abruptly surged and we switched it off. In pitch darkness we ghosted along, then picked up ominous little whiffs of breeze from the southwest. Within moments we were in a full-fledged squall, with heavy rain and winds—our worst burst of weather since the frontal passage we had encountered off Jacksonville, Florida, a year before. The wind opened a bad tear along a seam of our genoa jib; miraculously it did not blow out entirely before we replaced it with the working jib.

All night we pounded along, close-hauled, as miserable weather continued and Rio grew little nearer. By morning the swells had become large, building toward the heavy surf that coastal Brazilians call a *resaca*. When the visibility improved between heavy rainsqualls, we could see waves crashing strongly against the beaches of the resort towns along the coast north of Rio. Later in the day the rain stopped and the wind died. The engine surged each time we started it, and we began to fear that if we tried to use it now, it might give out entirely—or simply not start at all—if the wind dropped to zero and the mountainous waves began sweeping us toward the beach. For several hours we drifted, barely maintaining steerageway. Midafternoon brought a little northerly off-

View from *Sanderling*'s first anchorage
in Guanabara Bay, Rio de Janeiro.

shore breeze that ghosted us along somewhat faster. By dusk the heights
of Sugarloaf and Rio's other soaring peaks crept into view.

At 0108 on Sunday, April 10, we finally dropped the anchor off Rio's
unwelcoming yacht club. We celebrated with the last drops of some good
scotch that Mauricio Obregón had brought aboard in Antigua and with
our last bottle of good Barbadian rum. This was hardly the shutter-
snapping, triumphant entry into Rio that had been envisioned. But we
were there. We had done with 7,685 or so miles of sailing from Maine.

16

Beyond Brazil

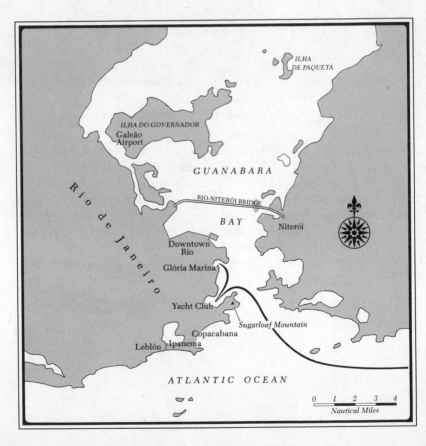

Ships entering Guanabara Bay during the seventeenth century.

NOW MY TASK WAS TO TRY TO LEARN SOMETHING OF THE CONDITIONS in Rio's Guanabara Bay. One hundred forty-seven square miles in size, containing one hundred thirteen islands, with eighty-one miles of shoreline, this body of water ranks among the world's spectacular natural harbors. From outside the narrow jaws of its entrance, one side of the view embraces the graceful curve of Copacabana Beach and ends at Arpoador Point, with the famous beaches of Ipanema and Leblón beyond, and in the distance the remarkable volcanic towers called Dois Irmãos (Two Brothers) and the Pedra da Gávea (Gávea Rock).

Sugarloaf lies off the port bow, the Corcovado with its famous Christ figure dead ahead. Below the mountain and a little to starboard, the city. In the distance the mighty bridge that spans the bay from Rio across to Niterói, another city of substantial size that lies between spectacular high cliffs on the bay's north coast. Inside the bowl of the bay are sandy beaches, calm waters, many pleasure craft and large ships at anchor and along the quays of the busy port. Both Rio's international airport, called Galeão (Galleon), and a downtown commuter-flight terminal face on the bay. How, I wondered, did conditions here compare with those of the Hudson or the Chesapeake, or to All Saints Bay in Bahia?

My reintroduction to the bay began with a helicopter fly-over kindly arranged by my old friend Márcio Moreira Alves, a senior official in the Rio de Janeiro state government. Together we drove up a steep knoll to a heliport behind the ornate Laranjeiras Palace, the President's residence in the days before the capital moved inland to Brasília, now the home of the state governor. The chopper lifted into the still air of early morning, banked sharply left, and overflew the port area, heading toward Galeão and the large Duque de Caxias oil refinery near the upper end of the bay. Then we circled clockwise, passing over Paquetá Island, a traditional tourist destination, then Niterói. Once past the harbor's narrow jaws we leveled off and ran the beaches to the end of Leblon, then turned back to land at a midtown clearing above the Palácio Guanabara, where the state governor works.

My notes while embarked on this ride convey something of the horrors I saw:

> Situation on islands near port: black ooze . . . black sewers (open) draining in . . . blue-black water . . . dead mangroves on dried-out mud flats . . . garbage dump alongside . . . then the refinery . . . one fishing boat out working . . . near many fish weirs the water iridescent from an oil slick . . . waves of scum off Paquetá and near the Marine training camp . . . garbage floating in great stripes and bands . . . open sewers leading out from the Intercontinental and Nacional hotels near Gávea.

Nothing could have been more shocking than to see close up, from the air, the ravages imposed by modern times on this striking body of water. In search of the details, I called on Victor Monteiro Barbosa Coelho, a senior civil engineer with many years' service at the Fundação Estadual de Engenharia do Meio Ambiente (FEEMA), the state environmental agency. "Forty years ago, when I was a small boy, my father had a little motorboat and we spent a lot of time on the bay," Coelho began. "It was heavily used then for recreation and fishing, and many people would take the ferry across to the beaches on islands like Paquetá. In, say, 1950 the bay was almost completely clean except for a little pollution around the port area. But then two things happened. One was that the population began to grow very fast. In 1950 there were 4.6 million people in the region, of whom about three million were within the ecosystem of the bay. In 1980 eight million lived on the bay, and today the number has passed nine million, and there was proportional growth in the need for sewage-treatment facilities. For financial and political reasons, this could not properly be addressed. Secondly, the

Duque de Caxias oil refinery, which opened in 1961, marked the beginning of accelerated industrial development. In 1960 we had about 5,500 factories around the bay. Now we have 10,000, of which half are significant sources of pollution. The Duque de Caxias refinery is still responsible for the greatest amount of point-source pollution. The liquid effluents it pumps into the bay contain great quantities of oil, grease, heavy metals such as cadmium and mercury, and organic matter—56 percent of all the industrial waste entering the bay. For a long time, Petrobrás, the government's oil company, simply ignored our complaints. Now they have agreed to comply, and other companies have applied pollution controls. Nevertheless, industries remain a principal source of all the bay's pollution. The situation has reached a state of emergency, not only for the sake of the bay's ecosystem, but also for the health of the people in the region."

In a paper he wrote in 1987, Coelho provided further detail about the growing crisis. The pollution problem had been aggravated by deforestation around the bay, leading to erosion and flooding during the periods of heavy rain that often occur during summer months. Only 17 percent of the region's domestic sewage was receiving secondary treatment; 58 percent was not treated at all. Sardine-processing plants and slaughterhouses contributed not only large volumes of organic matter but noxious odors as well. For want of adequate garbage collection systems in many sectors around the bay, the rivers carried large quantities of litter casually tossed into them. Fifteen of the rivers entering the bay were polluted. Coelho and others have documented the rapid siltation of the bay due to erosion. Ten percent of the bay has already been lost to landfill. More than half of it, Coelho told Marlise Simons of *The New York Times* in a 1987 interview, is one foot and a half or less in depth, and in danger of drying up. Oil tankers are said to violate regulations and flush their tanks at night within the bay. About the only problem the bay does not have is that of excessive nutrients from agriculture, still poorly developed in the region and using little fertilizer. But Guanabara Bay receives torrents of everything else, and because of its narrow entrance only a small central section of its total area gets any significant flushing from the sea. Garbage dump, cesspool, Love Canal—these were the words being applied to it.

The results of the onslaught have been disastrous to many forms of life. Commercial fishing dropped 90 percent from 1967 to 1987, the shrimp catch from 300 tons a year in 1961 to 24 tons a year in 1972 to zero in 1987. Mangroves are disappearing at a relentless rate. Though they are still heavily used, all beaches in the bay's interior are unsafe for swimming. So severe has the situation become, said Coelho's report, that the region's health and very economy are severely endangered; cleaning up the bay must form an integral portion of the state of Rio de Janeiro's economic development program.

The problem with the government's remedies for the bay—better laws, better enforcement, a massive program to construct sewers and sewage-treatment facilities—is that they cost vast amounts of money. Debt is a heavy burden: in 1986, 59 cents on every dollar that Brazil earned from exports went to repay foreign loans. All government functions and services are greatly squeezed, at a moment when needs have never been greater. The state of Rio de Janeiro's financial problems are exacerbated by the fact that its government, continually in opposition to the Brasília regime from 1971 until 1987, has consequently received less than its fair share of federal revenues. Much catching up is required before any progress can be achieved. In the past and in spite of all the nation's notorious weaknesses, Brazil and its engineers have performed with remarkable efficiency in the installation of a nationwide electric-power system. An open question is whether, even if the funds were available, the nation could respond as effectively to the challenge of cleaning up its coastal waters.

To the south of Rio, the Santos area is another center of pollution. It contains the fetid chemical-plant town of Cubatão, often cited as the world's most polluted place until the situation recently moderated somewhat thanks to the government's insistence that the industries overconcentrated there install new controls. If Guanabara Bay and Santos rank with the worst of U.S. industrial pollution, and they do, what kinds of comparisons can be made between other coastal areas in the two countries? For one thing, though industrialization has proceeded rapidly in Brazil since the 1960s, point-source toxic pollution from factories affects far less of the coastline than in the United States, where pulp and paper plants alone represent a problem from Maine to Florida. Second, since Brazilian farms are far less doused with chemical or organic fertilizers than those in the United States, nutrient pollution affects only small portions of the Brazilian coast. Ownership patterns also favor Brazil. Whereas U.S. developers are usually able within the law to crowd new condos right up against the high-water line on their own property, in Brazil a very different regime applies. By means of regulations handed down from the Portuguese king to guarantee public access to the beaches, a strip of land thirty-three meters in from the 1831 coast remains in government hands. Much of the coast has been controlled by the Navy, which recently concluded that it could not handle the mounting challenge of coastal management, and would prefer to hand over much of the responsibility to civilian officials. Still, the governing principle has spared Brazil's coast the kinds of assault launched at Ocean City or Myrtle Beach.

In Brazil commercial fishing remains by and large the province of the poorest of the poor. Few fishermen can afford to make investments in expensive commercial rigs and the business remains largely artisanal, a matter of canoes and *jangadas* and small motorboats. The government agency formally entrusted with national fisheries management cannot exercise effective control over most of the country's long coastline. But the primitive nature of the national fishery has itself been a way to limit predation of the stocks. Along many stretches of the coast, according to the ethnographers John C. Cordell and Margaret A. McKean, Brazil's own fishermen have done at least as good a job of self-policing as would be done if they were rigidly controlled by effective regulators. In many communities, the researchers found, the "informal" systems they have established are, even if difficult for an outsider to perceive, "just as real, socially binding, and ecologically consequential as standard catch quotas, seasons, and selective licensing programs." Another positive factor has been Brazil's isolation from other countries and markets. Factory ships from faraway places are seldom found offshore, let alone preying on inshore stocks.

As in the United States, the most general coastal problem that Brazil faces is the onslaught of a rapidly rising population. In 1964, when Flo and I arrived in Brazil, the population of the entire nation was on the order of 65 million, and it was growing at a rate approaching 3 percent. The 1989 population was approaching 145 million. Though the growth rate was down to 1.8 percent, Brazil was still adding 3 million new people each year. National policy has favored westward expansion, away from the coast, since the new capital was built at Brasília in the late 1950s. Nevertheless, the population continues to grow along the coast as well, particularly in large cities, where 70 percent of all Brazilians live (vs. only 30 percent in 1940). What is different in Brazil is the relative absence of coastal degradation in rural areas. From each large urban area the belt of disorderly development oozes outward as the population expands. At least along the extensive stretch of coast that we viewed from *Sanderling*, though, pristine quality took over at development's edge and remained dominant for scores or even hundreds of miles up to the outer border of the next urban agglomeration. Brazil's coastal problems are more concentrated, less widespread than those of the United States.

Put together, these arguments lead to the conclusion that, despite the casual and sometimes even venal way in which Brazil operates, its coastline remains in better overall condition than that of the United

States. Because of its great burst of industrialization, on the other hand, Brazil faces worse problems than even the large islands of the Greater Antilles. Closer to purity on the spectrum are the Windwards and Leewards, and at the very top are the Bahamas, where Nassau was the only place I could find with anything more serious than nuisance forms of pollution. Everywhere, on the other hand, growing numbers of people along the shore would cause things to continue getting worse unless new and tighter controls are imposed and new attitudes and behavior patterns emerge.

As *Sanderling* lay dormant in Rio, we pondered the question of what other conclusions had come from our experience. One, surely, was that we had seen fine examples of resiliency along the coast. The return of the Atlantic puffin to Maine islands, of the bald eagle to the Hudson River valley, of the brown pelican to the southeastern shores of the United States, are stirring examples of what nature can achieve if people alter their behavior in small ways. Unlike tropical forests, which once destroyed are not likely to recover the fullness of their original biological diversity, coastal and marine natural communities tend toward restoration. Coral reefs and mangroves will regenerate if given a chance. The white sea urchins of the Caribbean reproduce remarkably fast. If some species such as marine turtles will be slow to rid themselves of toxic poisons they have accumulated, others—notably clams and oysters—can regain full health with great speed.

Dune grasses, subaquatic vegetation in estuaries, the algae and seaweeds and other plant organisms of fundamental importance to marine environments, will grow again where the water is clean. The haddock and the cod are examples of fish now showing signs of recovery from decades of overfishing. It is a miracle that the lobsters of New England and the Virgin Islands, the crabs of the Chesapeake and All Saints Bay, have survived at all. Since mortality rates for many marine species are extremely high even without human intervention, they are often designed to withstand heavy attrition. Numerous finfish, sea turtles, the Caribbean conch, all compensate by laying vast numbers of eggs. Most die. A greater percentage would survive in a more favorable environment.

We saw much of the zeal and vitality with which gifted individuals are already out there on the barricades, doing their best to give nature a hand. From Philip Conkling and Steve Kress in Maine to Lena Ritter and Todd Miller in North Carolina, from Allen Putney and Yves Renard, Gabriel Charles and Paul Butler in the Caribbean to Tania Tavares and Victor Coelho in Brazil, the Atlantic coast has become increasingly populated by knowledgeable, dedicated individuals and institutions with

A classic cartographic view of the coast's sweep made in 1529.

lengthening lists of accomplishments to their credit. These people are a rather nicer lot on the whole than the discoverers and settlers who preceded them by five hundred years and who by and large were far less nobly motivated. Few are the examples of those who arrived from Europe during the sixteenth century, such as the Spanish missionaries on Georgia's St. Catherines Island or Cabral's crew during their scant week in Pôrto Seguro, who established any notable measure of rapport with the people or natural environments they encountered.

We saw many examples of fixes that can be accomplished fairly easily at the local level. As Brazil's "primitive" fishermen have shown, it does not take vast bureaucracies or heavy-handed controls to achieve effective management of marine resources. A few young scientists managed to shut down powerful industries polluting All Saints Bay in northern Brazil. The U.S. coast offers many fine examples of how citizens can act to reduce point-source toxic contamination. If adequate treatment of human wastes is built in as a high priority when communities begin rapid growth, the shock of this cost is far more tolerable than when older cities such as Boston take up the $6 billion task of making up for more than a century of neglect. Every citizen living near or on a coast can directly affect its health—by being careful about garbage and sewage, by refraining from using cars that leak oil or use leaded gasoline, by showing vigilance about local sources of toxic or organic pollution and about poorly planned real estate development projects.

Many of the coastal problems, however, have become far too diffuse to be soluble on the basis of even the most skillful local action. The growing role of acid rain as a source of coastal pollution ("sewage from the sky," Environmental Defense Fund scientist Michael Oppenheimer called it) demands that the issue be addressed not regionally but nationally and even internationally. Nonpoint-source pollution is almost as insidious. Community efforts cannot fully address new realities: storm-water runoff from superhighways, and excessive organic wastes flowing into streams, rivers, and estuaries from faraway towns and farms are major contributors to coastal woes. More than half of all U.S. estuarial pollution was, by 1988, coming from nonpoint sources.

Failure, or at least partial failure, will have to be accepted in some instances even if the rules get tougher. Cleaning up Guanabara Bay or the Chesapeake can at best be achieved on the basis of decades of work and hundreds of millions of dollars. It is unlikely that either of these jobs will ever be fully done. Perhaps all one can expect is for the decline to be arrested and gradual, limited restoration instituted. In the absence of additional measures, the Office of Technology Assessment's 1987 *Wastes in Marine Environments* report argued, "new or continued degradation will occur in many estuaries and some coastal waters during the next few decades (even in some areas that exhibited improvement in the past)."

In the United States, where the toughest problems are to be found, we are also seeing the most aggressive counterattack. In 1988, the Natural Resources Defense Council published, in its incisive *Amicus Journal*, an acerbic critique of current coastal regulations by Tulane University law professor Oliver Houck. The trouble with coastal management programs, he stated, is that they "are not designed to protect coastal resources. They are designed to produce tradeoffs." The principal shortcoming of the Clean Water Act's support for improved municipal sewage treatment, said Houck, is that the waste should never have been dumped into the water in the first place but treated by available technologies "as a resource to be reclaimed." Agricultural discharges, in Houck's view, are "firmly out of control," the National Estuary Program passed by Congress in 1987 no more than an enlarged version of previous failures, the NPDES discharge-permitting program badly in need of new criteria based on "best available technologies" rather than merely on limiting the flow of effluents.

The coast "is disappearing so rapidly that the measures needed to save it are almost at the limits of technology, to say nothing of economics and political will," Houck continued. "It is time to stop fooling around. A few parts of our coastline are holding their own, but most are deteriorating and some are in a state of total collapse. Either we act more forcefully to save America's most important ecosystem, or we should stop spending the money on halfway measures that simply forestall the inevitable."

Houck recommended a sweeping remedial effort, including tough new limitations on coastal development; the institution of "nondestructive technologies" to harvest oil, gas, and fish; an end to reliance on "water as a carrier and assimilator of human wastes" and to "the introduction of industrial pollutants into our sewage-treatment systems." Overall, Houck called for "the full leverage of federal aid to require sound conservation practices" to restore coastal water quality.

With regard to bays and estuaries, the proceedings of Save the Bay's 1987 Rhode Island meeting provide a draft agenda for national action. The group advocated a "subsidy-busting" program to remove incentives for coastal development; measures to reduce waste at the source rather than dispose of it; a renewed commitment to save and restore wetlands; the establishment of an "Aquafund" to complement the EPA's Superfund; and a return to "environmental law and order." The essential message of the Rhode Island group was to reiterate what was first whispered in the 1972 Coastal Zone Management Act: what happens on land is the key to the quality of adjacent waters, and to be effective any new rules or laws will have to obey this principle.

In 1988, a National Wetlands Forum, chaired by three state governors, including New Jersey's inventive Thomas Kean, issued a comprehensive report based on participation by hundreds of people in the public and private sectors. The report, published by the Conservation Foundation (convener of the Forum), called for a variety of detailed steps to achieve "no overall net loss of the nation's remaining wetlands base," and said also that "it is time for the nation to realize wetlands protection is good public policy."

At last, perhaps more out of fear than nobility of purpose, U.S. citizens may have started listening to exhortations such as these; a national constituency seemed to be forming, and prospects for national action seemed politically promising. A public beyond the committed few had finally become aroused. In the long run the result of this greater awareness will depend not so much on press coverage or political rhetoric, or even court decisions, as on how people end up reacting to their new knowledge—what they will be willing to accept, what sacrifices they will be willing to make. The most difficult thing for landowners to swallow, beyond the sheer cost of some remedial efforts, will be the need to surrender personal freedom, even power. In this regard, a key indicator will be the fate of Maryland's ambitious Critical Areas program (which in 1989 suffered from budget cutbacks) and other initiatives such as the proposed limitations on the development of Cape Cod and the New Jersey coast. One can only wonder what lessons the Brazilians, and the people of the Caribbean, might draw from the U.S. experience.

The voyage of the *Sanderling* took place during the infancy of a paradigm. Not only were coastal problems hidden for many years; they were not even remotely recognized as threats. In 1957, as astute a man as Judge Curtis Bok, an avid blue-water yachtsman (and father of the Harvard president), echoed the world's opinion in writing: "The sea is earth's primal antiseptic, taking its rot and ordure and debris at the littoral and destroying their infection." Now, dramatically, the notion of salt water as the great cleanser is being replaced by a reverse idea: that the mess we create on land poisons the adjacent seas and that this process has profoundly negative consequences for almost everybody. As of the late 1980s, the defenders of the Atlantic coast had a big new idea within which to frame their future actions.

If only there had been more time! I had wanted to visit Red Bay and other small towns along the north shore of the Gulf of St. Lawrence, where local people are now beginning to regard the seabirds—the auklets and murres and dovekies and razorbills—as integral parts of their environment rather than simply as objects to be caught and eaten. I had wanted to visit L'Anse aux Meadows, a desolate bay on the Newfoundland shore that may have been settled by Vikings and was doubtless a stopping-off place for a succession of early explorers from Cabot to Cartier. I had wanted to visit São Paulo and see Cubatão, then sail *Sanderling* south to the Váldez Peninsula on the Argentine coast with the cetologist Roger Payne, to witness the great congregation of breeding whales that reaches its peak there during the months of September and October. There was much yet to study, to experience, to see.

Now, one damp night in Rio, I stood under a glary floodlight at the entrance to the Glória Marina, where *Sanderling* had rested for a fortnight. Peter and Matt and Ned were gathered around, and so were Bob Heinemann and Barry Willson, who would whistle the boat back to the Caribbean and then to Florida, her final resting place under the WWF flag. We stood sheepishly about. As Bill Anderson had to me in Camden, I mumbled bits of last-minute advice to the new crew. I tried also to express the appreciation I felt to others who had come so far with me.

A few handshakes and embraces. It felt like a funeral. Then I dove into the waiting taxi and sped off to the Galleon airport.

Bibliography

"Christopher Columbus and the New World He Found," *National Geographic*, November 1975.

"Columbus and the New World," *National Geographic*, November 1986.

"Don't Go Near the Water," *Newsweek*, August 1, 1988.

"Our Troubled Coasts," *Oceans*, March–April 1987.

"Shrinking Shores," *Time*, August 10, 1987.

"The Dirty Seas," *Time*, August 1, 1988.

"Troubled Waters," *Business Week*, October 12, 1987.

Amsler, Jean. *Histoire Universelle des Explorations*. Vol. 2. Paris: Nouvelle Librairie de France.

Barbour, Henry. *The Three Worlds of Captain John Smith*. Boston: Houghton Mifflin, 1964.

Barbour, Philip. *The Jamestown Voyages under the First Charter, 1606–09*. London: Cambridge University Press, 1969.

Barbour, Thomas. *Naturalist at Large*. Boston: Little, Brown, 1943.

Beam, Lura. *A Maine Hamlet*. New York: Wilfred Funk, 1957.

Beitzell, Edwin W. *Life on the Potomac*. Abell, Md.: E. Beitzell, 1968.

Beston, Henry M. *The Outermost House*. Garden City, N.Y.: Doubleday, Doran, 1928.

Biggar, H. P., ed. *The Works of Samuel de Champlain*. Toronto: The Champlain Society, 1922–26.

Bok, Curtis. *The Newport-Santander Race 1957*. Privately published.

Boorstin, Daniel J. *The Discoverers*. New York: Random House, 1983.

Boyle, Robert H. *The Hudson River*. New York: W. W. Norton, 1969.

Bradley. A. G., ed. *Travels and Works of Captain John Smith*. New York: Burt Franklin, 1910.

Brereton, John. *A Brief and True Relation of the Discoverie of the North Part of Virginia*. London: George Bishop, 1602.

Brown, Ralph H. *A Historical Geography of the United States*. New York: Harcourt, Brace, 1948.

———. *Mirror for Americans*. New York: American Geographical Society, 1943.

Burrage, Henry S. *Early English and French Voyages*. New York: Scribner's, 1906.

———, ed. *Gorges and the Grant of the Province of Maine 1622*. Augusta, Me., 1923.

Bibliography

Caminha, Pedro Vaz de. *A Carta de Pedro Vaz de Caminha*. Rio de Janeiro: Livraria Agir Editora, 1965.

Capper, John, Garrett Power, and Frank R. Shivers, Jr. *Chesapeake Waters: Pollution, Public Health, and Public Opinion 1607–1972*. Centreville, Md.: Tidewater Publishers, 1983.

Carr, Archie. *The Windward Road*. New York: Alfred A. Knopf, 1963.

Carson, Rachel L. *The Edge of the Sea*. Boston: Houghton Mifflin, 1955.

———. *The Sea Around Us*. New York: Oxford University Press, 1951

———. *Under the Sea Wind*. New York: Oxford University Press, 1952.

Chao, Ling Nabbish, and William Kirby-Smith, eds. *Proceedings of the International Symposium on Utilization of Coastal Ecosystems*. Rio Grande, Brazil: Editora da Fundação Universidade do Rio Grande do Sul, 1985.

Clark, John. *Coastal Ecosystems: Ecological Considerations for Management of the Coastal Zone*. Washington, D.C.: The Conservation Foundation, 1974.

Conkling, Philip W. *Islands in Time*. Camden, Me.: Down East Books, 1981.

Cornell, Jimmy. *Ocean Cruising Survey*. Dobbs Ferry, N.Y.: Sheridan House, 1986.

Craton, Michael. *A History of the Bahamas*. London and Glasgow: Collins, 1962.

Cronon, William. *Changes in the Land*. New York: Hill and Wang, 1983.

Darwin, Charles. *The Voyage of the Beagle*. Leonard Engel, ed. Garden City, N.Y.: Doubleday, 1962.

DeBlieu, Jan. *Hatteras Journal*. Golden, Colo.: Fulcrum, 1987.

Defoe, Daniel. *A General History of the Robberies and Murders of the Most Notorious Pyrates*. Reprinted and with a new introduction by William Graves. New York and London: Garland Publishing, 1972.

DeVorsey, Louis, Jr., and John Parker, eds. *In the Wake of Columbus*. Detroit, Mich.: Wayne State University Press, 1985.

Doyle, Chris. *Sailor's Guide to the Windward Islands*. St. Lucia, 1984.

Duke, Thomas W., ed. *Impact of Man on the Coastal Environment*. Washington, D.C.: Office of Research and Development, U.S. Environmental Protection Agency, 1982.

Duncan, Roger F., and John P. Ware. *A Cruising Guide to the New England Coast*. New York: Dodd, Mead, 1967.

Dwight, Timothy. *Travels in New England and New York*. New Haven, Conn.: T. Dwight, 1821–22.

Eiman, William J. *St. Maarten/St. Martin Area + St. Kitts & Nevis Cruising Guide*. Philadelphia: Virgin Island Plus Charters, 1986.

Exquemling, John. *The Buccaneers of America*. Reprint. New York: Dover Publications, 1967.

Farb, Peter. *Face of North America*. New York: Harper & Row, 1963.

——— and John Hay. *The Atlantic Shore*. New York: Harper & Row, 1966.

Fields, Meredith Helleberg, ed. *Yachtsman's Guide to the Bahamas*. North Miami, Fla.: Tropic Isle Publishers, 1986.

———, ed. *Yachtsman's Guide to the Virgin Islands & Puerto Rico*. North Miami, Fla.: Tropic Isle Publishers, 1986.

Fisher, Diane, Jane Ceraso, Thomas Mathew, Michael Oppenheimer. *Polluted Coastal Waters: The Role of Acid Rain*. New York: Environmental Defense Fund, 1988.

Footner, Hulbert. *Rivers of the Eastern Shore*. New York: Holt, Rinehart and Winston, 1944.

Fox, William T. *At the Sea's Edge*. Englewood Cliffs, N.J.: Prentice-Hall, 1983.

Fuson, Robert H. *The Log of Christopher Columbus*. Camden, Me.: International Marine Publishing Company, 1987.

Gardyner, George. *Description of the New World*. London, 1651.

Goerch, Carl. *Ocracoke*. Winston-Salem, N.C.: John F. Blair, 1956.

Bibliography

Greenlee, William B., ed. *The Voyages of Pedro Alvares Cabral to Brazil and India*. London: Hakluyt Society, 1938.

Hakluyt, Richard. *The Principal Navigations, Voiages, Traffiques, and Discoueries of the English Nation*. 3 vols. London, 1589, and London, 1598–1600.

Hammond, Beth, et al. *Saving Our Bays, Sounds, and the Great Lakes: The National Agenda*. Providence, R.I.: Save the Bay, Inc., 1988.

Hariot, Thomas. *A Briefe and True Report of the New Found Land of Virginia*. London, 1588.

Harrisse, Henry. *The Discovery of North America*. London and Paris, 1892.

Hedeen, Robert A. *The Oyster*. Centreville, Md.: Tidewater Publishers, 1986.

Horton, Tom. *Bay Country*. Baltimore and London: Johns Hopkins University Press, 1987.

Houck, Oliver A. "America's Mad Dash to the Sea," *The Amicus Journal* (New York: Natural Resources Defense Council, Vol. 10, Summer 1988).

Howe, Henry F. *Prologue to New England*. New York: Farrar & Rinehart, 1943.

———. *Salt Rivers of the Massachusetts Shore*. New York: Rinehart, 1951.

Ives, J. Moss. *The Ark and the Dove*. New York: Cooper Square Publishers, 1969.

Jameson, J. L., ed. *Original Narratives of Early American History*. Reprint. New York: Barnes & Noble, 1967.

Jameson, John F. *Narratives of New Netherland, 1609–69*. New York: Scribner's, 1909.

Kalm, Peter. *Travels into North America*. 2 vols. London: T. Lowndes, 1772.

Kaufman, Wallace, and Orrin Pilkey. *The Beaches Are Moving*. Garden City, N.Y.: Anchor Press/Doubleday, 1979.

Kincaid, Jamaica. *A Small Place*. New York: Farrar, Straus & Giroux, 1988.

Klingel, Gilbert C. *The Bay*. Hatboro, Pa.: Tradition Press, 1987.

Klinkenborg, Verlyn. "Sir Francis Drake and the Age of Discovery." Monograph. New York: The Pierpont Morgan Library, 1988.

Leite, Serafim. *História da Companhia de Jesus no Brasil*. Lisbon: Livraria Portugalia, 1938–50.

Léry, Jean de. *Viagem a Terra do Brasil*. São Paulo: Livraria Martins, 1967.

Loomis, Alfred F. *Ranging the Maine Coast*. New York: W. W. Norton, 1939.

Lorant, Stefan. *The New World*. New York: Duell, Sloane & Pearce, 1946.

MacLeish, William H. *Oil and Water*. Boston and New York: Atlantic Monthly Press, 1985.

Maltby, Edward. *Waterlogged Wealth*. London and Washington, D.C.: International Institute for Environment and Development, 1986.

Matthiessen, Peter. *Men's Lives*. New York: Random House, 1986.

McClymont, James Roxburgh. *The Discoveries Made by Pedro Alvarez Cabral and His Captains*. Hobart, Tasmania: J. Walch & Sons, 1909.

McKee, Gwen, ed. *A Guide to the Georgia Coast*. Savannah, Ga.: The Georgia Conservancy, 1984.

McKenzie, William J. *A Visit to South America*. London: Stanley Paul, 1922.

McManis, Douglas R. *European Impressions of the New England Coast, 1497–1620*. Chicago: University of Chicago Department of Geography, 1972.

Meinig, D. W. *The Shaping of America, Vol. 1, Atlantic America, 1492–1800*. New Haven and London: Yale University Press, 1986.

Metcalf, Paul. *Waters of the Potowmack*. San Francisco: North Point Press, 1982.

Millemann, Beth. *And Two If by Sea: Fighting the Attack on America's Coasts*. Washington, D.C.: Coast Alliance, 1986.

Morison, Samuel Eliot. *Admiral of the Ocean Sea*. Boston: Little, Brown, 1942.

———, ed. *Of Plymouth Plantation, 1620–1647*, by William Bradford. Boston: Houghton Mifflin, 1965.

Bibliography

————. *Samuel de Champlain*. Boston: Atlantic–Little, Brown, 1972.

————. *Spring Tides*. Boston: Houghton Mifflin, 1965.

———— and Mauricio Obregón. *The Caribbean as Columbus Saw It*. Boston: Atlantic–Little, Brown, 1964.

————. *The European Discovery of America: The Northern Voyages*. New York: Oxford University Press, 1971.

————. *The European Discovery of America: The Southern Voyages*. New York: Oxford University Press, 1974.

————. *The Story of Mount Desert Island*. Boston: Atlantic–Little, Brown, 1960.

Mota, Avelino Teixeira da. *Novos Documentos Sobre uma Expedição de Gonçalo Coelho ao Brasil*. Lisbon: Junta de Investigações do Ultramar, 1969.

Mueller, G. O. W., and Freda Adler. *Outlaws of the Ocean*. New York: Hearst Marine Books, 1985.

National Wetlands Policy Forum. *A Legacy for the Future*. Washington, D.C.: The Conservation Foundation, 1988.

Nobrega, Manuel da. *Cartas do Brasil*. Rio de Janeiro: Oficina Industrial Gráfica, 1931.

Obregón, Mauricio. *Argonauts to Astronauts: An Unconventional History of Discovery*. New York: Harper & Row, 1980.

Ogburn, Charlton. *The Winter Beach*. New York: Morrow, 1966.

Oppel, Frank, ed. *Tales of the New England Coast*. Secaucus, N.J.: Castle, 1985.

Parry, J. H., and Philip Sherlock. *A Short History of the West Indies*. New York: St. Martin's Press, 1956.

————. *The Discovery of South America*. New York: Taplinger, 1979.

Pilkey, Orrin H., Jr., and William J. Neal, Orrin H. Pilkey, Sr., and Stanley R. Riggs. *From Currituck to Calabash: Living with North Carolina's Barrier Islands*. Durham, N.C.: Duke University Press, 1978.

Plummer, Henry M. *The Boy, Me, and the Cat*. Rye, N.H.: C. Chandler Co., 1961.

Price, A. Grenfell. *White Settlers in the Tropics*. New York: American Geographical Society, 1939.

Putney, Allen D. *The Wider Caribbean: A Study in Diversity*. St. Croix, U.S. Virgin Islands: Unpublished, 1981.

Pyle, Douglas C. *Clean Sweet Wind*. Preston, Md.: Easy Reach Press, 1981.

Quinn, David. *Set Fair for Roanoke*. Chapel Hill and London: University of North Carolina Press, 1985.

Reiger, George. *Wanderer on My Native Shore*. New York: Simon & Schuster, 1983.

Roberts, W. Adolphe. *The Caribbean and the Story of Our Sea of Destiny*. New York: Negro Universities Press, 1940.

"Sailors Narratives of Voyages Along the New England Coast, 1524–1624." Notes by George P. Winship. New York: Burt Franklin, 1968.

Sauer, Carl O. *Land and Life*. Berkeley: University of California Press, 1967.

————. *Northern Mists*. Berkeley: University of California Press, 1968.

————. *Sixteenth Century North America*. Berkeley: University of California Press, 1971.

————. *The Early Spanish Main*. Berkeley: University of California Press, 1966.

Schlee, Susan. *On Almost Any Wind*. Ithaca, N.Y.: Cornell University Press, 1978.

Schoenbaum, Thomas J. *Islands, Capes, and Sounds*. Winston-Salem, N.C.: John F. Blair, 1982.

Scott, John Anthony, ed. *Settlers on the Eastern Shore*. New York: Alfred A. Knopf, 1967.

Semmes, Raphael. *Captains and Mariners of Early Maryland*. Baltimore: Johns Hopkins University Press, 1937.

Bibliography

Sherry, Frank. *Raiders and Rebels*. New York: Hearst Marine Books, 1986.

Simon, Anne W., and Paul Hauge. *Contamination of New England's Fish and Shellfish*. Washington, D.C.: The Coast Alliance, 1987.

Simons, Marlise. "The Bay's a Thing of Beauty; Pity It's a Cesspool," *The New York Times*, September 16, 1987.

Simpson, Dorothy. *The Maine Islands in Story and Legend*. From material compiled by members of the Maine Writers Research Club. Philadelphia and New York: J. B. Lippincott, 1960.

Smith, Bradford. *Captain John Smith*. Philadelphia: J. B. Lippincott, 1953.

Southey, Robert. *History of Brazil*. London, 1810.

Stick, David. *Roanoke Island: The Beginnings of English America*. Chapel Hill, N.C.: University of North Carolina Press, 1983.

Stone, Roger D. *Dreams of Amazonia*. New York: Elisabeth Sifton Books/Viking Press, 1985.

Stone, William T., and Fessenden S. Blanchard. *A Cruising Guide to the Chesapeake*. New York: Dodd, Mead, 1983.

Tate, Thad W., and David L. Ammerman. *The Chesapeake in the Seventeenth Century*. New York: W. W. Norton, 1979.

Teal, John and Mildred. *Life and Death of the Salt Marsh*. Boston: Atlantic–Little, Brown, 1969.

Thayer, Rev. Henry A. *Sagadahoc Colony*. Portland, Me.: Gorges Society, 1892.

Thevet, André. *The New Found Worlde*. London: Thomas Hacket, 1568.

U.S. Congress, Office of Technology Assessment. *Integrated Renewable Resource Management for U.S. Insular Areas*. Washington, D.C.: U.S. Government Printing Office, 1987.

————. *Wastes in Marine Environments*. Washington, D.C.: U.S. Government Printing Office, 1987.

U.S. Department of Commerce. *NOAA Estuarine and Coastal Ocean Science Framework*. Washington, D.C.: NOAA Estuarine Programs Office, National Oceanic and Atmospheric Administration, 1987.

Upton, Joe. *Amaretto*. Camden, Me.: International Marine Publishing Company, 1986.

Vasconcellos, Simão de. *Chrônica da Companhia de Jesus do Estado do Brasil*. Lisbon, 1663.

Vespucci, Amerigo. *The Letters of Amerigo Vespucci*. Sir Clements Markham, ed. London: Hakluyt Society, 1894.

————. *The Vespucci Reprints*. Princeton, N.J.: Princeton University Press, 1916.

Vigneras, L. A., ed. *The Journal of Christopher Columbus*. Cecil Jane, trans. New York: Clarkson N. Potter, 1960.

Warner, William W. *Beautiful Swimmers*. Boston: Atlantic Monthly Press, 1976.

————. *Distant Water*. Boston: Atlantic Monthly Press, 1983.

Weddle, Robert S. *Spanish Sea: The Gulf of Mexico in North American Discovery, 1500–1685*. College Station: Texas A&M University Press, 1985.

Whipple, A. B. C. *Vintage Nantucket*. New York: Dodd, Mead, 1978.

White, Rev. Andrew. *A Brief Relation of the Voyage unto Maryland*. London, 1634.

Wood, William. *New England's Prospect*. London: T. Cotes for J. Bellamie, 1634.

Wroth, Laurence C. *The Voyages of Giovanni de Verrazzano, 1542–1528*. New Haven: Yale University Press, 1970.

Index

Index

Index

Index

Index

Mustique, Grenadines, 257
Myrtle Beach, S.C., 108, 277

Nags Head, N.C., 88
Nantucket Conservation Commission, 43
Nantucket Conservation Foundation, 42, 43
Nantucket Island, Mass., 40–4
Napoleon, 159, 174
Narragansett Bay, R.I., 6, 51–2
Nassau, New Providence Island, Bahamas,
    120–1, 124, 278
Natal, Braz., 247
National Audubon Society, 22, 23
National Estuary Program, 281
National Flood Insurance Program, 7
National Geographic, 72, 76, 130, 134, 135,
    137
National Marine Fisheries Service, 100
National Oceanic and Atmospheric Adminis-
    tration (NOAA), 6
National Park Service, 92, 113
National Parks Trust (BVI), 180, 182
National Pollutant Discharge Elimination
    System (NPDES), 6, 52, 281
National Wetlands Forum, 282
Naturalists' Society (St. Lucia), 203
Natural Resources Defense Council
    (NRDC), 58, 59, 79, 281
Nature Conservancy, 8, 25, 31, 74–5
Nelson (Haitian boat boy), 159, 161
Nelson, Ripley, 42
Nelson's Dockyard (Antigua), 187
Nevis, 186
New Bedford, Mass., 44–7
New England, 17–34, 36–38, 49–53, 278
New England's Prospect (Wood), 21, 33–4
New Environmentalism, 72
New Jersey, 60–1, 282
New Providence Island, Bahamas, 120
Newsweek, 8
Newton Cay, Bahamas, 132
New World Museum (San Salvador, Baha-
    mas), 134
New York City, 54–5, 57, 58, 59
New York Harbor, 55
New York Nautical, 219
New York State, 53–60; Department of En-
    vironmental Conservation, 58, 59, 60
New York Times, 275
New York Zoological Society, 111
Nicholson, Desmond, 188–9, 191
Niña, 260

Niterói, Braz., 273
Noble, Edward John, 111
Nobrega, Fr. Manoel de, 264
Nonesuch Bay, Antigua, 188
nonpoint-source pollution, 280
Noonan, Pat, 75
Norbury's Landing, 61
Norfolk, Va., 84, 85, 86
Norman Cay, Bahamas, 122, 125
North Carolina, 87–97, 99–108; Dredge and
    Fill Act, 99; Marine Fisheries Commis-
    sion, 99, 105
North Carolina Coastal Federation, 101,
    105, 107
northern gannets, 108
Northern Voyages (Morison), 89
North Haven, Me., 17
North River sewage treatment plant (New
    York), 58
North Sound, Virgin Gorda, BVI, 182
Norumbega, 17, 18, 19
Nunes, Fr. Leonardo, 264
nutrient pollution, 4, 276

Oakes, Sir Harry, 121
Obregón, Javier, 127–47 *passim*
Obregón, Lita, 127, 130, 139, 142, 144
Obregón, Mauricio, 127–47 *passim*, 151,
    189, 191, 271
Ocean City, Md., 69–71, 92, 277
Oceanic Society, 7
Ocracoke, N.C., 94–7
Ollivierre, Athneal, 209
Oppenheimer, Michael, 280
Oregon Inlet, N.C., 91–3, 96
Organization of American States, 213
Orient Bay, St. Martin, 185
Outer Banks, N.C., 88, 91, 94, 99, 101
Outermost House, The (Beston), 36
Outward Bound, 25
Oyster, Va., 74
oysters, 37, 51, 54, 64, 65, 68, 76, 102–3,
    105, 106, 110, 278

Pamlico River, N.C., 87, 102
Pamlico Sound, N.C., 90, 91, 94, 99
Panama, 120
Paquetá Island, Braz., 274
Paradise Bay, Cambridge Cay, Bahamas, 125
parrots, 194–204 *passim*, 209–10, 270

Index

Pasquotank River, N.C., 87, 88
Patuxent River, Md., 73, 74
Payne, Roger, 283
PCBs, 46, 57, 59, 67
Peace and Plenty Hotel (Exumas, Bahamas), 218
Peace Corps volunteers, 178, 191, 199, 210
peat mining, 101
Pedro, José, 45
Peltier, W. R., 5
Pennsylvania, 64, 65, 72, 73, 79
Penobscot Bay, Me., 17–18, 19
Penobscot River, Me., 18, 19, 22
peregrine falcon, 74
Perkins, Bill, 14, 38
Permuda Island, N.C., 102, 103–5
Peso, Marlene C., 254, 255
Peters, Klaus, 256–8
Petrobrás, 247, 275
Philemon (Haitian guide), 159–60
Philipsburg, St. Maarten, 184
Pigeon Island, St. Lucia, 203
Pilgrims, 36
Pilkey, Orrin, H., Jr., 69, 92, 93, 97
Pilot Charts, 219
Pindling, Sir Lynden O., 122
Pinzón, Vicente Yáñez, 260–1
piping plover, 70, 71
pirates, 94, 119, 120–1, 155, 156–7, 160, 174
Piscataway Indians, 63
Plante, Christina, 202
Plummer, Henry M., 122–3, 127
point-source pollution, 276
Polcaro, Joseph, 39
Ponce de Léon, Juan, 120
Popham, George, 20
population growth, 9, 80, 274, 277
Port-de-Paix, Haiti, 155–7
Porter, Eliot, 18
Portland, Me., 26, 33
Pôrto das Dunas complex (Fortaleza, Braz.), 245
Pôrto Seguro, Braz., 261, 262, 264, 265–7
Portsmouth, Dominica, 197, 199
Portsmouth, Va., 85
Portuguese explorers and settlers, 18, 256, 260, 261–4
Potomac River, Md.–Va., 8, 65, 79, 80
Praia do Forte, Braz., 256, 257
Prince Rupert Bay, Dominica, 197, 198
Prohibition, 121
Projeto Tamar (Braz.), 256
Provincetown, Mass., 36–7

Prudential Insurance Company of America, The, 101
Pseudopatystoma coruscans, 254
Puerto Escondido, Dom. Rep., 163, 165
Puerto Naranjo, Cuba, 148–50
Puerto Plata, Dom. Rep., 162–4
Puerto Rico, 168–71
Pulsifer, Lydia, 188
Pungo River, N.C., 87
Putney, Allen, 177–85 *passim*, 188, 195, 211, 278
Putney, Lilia, 177
Putney family, 177–8

Q (quarantine) flag, 124, 155
Quakers, 182

Ragged Island, Bahamas, 139, 140–2
Raiders and Rebels: The Golden Age of Piracy (Sherry), 121
Raleigh, Sir Walter, 20, 88, 89, 90, 91, 120
Ranging the Maine Coast (Loomis), 3
Rare Animal Relief Effort (RARE), 196, 210
razorbill, 23
Reagan, Ronald, 6–7, 72–3
Recife, Braz., 243, 248, 249–50, 261, 266
Recôncavo region, Braz., 253–5
Red Bay, Nfld., 282–3
Red Hook Bay, St. Thomas, 176
red knots, 61
red-necked parrots, 195–6
red tide, 106; *see also* algal blooms
Renard, Yves, 204, 205–6, 207, 208, 278
Revere, Paul, 17
Revolutionary War, 56
Rhode Island, 51–2
Rhône, 181
Rice, Bernice, 105–6
Rice, Bill, 105–6
Richmond Island, Me., 33
Riding Rock Inn (San Salvador, Bahamas), 133
Riehemann, Steve, 221–2, 226–34 *passim*, 238, 245, 246, 247, 251
Riggs, Stanley, 92
Rime of the Ancient Mariner, The (Coleridge), 115
Rio das Cachoeiras, Braz., 265
Rio de Janeiro, Braz., 241, 243, 271, 273–4, 276

Index

Index

The author and publisher would like to thank the following for kindly providing the illustrations used in *The Voyage of the Sanderling:* John G. Alden Inc. of Massachusetts for the *Sanderling* plans on page 14; the Library of Congress for the maps by Alonso de Santa Cruz, Thomas Hood, Homem-Reineis, and Diego Ribero on pages 19, 156, 242, and 279 respectively; the Bettmann Archives for engravings on pages 21, 56, 90 (right), 121 (left); Duryea Morton for the photograph on page 24 (right); Peter Ralston for the photograph on page 24 (left); the Old Dartmouth Historical Society for the photograph on page 37; Cary Hazlegrove for the photograph on page 41; Dale Leavitt for the photograph on page 47; Jerry Howard for the photograph on page 52; the Chesapeake Bay Foundation for the photograph on page 66; Judy Johnson for the photograph on page 69; Harr, Hedrich-Blessing for the photograph on page 80; the National Maritime Museum, Greenwich, London, for the engravings on pages 89, 185, 252, 273; the British Museum for the engravings on pages 90 (left), 121 (right), and 263; the Winston-Salem *Journal*/David Rolfe for the photographs on pages 93, 100, 103; the North Carolina Coastal Federation for the photograph on page 104; the John Carter Brown Library of Brown University for the map by Joseph Acosta Miranda on page 115; Hassel for the photograph on page 131; Javier Obregón for the photographs on pages 134 and 135; the New York Public Library for the engraving on page 167; the Caribbean Conservation Association for the photograph on page 205; Peter Walsh for photographs on pages 208, 223, 234, 269, and 271; and Matthew Huntington for the photographs on pages 246 and 266.

ABOUT THE AUTHOR

Roger D. Stone, formerly chief of the Time-Life News Bureau in Rio de
Janeiro and president of the Center for Inter-American Relations, was
vice president of the World Wildlife Fund from 1982 to 1986 and Whitney
H. Shepardson Fellow at the Council on Foreign Relations for 1990. He is
currently a senior fellow of the World Wildlife Fund and the Conservation Foundation. His last book was *Dreams of Amazonia* and his forth-
coming work, *The Nature of Development,* is scheduled for publication
in 1992.